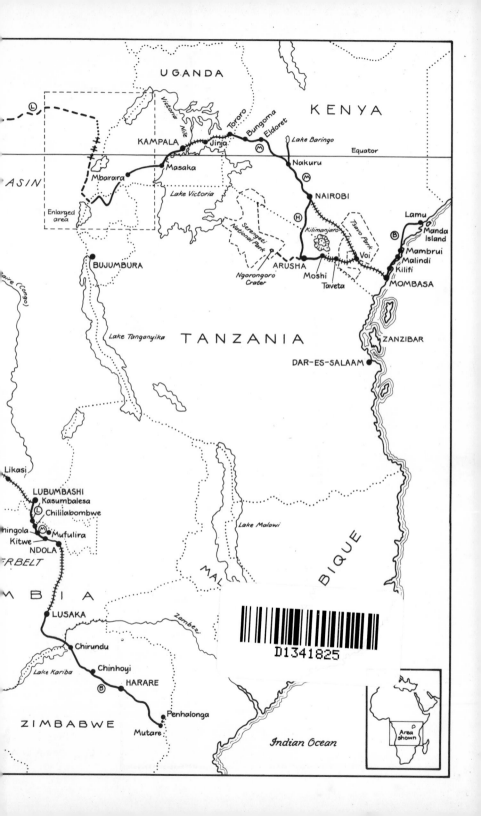

A Family Outing in Africa

A Family Outing
In Africa

Charles and Janie Hampton
and
their children

**MACMILLAN
LONDON**

to our parents

First published 1988 by
MACMILLAN LONDON LIMITED
4 Little Essex Street London WC2R 3LF
and Basingstoke

Associated companies in Auckland, Delhi, Dublin, Gaborone,
Hamburg, Harare, Hong Kong, Johannesburg, Kuala Lumpur,
Lagos, Manzini, Melbourne, Mexico City, Nairobi, New York,
Singapore and Tokyo

British Library Cataloguing in Publication Data

Hampton, Charles
A family outing in Africa.
1. Africa—Description and travel—1977-
I. Title II. Hampton, Janie
916'.04328   DT12.25

ISBN 0-333-44190-7

Typeset by Columns of Reading
Printed in Hong Kong

1

Janie. . .

We put off the sale of our belongings until the very day we left our home in Zimbabwe. It was pouring with rain but we had to go ahead. The market-place was at the bus-stop, where a tin-roofed Tea Room and some women selling fruit and vegetables catered for the passengers. Mr Kutiwayo, the milkman, stopped us as we bumped down the track and asked to have first pickings. He took the paraffin stove, a pan and a plastic dustbin we had stored water in.

Orlando went into the Tea Room and called:

'*MaJumble, tengai maJumble.*'

Nobody showed much interest. They went on eating their *sadza*, a stiff porridge made from maize flour, which they dipped into a bowl of stew. The women came to finger our old clothes. The rain drummed on the roof and splashed up off the ground.

Then a bus arrived and the children ran into the muddy road and shouted. The driver switched off his engine, a signal for the whole bus to empty excitedly. Passengers jammed in the doorway and someone scrambled out of a window. We were besieged by eager hands waving our belongings and demanding a price. The bus driver bought a hammer and a bag of nails, a shirt and two pairs of Y-fronts.

An old man appeared wearing an ancient solar topi adorned with a red and black typewriter ribbon.

We had set aside a box of groceries to give away but somehow it got sold too – half a bottle of tomato ketchup for five cents, a bag of salt for six. Some odd socks went for one cent each. A skirt got ripped in half. We nearly sold the jack and spare tyre from the car. Joseph handed out things for free and was parting

1

with his shoes when I caught him just in time. At length, the driver climbed back behind his wheel and our customers disappeared over the horizon.

We had agreed to sell the car to one of Charlie's teaching colleagues who had already paid a deposit and started driving lessons. We no longer lived at the school because a new term had begun. A twisting dirt road led to Saint Augustine's. The steep hills were largely uninhabited: the whole area, less than ten miles from the border with Mozambique, had been tense and dangerous during the war. Halfway along we had a puncture. While I struggled with the wheel-nuts, a crowd of ragged children stood and watched me. We needed to get to the bank in town before three and I was in no mood for an audience.

At Saint Augustine's, Mr Chirima shook his head when he saw the hole in the tyre but he paid up the rest of the cash. We made our sad farewells. The mission had been our home for the past four years. Rosie, my closest friend, was in tears. Phillip, the orphan who had become a part of our family, stood awkwardly twisting his shirt-tail.

'You must write to me every day from England.'

'Of course we will write often. And you must write too and work hard. Your school fees will be paid and there's money for clothes and the holidays. One day, we shall come back to visit you. Goodbye!'

'Goodbye.'

The Principal drove us to town in his pick-up. It was drizzling by now and we felt thoroughly miserable.

I had to knock at the back door of the bank to collect our traveller's cheques. With an afternoon to kill before our train left for Harare, the capital, we set out to find a young German couple who had recently arrived from Europe in their own truck. I wanted to glean all the information I could, especially about Zaire, the country on our route about which we knew least.

We planned to travel northwards in a great arc that would take in the west coast at the Zaire/Congo estuary and the east coast in Kenya. This meant crossing Zambia, Zaire and Rwanda. If the situation in Uganda proved too risky, we would make a detour south through Burundi and Tanzania, reaching Kenya that way.

We had various objectives. The romantic 1000 mile journey up

2

the great Zaire river was clearly what explorers did. Charlie wanted to climb Kilimanjaro. We hoped to meet the pygmies of the Ituri forest and to stay with teachers, missionaries and health workers in remote areas.

Main Street in Mutare is long and straight. Shops and super-markets give way to flats and then to private houses and a high school set in spacious grounds. It was the first time we had tried to walk anywhere with our rucksacks. They were far too heavy and when I put Joseph's in place, he fell over backwards, his legs waving in the air.

'How much further is it?'

'Not far now.'

'Do we have to go?'

'Yes, this is important.'

'But I'm tired.'

'How do you expect to walk home to England if you can't even make it up Main Street?'

'I don't want to.'

'Neither do I,' said Orlando. 'How far is England anyway?'

'It's a long long way,' said Daisy. 'I should think it's hundreds of thousands of miles.'

'How long will it take, Mum?'

'Just a few minutes more, darling. I promise you can have a cool drink when we get there.'

'Mummy! That's not what I meant.'

'We shall get home in time for the summer holidays.'

'Where are we going to live?'

'I don't know at the moment. It depends on your father.'

Charlie was in England for a fortnight, seeing about his future.

'Look, here we are!'

An armoured truck with German plates was parked in the road. The house was covered in a mass of red, orange and purple bougainvillea. A young man came to the door.

'Hello,' I said. 'I rang earlier. I believe you've just driven through Zaire. Can you tell us all about it?'

'You may come in,' he replied, 'but we have to go out ourselves in ten minutes.'

I was disappointed. How could they tell me anything in ten minutes? But they did.

3

'What was Zaire like?'

'Oh, it was fine.'

'Was there any food there?'

'I expect so. I don't know. We carried all our own food from Germany.'

'Were the people friendly?'

'They may have been. We did not meet many. We had no cause to.'

'I have heard that Zaire contains many thieves. Did you have things stolen?'

'We always slept in the truck for safety. We never left it alone.'

'What can you tell me about your journey?'

'It was okay. We had no problems. There was not much water in Chad, but we have large water carriers.'

'Thank you very much. Could the children have a drink of water please?'

We had already decided that public transport was the best way to learn about a country, meet its people and have an adventure. This conversation confirmed it.

Passenger trains in Zimbabwe move slowly and in the cool of the night. The trip to Harare takes three hours by car and ten by train. The station was empty when we arrived at six to buy our tickets.

We usually travelled third class. You can't book but the couchettes are almost as comfortable as second and very good value. Fourth class isn't much fun because you have to sit up all night and drunks can be a problem. On this occasion, with a few dollars to burn before we left Zimbabwe, we decided to be extravagant and go second. The white man who sold the tickets would not agree.

'You can't take children in second class. It's not right.'

He got out his booking forms and looked down the names written by each number. Africans and Europeans were in separate compartments. There were no empty ones left.

'Would you mind if . . . ?'

'No, we don't mind sharing a compartment with blacks, do we kids? In fact, we would rather.'

On my last trip I had been put in a double bunk with a white

4

woman who talked the whole night about her fear of African men, and I didn't get any sleep.

'The train is pretty full already.'

He went away and consulted another register.

'This is your number. It won't leave for another two hours. Bring the children into my office.'

He sat us down and told us how he and his mates could have won the war against the 'terr's'. He reckoned Ian Smith had sold out to the blacks.

'Some of them are becoming quite civilised, I grant you. You wouldn't believe the furniture they buy on tick. And the cars they bust up after a few beers! The African cannot hold his drink. I heard a *kaffir* talking in the bar here; went to the tribal trustlands the other week, hit a cow and wrote off a Mazda. Where do these guys get the money?'

'They work hard for it.'

'But can they do these jobs? What do you read in the papers? They're bloody inefficient, hey? Their brains can't cope with it.'

'My husband taught A levels to the people you call terr's. They got excellent results.'

'Anyone can pass in these new subjects: Shona, what use is that in the wide world?'

'He taught them English and Economics. They got As and Bs.'

'The world is changing. But why should I have them living in my street, you tell me that? They're not like us.'

When we got onto the train we found our compartments were first class. I took the tickets back. 'There seems to be a mistake. We asked for second.'

'Don't you worry, it's all taken care of.'

Charles. . .

We had arranged to spend our last three days in Zimbabwe with Pat and Hugh Lewin. Hugh is a South African who spent seven years in prison for his part in sabotaging electricity supplies. His book *Bandiet* gives a vivid account of his experiences. Their house stood on a rocky hill where the outermost limits of the city met the bush. It had smooth, shaded lawns and a pool set among aloes and thorn-trees. I marvelled at the contrast with February in London. Three bumptious little dogs called Tombi,

5

Sissi and Tsoki were yapping and tugging at my trousers. They chased a rubber ball with crazy abandon, tumbling over their stubby legs and diving paws first into the pool. I stripped off and leapt in after them.

When it came to a dip, my children were never far behind.

'Let's swim in our nude!' said Joe and jumped on my head with a wild shriek.

Pat came home at six-thirty and was immediately called to the phone. She is a lecturer in law at the university and runs a free legal aid scheme. It was intended to be a teaching opportunity but there is no other comparable help in the country and she has to turn many applicants away.

I felt slightly awestruck in the Lewins' home. Hugh was about to leave on a research tour for the World Council of Churches. Pat complained about the actions of some government minister which fell outside the law. Naomi Mitchison, the author, had left the day before. A genial Anglican called Walter Makhulu came to supper. He charmed Daisy and the two Lewin girls by using English, Zulu, Shona, Afrikaans, Greek, French and Russian.

'Is he drunk or showing off?' asked Orlando.

'Neither, darling,' replied Janie. 'Don't you realise he's an archbishop?'

Walter told us about people's reactions to his purple shirt. Some became aggressive, like the man who had left the Roman priesthood in order to marry. Others put him on a pedestal or simply gawped.

Walter's home is in Botswana and the conversation at supper turned to the murder of Jeanette Schoon and her small daughter with a parcel bomb. Janie and I had stayed with the Schoons in Gaborone when we were interviewed for their job with a British development agency. Jeanette's husband, Marius, had been in prison with Hugh and the bomb was clearly meant for him. The South African government particularly dislikes Afrikaaner revolutionaries.

Pat and Janie cleared away the plates. Walter and Hugh had grown sombre. I felt insignificant beside them but nonetheless caught up in their concern. For six weeks over the Christmas of 1982, virtually all the petrol supplies to Zimbabwe had been

6

withheld by Pretoria. We were working in a politically charged atmosphere. South Africans who had been the victims of violence came to stay at Saint Augustine's.

Outside our work, the only influence we could exert was through our relationships. Zimbabwe had until recently been a racialist state where white spoke to black in tones of command, impatience or irony. In certain places, just being polite and friendly was enough to elicit surprise. Through Rosie, Phillip and their familes, we learnt to love and be loved. We entered their homes as guests and apprentices in their art of living. We found a world of delight. It gave us the trust we needed to embark on our journey.

2

Charles. . .

Hugh drove us into town early on the morning of Wednesday, February 20th. It was the first day of Lent. At Saint Augustine's, Father Keble Prosser would be dipping his middle finger into moistened ashes and anointing 800 students on the forehead.

The *msika* – bus-station – was a cheerful Babel. Competing crews grabbed our sleeves and yelled their destination in our faces. Dense clouds of black smoke belched out round our feet. Inside the departing buses, tightly packed bodies swayed against the windows.

Passengers do not cling to the outside in Zimbabwe nor do they ride on the roof. It is a relatively prosperous country. Instead the buses carry a mattress or two, a goat tied by its legs, chickens in a cage, bicycles, a threaded stack of baskets which stream in the wind, sacks of mealie flour, crates of beer and bundles of personal belongings.

The buses link the wage-earner in the city with his parents, his wife and his children in the homeland. They extend markets and marriage prospects. They carry news and mail. Zimbabwe's main roads are excellent, a pay-off from the Rhodesian war effort.

Janie. . .

We had just joined the queue for the Lusaka bus when a boy's voice exclaimed:

'Hello Daisy!'

It was Shakey and Leonard with their parents, returning to Malawi after five years at the gold mine near Saint Augustine's. Shakey, semi-crippled by polio, walked three miles uphill to

8

school. He was in Daisy's class. We fell about laughing at the coincidence and nearly left my rucksack behind.

Our bus was just comfortably full and it departed promptly at eight o'clock without any of the customary roaring and blaring. This nearly caused an upset.

'*Maiwe, tichamboenda!*' – Heavens, we're going.

'*Mai Sarudzai, kaskera!*' – Mother of 'Be Choosy', hurry.

'*Handina matikiti!*' – I haven't got the tickets.

'*Iwe, dhiraivha, garai, chigarai!*' – You, driver, wait, please wait.

We drove out through the milling crowds, past the rank of battered taxis, past street-traders and men waiting hopefully outside factory gates. *Hapana basa*, said the signs. There is no work here. Try again tomorrow. The side-walks were littered with broken glass and mud-spattered weeds, but overhead flamboyant blooms spread in glory against the morning sky.

Charles. . .

We skirted the city centre, 1950s' Coventry in the sunshine; safe but dull. A square mile of office blocks, shopping malls, parks, cinemas and bars. The ministries fit in where they can. 'Education' is above a hotel. Only Parliament, the Law Courts and the Cathedral make a modest attempt at grandeur.

I watched the street names go past. Rhodes, Gordon, Nyerere, Samora Machel. Old heroes and new. The statues from settler history could easily have been destroyed but now they occupy a shady garden at the National Archives. Renaming proceeds at a gentle pace but any change is unwelcome to some.

My first fortnight in the country had been spent among white acquaintances. It was November 1980 and there was widespread paranoia on the cocktail-party circuit . . .

'There will be a civil war within nine months, you mark my words. Robert and old Josh are at each other's throats.'

'Harry caught a burglar last night. He was fishing for the silver through the security bars. Harry swears he was using a salmon rod.'

'Have you heard the Swanepoels are gapping it?'

'I must have been to drinks at the airport a dozen times this month.'

There were other signs of a society turned upside-down. I was in a lift with an African in torn overalls who gave me a nervous smile as it shot upwards.

'It's my first time to be in this thing,' he said.

At Christmas, 1981, one of my students invited me to his home in a township. Mile upon mile of identical concrete cabins. Floodlights at the centre of each block. One road in and one road out.

'How do I find 11097, New Canaan? I have been going round and round for hours. *Batsira ini shamwari* – Help me friend!'

'11097. That is Mr Chirombo. I will show you. He is my uncle.'

A low hedge. Borders of orange marigolds. Inside, a lumpy sofa, photographs of the family taken in a studio, a TV sharing a light socket with a fridge.

'Do you beat my son George, Mr Hampton?'

'No, I don't SaChirombo.'

'Then you must. He is so lazy, so very lazy. You must beat him a great deal.'

From the Saint Augustine's school magazine:
'*Local pastimes.*'
A two weeks' stay at our school certainly unveils to a stranger the remarkable yet fascinating variety of pastime activities. These range from simple chats among students of both sexes to much more meaningful ones of broad aspirations such as visiting places of interest.

Boys and girls are often seen in pairs walking leisurely about the school and conversing happily. Sometimes they amuse themselves at the swimming-pool. In open convenient places, groups of mixed sexes often admire the glorious, deep crimson rays of the sun. In summer students race-swim with great enthusiasm.

Some boys play football while girls laugh out their happiness while playing netball. Others simply watch. This is acceptable and is natural because interests vary. Nevertheless the tuck-shop remains unparalleled. People of various status visit it. There people smile, talk loudly, smoke, drink, look at each other interestedly; and all this establishes an atmosphere of great fondness, enthusiasm and happiness.

There are various clubs too. Some are the Journalists, the

Geography, the Student's View, the Dancing, the Student Christian Movement, the Sports and the Audio-Visual club. All these provide a variety of experiences essential for social and academic development.

Nevertheless the surrounding terrain demands attention. The green hills are inviting. The course of the Tsambe river and its waterfalls are attractive. The vast gum-tree plantations vie with the distant bluish horizon. Not wishing to lag behind other natural wonders, the rocks lure people to come and wonder at their form.

Why leave? Why leave at all?

I suppose things had come to a head three months earlier. October, the suicide month, when the heat and pressure build up before the explosion of rain.

The Bishop, Elijah Masuku, wanted the Principal to leave so that he could put a Zimbabwean in charge of the mission. Father Prosser did not want to go. He was not opposed to the idea of handing over – his support for the liberation struggle had made him a national figure – but he believed that the time was not ripe. His school, along with many others, had been forced to grow very rapidly since independence. Teachers were hard to find. Those he had were under great strain, losing their marking and preparation periods and finding it difficult to maintain discipline. It was clear that his experience and management skills were needed as never before. The Bishop was however a very determined man and disaffection spread among the staff.

I was a housemaster and white so it was generally assumed that I took the Principal's side. In fact, I couldn't make up my mind. It was clearly right that a Zimbabwean should run the school. I loved my job but, after four years, was I in danger of becoming a permanent fixture?

What tipped the balance for me was an unease about imposing European culture on the students. Father Prosser seemed to feel it was necessary to maintain his authority. One Easter, for example, the choir was asked to sing the responses in Latin to a setting by Palestrina. I was choirmaster and applied myself enthusiastically to the job. The result of a lot of hard work was fairly ridiculous.

I could not blame the Principal. When he had first arrived in the 1960s, Saint Augustine's was a thriving English religious

11

community with a priory and a convent. Now he was the only one left. The sisters had fled in 1978, during a crisis in the war. The Community in Yorkshire recalled the other fathers in 1983. Alone and in need of help, Father Prosser turned inwards to his faith and to the past. Those who knew him felt sad, because he was always a courageous defender of African rights.

My own position became increasingly difficult. I was caught in the middle. Leaving or staying – both were acts of betrayal.

The bus is grinding up the Chinoyi road now, through the northern suburbs. It's another world, this end of town. Hibiscus and honeysuckle screen the tennis-courts and soften the harshness of the security fencing. *Chengerai Imbwa!* Beware of the Dog! Dobermans and Rhodesian Ridgebacks, trained to bite black skin.

Today's *Herald* is open on my knee.

A team of inspectors from The Ministry of Trade and Commerce yesterday seized over 2000 tennis balls priced at $10.480 from Harare shops [i.e. £2 per ball]. *Reliable sources said 1,929 balls were seized from a shop in Baker Avenue, 25 from another shop in Stanley Avenue. . .*

I can hear the howls of complaint! But what was the real price of importing tennis balls to be thwacked across green lawns? I thought of the football pitch at Saint Augustine's, a sandy field that took the skin off your knees and flooded every summer. I thought of the schools built by parents out of sticks and mud: the children who played in the street, kicking a plastic bag stuffed with newspaper.

The bus rattles past fields of tobacco. A rope has worked loose and is whipping angrily against the tin roof. Opposite me is an advertisement in mock Soviet lettering:

Kariba Batteries. More Power to the People.

Shakey, Orlando and Daisy are chattering about the school-mates they have left behind.

The battle between Father Prosser and the Bishop got steadily worse. The Community wanted him back and when he refused, they threatened him with expulsion. The local peasants, convinced that the Bishop meant to drive them from their land,

12

demonstrated in Father Prosser's favour. For a week, the mission was blockaded by gangs. The national press carried the story and the Cabinet in Harare was said to be split.

I was still sweating it out in the choir gallery but I knew my presence was no longer welcome. I had introduced African music and rescued them from *Hymns Ancient and Modern* but who was I to make the choir a present of their own tradition?

I asked myself if the education I handed out was truly liberating. Did it simply replace an old set of alien values with a fresher version? For that matter, was I independent myself? How would I fare without the kudos of being a teacher? It was worth finding out.

3

Charles. . .

We stopped at Chinoyi to buy fruit and brave the toilets. Boys crowded round the bus, touting 'mealies'.

'Magwere, masweets, machewingum!'

Someone threw a slippery mango skin out of a window, narrowly missing Janie's neck. Two Asian women looked round and shook their heads.

The road to the north-west went through rich farmland for a hundred miles. Then, skirting the eastern end of Lake Kariba, it twisted through dry lumpy hills and descended into the baking hot valley of the Zambezi river. Elephant droppings steamed in the middle of the road. The bus startled a rhino which crashed away through the spindly trees.

We reached the border at one o'clock and gratefully drank a tray of Cokes. The customs officials were polite but firm. Everything had to be unloaded for inspection. The driver said that the Zambians would be the same and he advised us to carry our bags across the bridge. They were so heavy that even this distance made our legs wobble. The river was brown and fast flowing. A boy was fishing from a dugout canoe moored to the bank. . .

1D English, last period Wednesday afternoon.

'Hello 1D.'

'Good afternoon sir.'

'You can sit down. Open that window please. Munyaradzi, do up your shirt. Take out Wilson Katiyo, *Going to Heaven*. What page have we got to?'

'Seventy-two, sir.'

'Thank you Itai. Read for us please. You will remember that Alexio is escaping from Rhodesia.'

Despite his inaction, the searchlight remained fixed on him. Alexio started, hearing a man's voice command him to remain where he was: 'If you move we'll shoot!' The warning was blurted through a mechanical loudspeaker. More out of instinct than thought, Alexio took that as a command to do everything he could to get away. He hadn't gone ten feet before a shot cracked and a bullet embedded itself in the log. The warning was repeated again. Out of shock Alexio tumbled down off the log into the river. Never had there been a time he felt so sure he was going to die. Under water he would have cried if he could. There was no time to think. All he could do was to remain under water and drown or go up and be shot. Having gone under, he could only come up. When he went under again, he hit the bottom of the river. With a survival instinct, hoping to try and swim, he stood up. To his great surprise, the water level was up to his waist. Bullets were raining all around him. Panic-stricken, he tried to run out of the river.

'Where's Dad?'
'He's still on the bridge.'
'Charlie! Come on, we'll be last in the queue!'

Janie. . .
The Zambians discovered very quickly that most of our fellow passengers were trying to make a small profit on the trip. Rows of socks, shirts, flip-flops, knitting wool and toys were spread out under protest, while the duty was totted up or the goods were confiscated. Inside the immigration hut, it was very hot. Kenneth Kaunda's photograph hung at an undignified angle. A number of whites, who had arrived in fast cars, clearly felt they should be processed ahead of the bus queue. The official was polite but his faculties were in low gear. Charlie scribbled on forms at a crowded counter. Orlando decided his help was needed:
'You haven't filled that in. Why not, Dad?'
I took him outside but the only patch of shade was scattered with smelly rubbish. We waited. Daisy and Joseph went off to

15

search for drinks but came back empty-handed. Orlando became vengeful. People stared at us. My head was throbbing.

The customs man came over and the children crowded round him and explained all about our journey. He was so charmed that he chalked our bags without opening them. We had our own supply of razor-blades, biros and digital watches, so I was very relieved. At three o'clock the driver finally sounded his horn and we climbed back on board.

Charles. . .

What a relief to be moving again: a cool breeze, a sense of purpose. On a previous visit to Zambia in a car, we had confidently accelerated down the highway, only to screech to a halt on the lip of a crater. Buses can cope better with these conditions but it was nearly six before we entered Lusaka. The signs of economic distress were all around us. The tall buildings on the Cairo Road rose out of a wide plain. Its flatness hid thousands of random mealie patches and shanties. Each business we passed was like a fortress.

'I like the way they decorate their walls with pretty bits of glass,' Joseph commented.

The terminus was a surprise. It was like a miniature modern airport with staircases poised in mid-air to unload cargo from the roof of the bus. Large signs in the conventional European white on blue indicated toilets, telephones, information services, a bank and police – none of which were functioning. Janie discovered an informal currency market and exchanged ten Zimbabwean dollars for fifteen kwacha. We had quarrelled on the bus over a cooked chicken which she wished to eat there and then and I wanted to save for supper. She won and she was right. With night approaching, we needed energy and patience to find a room.

Africa on a Shoestring recommended the Sikh Temple and the Salvation Army. A man claiming to be a taxi driver commandeered us and squeezed us into his Renault 4. He said he was a Christian and would take us to the Citadel. Three times in the short journey, the tailgate flew open and our bags dropped out into the road. The children chattered happily about our journey.

'Whatever do you wish to go to Zaire for?' said the man.

'There is enough confusion here. In Zaire, it is total confusion.'

We came to a halt beside a high concrete wall with its own pretty glass icing. Daisy stepped out of the back door and disappeared completely. She emerged from a five-foot storm drain, covered in prickles but laughing.

Janie asked the driver to reverse up to the gate. He said he had run out of petrol and wanted paying. We gave him a five-kwacha note and he went to look for change, leaving Janie with his car-keys.

'You can trust me to return soon, madam. I am a Christian.'

Meanwhile, I found a way into the compound and located the commanding officer, an Australian called Captain Creek who gave us a verandah and an area for our tent. While we were boiling some tea, his young son came to question Orlando.

'What are you doing?'

'Travelling home to England with my parents.'

'Are you going to the airport tomorrow?'

'No, we're not flying back. We're going by road.'

'Why?'

'Don't ask me. They want to, that's why.'

'Are you a tourist?'

'Shucks no. I'm a terrorist.'

Captain Creek told us to leave the electric light on in case a *tsotsi* – thief – came over the wall. By eight we were all asleep.

4

From an editorial in *The Times of Zambia*, 21/2/85. . .

About this time last year, Minister of Lands and Natural Resources Mr Fabiano Chela received a very important report on the 'National Conservation Strategy for Zambia' prepared by an international organisation.

Soil erosion is of particular concern not only to farmers but to township dwellers as well. Roads in townships have been reduced to huge yawning gutters, and the most disturbing thing is that local authorities do not seem to be doing anything about this deplorable situation.

Residents who own vehicles, buses or taxis can't drive them because roads are full of pot-holes, gullies and even pools of standing water, which are breeding grounds for mosquitoes.

Is this the right way to treat people who are always being asked to pay, in these days of belt-tightening, rent and rates through the nose? Councils should not only be interested in receiving revenue from the people. They must be just as interested in providing services for the goose that lays the golden egg.

Come on councils. Let us get on with the job and fill those gutters and end the anguish of the people who have to bury their dead every other day because of malaria and other diseases which could be prevented if the right environment prevailed.

And while we are at it, what are the councils doing about lightening up streets? In Ndola's Independence Avenue, the very road where the council has its offices, nights are just black chasms. Pedestrians are afraid to walk and motorists are afraid to stop at stop signs for fear that someone may pounce on them from the dark ditches.

Charles. . .

All night long, trains clanged and boomed nearby. I dreamt my father took me out on the Solent in a small boat. We capsized and I was treading water for hours until my back ached so much, I woke up. I was lying on the concrete floor. It was six-thirty. The others were stirring too. We brewed a drink, left our bags with Captain Creek and made our way to the station.

It was the dream of Cecil Rhodes to colour the map of Eastern Africa pink from top to bottom. Lusaka's main street is still called the Cairo Road. The concrete tower blocks, relics of the sixties' copper boom, are sprouting weeds. The plate-glass is cracked. The shops are almost empty.

Our plan was to make for the copperbelt, 250 miles to the north. We had contacts in the towns of Chingola and Chilila-bombwe who would help us to cross into Zaire. We booked seats on a train leaving for Kitwe at one o'clock.

'Tomorrow I'm going to be seven,' Joseph said to the ticket clerk.

'Then tomorrow you must pay full fare,' he replied.

In the foyer was a departures board with a painting of a train and the word 'gone' chalked alongside the down express to Luangwa. Every now and then, the schedules become so disorganised that the whole system takes a day off and starts again.

We decided to visit an acquaintance at the Anglican cathedral. It is a brash, modern building with windows stained in primary colours. Twenty years after independence, Union Jacks and Ensigns still hang from the walls. Services in the vernacular are held only on Sunday afternoon. The dean, a chartered surveyor in a previous embodiment, made a series of profitable invest-ments on the property market. He left recently but another Englishman has taken his place.

The train to Kitwe took twelve hours and cost about £15 for the whole family in second class. The carriages swayed and bumped a great deal. The seats reclined like a dentist's chair: we were puzzled by their random layout until we discovered they were on giant swivels and could face in any direction. The toilets were the grandest I've ever seen on a train. Separate facilities for men and women, wash-basins in open cubicles and a drinking-water dispenser opposite. Daisy accidentally pulled the plug out of our water carrier and we had to make embarrassed apologies as water sloshed from one end of the carriage to the other.

We ate a picnic of bread, spam, tomatoes and cucumber for lunch, and *sadza* with meat from the restaurant for supper. In between times, we dozed and read and played paper games. The children made friends with a Zambian called Jimmy. He wore a T-shirt which said, 'I'm HIS because HE deserves the finest'. He told them he was Scottish, had studied in California, travelled for a living and threw away his clothes when they became dirty.

The lights failed soon after dark and it took us ages to find a candle. We still had to establish a system for packing our bags.

The copperbelt appeared soon after midnight. Molten slag glowed on the spoil heaps and flames billowed from distant chimneys. At Kitwe, the passengers made a dash for the waiting-room and bedded themselves down for the rest of the night. We took a look at the hard benches and smelly floor and decided to try our luck elsewhere. Jimmy shouldered one of our bags and led us to the Hotel Nkana. We were relieved to find the streets well lit but we kept to the middle of the road. A porter let us in and offered us a room with three hard but clean beds and no light for forty-five kwacha. Janie had managed to change a ten pound note for eighty kwacha with an Asian in Lusaka, so we felt able to afford it.

Janie. . .
Breakfast the next morning was served in a large dining-room painted blue and orange. We looked at the menu and chose 'Continental: a choice of toast, croissants and scones served with honey, jam and marmalade: fresh tea and coffee'. At the top was printed, 'The essence of culinary art is time. Please indulge us with your patience', and at the bottom, 'We cannot guarantee availability of commodities'. It took twenty minutes for our food to arrive. The waiter explained they were having trouble getting the water to boil. When it did arrive, the tea and

coffee were indistinguishable and the bread had been turned into rusks by the passage of time. We abandoned it and went out to the post office.

In my notebook, I had the box number of Ernie van Leeve. Ernie had visited Manicaland the year before as a contestant in a motor rally. I was reporting on the event for a Zimbabwean magazine and joined the drivers in the bar of a local hotel. After a few drinks, Ernie asked me to return to Zambia with him. The bait was a share in the fabulous wealth of his emerald mine. I said I couldn't very well leave my husband and children. 'Never mind,' he replied, 'bring them too!' I said I might just hold him to that. His engine blew up spectacularly the next day and he flew home.

While Charlie searched the Chingola directory for Ernie's phone number, the children and I went window-shopping. The stores were mostly kept by Asians. They sold everything from blankets and rolls of material to tin trunks and fishing-line. In one window, protected from the sun by orange polythene, the saris and dresses were displayed on bald, chipped, handless pink dummies. We joined a queue for delicious mango ice-creams and chatted to a group of black Hare Krishna followers with saffron robes and shaved heads. They were having the usual problem raising funds and public consciousness. We emptied our pockets of fifty-eight Zimbabwean cents.

'I've found it! W.J. Engineering,' called Charlie, waving a scrap of paper. 'They're not answering the phone though.'

'Let's go and catch a bus.'

We collected our luggage from the hotel.

'The bus depot is just down the road,' the receptionist said.

She described the turnings carefully to us and added, 'You can't miss it.'

Orlando was protesting that he couldn't walk.

'Why can't we take a taxi?'

'If we walk, we'll have money for a nice lunch,' I said.

'I don't care about lunch. This thing's impossible to carry. I want to take a taxi.'

How do you explain to a child in front of an interested crowd that you are hoping your black-market funds will last a few more days until you leave the country? Mercilessly, we pushed him out into the sunshine.

We got lost almost at once. Charlie said his pack was so heavy that he had to keep going. He strode off through a market with Daisy and Joseph panting at his heels. I made the mistake of drawing Orlando's attention to some home-made toy cars. He lost all appetite for going any further and announced he was on strike. I was hot and straining under my load too and I felt like leaving him there. Twenty yards further on, I stopped to inspect a traditional healer's stall with snake-skins, monkeys' tails, eagles' feet, dried herbs and bottles of potion. Two young men came running up behind me, one carrying Orlando and the other his rucksack.

'Madam, here is your son! You must not leave him, it's very dangerous. There are kidnappers. He may disappear.'

Orlando scowled.

'Where is the bus to Chingola, please,' I asked.

'Come with us,' said one.

'We will show you. It is not far.'

They led us out of the market, through narrow mud-walled streets, past the wire of a police compound and a beer-hall. Finally we heard the familiar klaxons and the roar of revving engines.

'Hello Mum,' shouted Daisy. 'Over here. You're just in time.'

We ran across the muddy ground, shaking off the attentions of rival touts and tried to squeeze into the back of a minibus.

'There isn't room for us, surely!' I said.

'Plenty, plenty room,' said the driver. 'Hop in quick.'

Orlando. . .

I was fed up of being squashed and hot. I tried to stick my head out of the window but the man who loaded things onto the roof said it was dangerous. It wasn't fair. He sat with his whole body out of the window. Then we heard a loud bang and Dad said a tyre had burst. The bus tried to go on. Then it decided to stop. We all got out for a bit. Joe and I looked for emeralds in the gravel. Luckily, it wasn't far to Chingola. We never did get a proper lunch. Mum bought us a tiny hamburger and a Coke. We waited at the bus-stop while she went to find Ernie.

5

A sign beside the road:

*UNIP. Chingola Region. Welcome to Central Constituency –
the hub of good & clean politics. We believe in the principles of
Zambian Humanism.*

Janie. . .
Daisy and I soon found W.J. Engineering on a corner near the
bus-stop. The doors were barred and padlocked but I discovered
a mechanic next door.

'You want Bwana Leef? He went many months ago.'

'Where?'

'Maybe Lusaka, maybe Kitwe, or down south. He move
around. We ask my bwana. Maybe he know.'

We were shown into the office of Mr James who remained
seated behind his desk, a cigarette burning in the ash tray. He
looked none too pleased at being asked to find Ernie by an oddly
dressed female with a child in tow.

'We're on our way to Cairo,' was all I could think to say. He
didn't seem impressed. 'We just need somewhere to pitch a
tent.'

'Have a cool drink. Samuel, bring us two cool drinks for the
madams.'

Daisy tittered. It made us sound like prostitutes.

Mr James took a drag on the cigarette and reached for the
phone. Four calls later, he shook his head.

'Ernie is definitely out of town,' he said. 'Now I'll tell you
what I'm going to do. He has a partner, Mario Sportelli. His wife
has agreed to look after you.'

23

He looked doubtfully at us.

'Thank you,' we said.

He stood up and hitched his shirt into his shorts.

'There's a pick-up outside.'

'My husband is at the bus-stop with the other children.'

'How long are you staying in Chingola?'

'Not more than a couple of days.'

'Then it's on to Cairo, hey?'

'Yes.'

We drove round and he looked disbelievingly at the pile of rucksacks with Joseph sitting on top, shaded by our multi-coloured golf umbrella.

'Come on young man, in the back.'

We sped out to a suburb and stopped beside a spacious bungalow behind a high fence.

'This is Sportelli's place.'

The garden was parched and untidy. There were children's bikes, rusty swings, a car under repair and an old tractor. A chorus of barks came from a shed. An African maid, her head wrapped in a white scarf, paused and looked up from the wash-tub outside the kitchen door. A plump brown woman and an attractive teenage girl came out of the house.

'Hello,' I said. 'I'm Janie.'

'Rosa, Rosa Sportelli. Very pleased to meet you. Please to come in.'

'We just wondered if we could pitch our tent in your garden for the night.'

'Yes, of course, no problem. Why not you come in the house? Too much rain outside.'

'Well, if you're sure.' It couldn't have rained for weeks.

'Yes, I sure. Miriam, you can sleep with the boys. Yes! I say so! I have two boys as well. They are at school – home soon. How old are your children? What is your name? Dezzy . . . Daisy? Miriam, this is Daisy. Look, you can have this room and your children sleep in here. Hello Charlie, I am Rosa. We have video. You like football? Mario, he like very much. Italia win the World Cup, we have. You make yourself at home with Rosa. I just make pizza – tomato, formaggio, peperone; it's fresh, I buy today, you like?'

Joseph. . .
It was my birthday. I had it in the copperbelt. I got some transfers, a packet of chewing-gum and a pen that writes in gold. We watched a video about space invaders. It was good.

Charles. . .
Mario came home and we sat around the kitchen table, drinking coffee and smoking cigarettes. He told us what had happened to the emerald mine.

Ernie and Mario first muscled in on the business as contractors for Prince Ushindi. The Prince was hopeless at finding emeralds. The whole countryside was covered in slit trenches and he couldn't afford to pay his two hundred labourers. Ernie and Mario bought a stake from him for Kw 14,000 (about £6,000). They were both supremely happy prospecting in the bush, dodging the government troops who were hunting smugglers from Angola. Emeralds are worth £2 million a kilo. You find them by panning gravel and then going down a few metres. It was not long before they struck a vein.

Ernie went to Lusaka and submitted a sample for auction. He then went to Zimbabwe to take part in the car rally. When he returned, it was to find the whole area cordoned off by the army, their machines interned and their permit revoked. For nine months, they waited for a new licence. It was unlikely they would ever regain their concession but Mario smiled.

'Maybe Ernie come back, maybe not. He is philanderer. I find more emeralds. No problem. I smell them.'

Orlando. . .
When we went to bed, I couldn't get to sleep because I was very frightened. A monster was outside the window, grunting and laughing at me in three different languages. I went to Mum and Dad. Dad came and pulled back the curtain. He got a shock too as he thought I was imagining things. We saw two white eyes and grinning teeth. It was the nightwatchman.

Daisy. . .
We had great fun at the Sportellis. Miriam, Alex and Christian

25

were very nice. We played pirates in their swimming-pool. It was very old, cracked and dirty. The water was bright green and had frogs in. We used an old door for a boat and brooms for paddles. We also played football. Alex kicked the ball in Dad's face and by mistake broke his specs.

Janie. . .

On Sunday morning, Mario drove us to the Catholic church. There were two Polish priests and pink plaster statues of Mary, and of Jesus dressed as a monk. The church was full. Much to his surprise, Charlie was asked to read the lesson by the choir-master. The sermon was about Noah, the flood and baptismal waters. Afterwards, the priests handed out flour and butter to the women in the congregation and asked them to make sponge cakes for a church bazaar. This was a great act of faith because these commodities were expensive and hard to come by.

Mario collected us and took us on a tour of the Ngacha mine compound. It is one of the largest open-cast mines in the world, three miles wide and one mile deep. Everyone in Chingola worked for the mining company. When not prospecting for emeralds, Mario was a freelance engineer. Rosa ran an ice-cream shop.

We drove down wide roads past clubs catering for hockey, football, shooting, swimming, tennis and even flying. We tried to enter the golf club for a drink but were turned away because Charlie was wearing sandals.

'Supposing Jesus turned up for a round of golf. Would they bar him as well?' he said crossly.

'You don't usually play golf in sandals, Dad,' said Daisy.

We got back in the car and went down Pope Drive into Oppenheimer Avenue. The white residential area was sealed off with concrete bollards across the approach roads. The Royal Ancient Order of Buffaloes allowed us into their bar. Mario greeted his friends and we ordered cold beer. Out of habit, he held his bottle up to the light before pouring it. There are all sorts of stories about the objects found inside Zambian beer. My favourite is a toothbrush.

Back outside, the car had developed a puncture. Mario stopped a passer-by who took us home.

Janie's horoscope in *The Times of Zambia*, 25/2/85:

> *PISCES. Do not allow things you no longer need to accumulate. Do not waste time on trivialities. Leave yourself time to enjoy life. Work is not everything. Be more moderate.*

Charles. . .

In Zimbabwe I used to travel around collecting hymns in Shona and Ndebele for the choir to sing. Along the way I discovered African spirituality. For ten years I had been a weekly attender at a parish church while a large part of me remained cynical and detached. It was worshipping in a language I didn't understand that brought on a change of heart. I was cut off from 'religion' as I had known it. The rhythms of the drums, the dancing and singing were spontaneous and uninhibited. Father Prosser muttered warnings but I knew I had to trust my instinct and explore where it led.

One evening among friends I was reading the story of Abraham and the sacrifice of Isaac when a fear gripped me that Orlando too would meet with a fatal accident, unless – unless what? I couldn't say exactly. I felt very confused. I was overcome by a strange light-headedness, at once pleasurable and frightening. All the wrong and hurt in my life coagulated into a grey, abstract feeling. It floated away from me. I was scared. That hurt was a part of me and I didn't like to lose it. I was shaking with tears by this time. I remember gasping over and over again, 'It's real, it's real!' I was astonished because the words of the Bible had jumped off the page and grabbed me by the throat. My friends hugged and comforted me and, after twenty minutes or so, I grew calm.

When I woke up the next morning, I was filled with wild and uncertain yearnings. I wanted to take a broom to my life and sweep it clean. The crude force of God's challenge took my breath away. I had been promised excitement, a re-awakening!

It was then I decided to apply to join the Anglican ministry. I gained admission to a theological college and went to the selection conference which assesses the nature of your vocation and your readiness for training. The result of this interview was waiting at our next mailing address in Kinshasa.

Janie. . .

Rosa's life revolved around her house, her children and her friend Maxie. Mario had to go to Lusaka the next day, to act as witness in the trial of a magistrate who had accepted a bribe to have Mario arrested, so that the Sportellis could be evicted from their home. Rosa took us round to meet her pal and have a clean swim. Maxie greeted us from a sun-lounger on her patio.

'Hello, do come up my dears. I've just had a phone call from Josephine. She wanted to know who the new white family were in church. Yes, I said, I know them. They're staying with Rosa. They're from Rhodesia. He's going to be a priest.

'"A priest!" she said. "He has a wife and children! He can't be a priest."

'Well, I said, I expect that's why he's going to be an Anglican priest. Do you know, she was rather cross.'

We had just settled down with more drinks when Maxie's large husband Bokkie came home in a Range Rover. He raised a hand in greeting and disappeared into the living-room. A few minutes later, he emerged in a pair of trunks and fell into the pool which spilt over the flowerbeds.

Rosa was telling us about Miriam's boarding school in South Africa. She said the road we had come down from Kitwe was infested with bandits and too dangerous to travel. Rosa and the other parents chartered a plane for their children from Ndola. The schooling cost them 12,000 rand – about £4,500 a year.

Maxie was born in South Africa but she had lived in Zambia for thirty years.

'I couldn't go back there to live, Janie. You see, I don't agree with apartheid. Nor do I think black majority rule works. Never! Just look at this country. Last week they ran out of cigarette papers if you please. And another thing, Janie, I don't hold with mixed marriages. As God is my witness, I am no racist, but I would not allow my children to marry an African. I've seen it and it just doesn't work.'

'Oh Rosa, Josephine has found some oil for you. Yes. It came in last Tuesday apparently. Her little man finally ran it to earth on Friday.'

'Do you need cigarettes, Maxie?'

'Not at the moment, thank you. You got some this morning, didn't you Bokkie dear?'

Bokkie was resting on his elbows at the edge of the pool. He reached over and lit one now. 'Only a hundred. They're asking five dollars a pack.'

'Who is?'

'That Greek, Demetrios.'

'I told you to try Jason.'

'Jason's out of town. His missus is sick.'

'Not again!' said Rosa. 'Janie, are you cold?'

The sun was disappearing behind the hill.

'I think we'd better go back to Rosa's and pack our things,' I said. 'We must leave tomorrow.'

'You no go,' said Rosa indignantly. 'You stay.'

'Our visa runs out on Wednesday,' said Charlie. 'Mario is trying to find us a lift to Lubumbashi.'

'What in God's name do you want to go there for?' said Maxie.

'We want to take the train and boat to Kinshasa.'

'Jeez! And then fly home?'

'No, then we carry on up the Congo.'

'Boy, you people are looking for adventure.'

'I wouldn't go there if I were you,' said Bokkie.

'Why not?'

'It's a nasty place, that's why.'

Charles. . .

Despite a common interest in mining copper, Zambia and Zaire are not on good terms. The mistrust which used to make such a wide gulf of the English channel still lingers round that border. British colonial types disapprove strongly of the Belgians and twenty years of independence have been plagued by banditry and smuggling. Zambians wishing to cut across the Zairean pedicle between Mufulira and Chembe are hassled by police at border posts and road-blocks. The expatriates in Chingola and Chililabombwe try to disregard the 'Congo'. It is to them a peripheral presence: anarchic, menacing and unpredictable. Better the crumbling remains of Pax Brittanica than someone else's bloody mess.

No local could be expected to drive us to Lubumbashi. What we needed was an itinerant businessman; someone with broader horizons and preferably some previous experience.

On Monday morning, Mario rang from Lusaka to say a truck going to Lubumbashi would pick us up at three. We got ready and waited but no one came. At sundown, Rosa said she would go and tell the maid to put the sheets back on our beds. We had some minestrone soup and watched another video. An excited party of Greeks in their dressing-gowns came round, hunting for cigarettes. At one a.m. we were woken by headlights and the sound of a large engine. A tired Englishman appeared at the door.

'You Mrs Sportelli?'

'No, I'm Janie Hampton.'

'Ah, you're just the person I'm looking for. You want to go to Zaire, is that right?'

'Yes. There are five of us actually.'

'It'll mean a bit of a squeeze. I've only got a cab.' He pointed into the road. 'It's an artic' you see.'

Rosa appeared in her dressing gown.

'You Alan, yes?'

'Yes.'

'You take these people?'

'Well, if they want to come.'

'You go now, this minute?'

'No, in the morning. I've been on the road since breakfast-time.'

'Where you put your lorry?'

'I'm going in search of a hill. The battery's flat.'

'Where you sleep?'

'In the cab.'

'No it's no good. You sleep here.'

'That's very kind but I dare not leave the lorry.'

'If you stay in the cab, they take you *and* the lorry.'

'So what do you suggest?'

'Put it by the fence. In the morning we push. There is slope here.'

She went into the garden and shouted.

'Henry, Josephat!'

The nightwatchmen came out of the darkness in their yellow oilskins.

'You watch the truck okay?'

'Where madam?'

'In the road of course. You guard it careful now.'

'Eeeh! In the road?'

'Madam, it's too dangerous there.'

'Henry, what you think I pay you for, eh?'

'You not pay me to be in the road, madam. I guard the house.'

'If you no watch that truck, you no job tomorrow. I no too fright to walk about the street. If bandits come, you shout and we all help.'

Alan manoeuvred the lorry up against the fence while the alsatians barked and snapped at the wheels.

Before he locked it, I climbed up to gauge the size of the cab. It was awfully small.

6

Charles. . .

We left at seven the next day. It took some time to insert Joe and a rucksack into the small remaining space between dashboard and sunshield.

After a night's rest, Alan was a determinedly cheerful bloke, accustomed to choosing his words carefully. He earned a living buying clapped-out trucks at auction in Johannesburg, driving them through Zimbabwe and Zambia and selling them for black-market dollars in Lubumbashi. It was better to carry out repairs in Lusaka than in Zimbabwe for some reason, so he was adept at nursing old crocks and quite resigned to breakdowns.

'If they stop within a hundred miles of Jo'burg,' he said, 'I just forget about them, hitch back to town and start again.'

This was his last run before retirement. At the age of thirty-four, he had made enough to buy an apartment in Monte Carlo and settle down. It must have been an anxious career. He told us that he had been arrested several times, not on charges of illicit trading or evading customs but as a spy. He relied on quick wits, a broad smile and diehard patience. We hoped his luck would hold.

A few kilometres outside Chililabombwe, we came to a road-block. A gumpole lay across two oil-drums and half a dozen soldiers sat round a fire under a flimsy shelter, their rifles to hand. One of them came over and peered into the cab.

'Where are you from? Where are you going?'

Joseph twisted and squinted down from his perch.

'To Zaire!' he said proudly.

The soldier grinned and waved us through. The tension in the cab relaxed.

'Are we in Zaire now?' asked Orlando.

'No, there's another kilometre or so yet.'

'Will there be more road-blocks?'

'Yes,' said Alan, 'it's anyone's guess how many. They're looking for emerald smugglers and every unit likes to be in on the act. Sometimes there are ten blocks or more. Getting through can take all day.'

Sure enough, we passed three more in quick succession. As the Zambians waved us down, a momentary look of doubt would cross their faces until they heard our brakes being applied. They took their time in walking over, avoiding eye contact until they were inches away at either window. Some asked us to get out but the task was clearly unreasonable. It was Alan who smoothed our way, smiling and shaking hands.

At Kasumbalesa the border posts were separated by a few hundred metres of ragged tarmac and we joined a queue of vehicles at the far end. Alongside us, a Boer in stetson and cowboy boots was arguing next to his cattle-truck, impotent fury writ all over his face. The official, a clipboard tucked under his arm, was explaining patiently that he must return to Zambia. As soon as we climbed down, a crowd of ragged children began taunting Orlando and Daisy, who stuck out their tongues in reply. A small boy shot out and whipped Orlando's hat off his head. Alan had warned us not to leave the luggage unattended even for a second. Was this a trick? An off-duty soldier, his massive face the colour of wet ash, swayed into Janie and asked her blearily for 'tips'. I hastened after Alan, grasping the passports and inoculation certificates. At the door of the immigration hut, he turned and grinned.

'I hope your French is good!'

We entered a narrow corridor, lined with a series of small windows like in a ticket office. They were set at an inconvenient height which rapidly brought on backache. Our visas were scrutinised and stamped. I declared some but not all of our American dollars. At the third window, I was surprised to glimpse Alan inside the office, sitting next to an official who was opening a quart of beer with his teeth. I was just wondering if I could join them, when a hand seized my arm and ushered me through a door into the presence of the *Chef Sanitaire*.

This gentleman waved me to a seat in front of a cluttered desk and asked politely to see my certificates. He had to ask twice because I found his guttural accent hard to follow. I apologised and handed them over. On a corner of the desk-top, covered in a thin layer of dust, lay a heap of yellowing files. Beneath them, and partly concealed, I noticed one of those ancient syringes with the capacity of a large tube of toothpaste, its glass cylinder encased in a chrome-plated frame with an evil-looking plunger. Anxiously I glanced around for a wash-basin. There was none. The *Chef Sanitaire* looked up from the documents and asked a further impenetrable question. He was tapping the certificates, flicking them through his fingers and holding out an empty palm. Something was missing.

'*Où est le typhoid? Le typhoid?*'

I reached over and took them from him. There were stamps for cholera, yellow fever, smallpox and tetanus. The latter had been included in a vaccine cocktail prepared for us in Zimbabwe. The nurse had written '+ ATT 0.5 ml.' beside the cholera dosage. These letters looked hopeful. Anti-tetanus-typhoid. That must be it! I began to explain these symbols to the chef with passionate conviction. (I was in fact quite wrong.) He remained unimpressed. I could not enter Zaire with my family unless we all received the typhoid injection first. He reached over and picked up the syringe, waving it at me to make sure I understood. Never in a month of Sundays, I thought, will Janie allow that thing to be stuck into her children.

'How much will it cost?' I asked.

He looked doubtfully at me. 'Twenty-five American dollars.'

I dug into my pocket and pulled out fourteen, laying them carefully on the desk.

'It's all I've got,' I lied.

He shrugged, picked them up and began to search in a drawer for the vaccine.

'But there's no need for the injection,' I said, pointing again to the ATT. 'We've already had it.'

There was a long pause.

'You don't want another?'

'No, but I'll pay you for a stamp.'

He shrugged again and pulled out an ink-pad. Thump, thump, thump, thump and thump.

'*Voilà, monsieur.* Welcome to Zaire. Pay attention to the robbers.'

34

He rose, unsmiling. We shook hands and I left.

Back outside Alan and Janie were enjoying a cigarette on the front bumper and waiting for customs clearance. The soldier had grown bored and gone in search of other prey. The Boer did indeed return to Zambia, swearing vengeance. Orlando had managed to retrieve his cap.

The customs officer arrived, a briefcase under his arm, and motioned us into the cab. It was Alan's drinking partner. To our astonishment, he climbed in with us.

'Ouch! He's sitting on my hair,' said Daisy.

'My arm's trapped,' said Orlando.

'Gedorff!' protested Joseph.

Alan explained that his friend would see us through the road-blocks which were much worse on this side. The army or the police might try to steal the truck! The official peered glumly through the scratched windscreen and said nothing.

The first two confrontations went smoothly enough. While the papers were scrutinised in the road below, Alan muttered something and his partner fished in his pocket. A rapid crackle followed as the money changed hands. The barrier was lifted and very gently we continued on our way. Janie asked how much had been paid.

'Z 30 – that is Zaires. There are fifty to the pound, so it cost us sixty pence.'

'The note looked enormous.'

'There are no coins. Money is bulky here.' Alan nodded at the briefcase.

'But sixty pence. I mean, what's the worry?'

'It's a lot in Zaire. A soldier's salary will be about five or ten quid a month, *if* it arrives. They ask for what they think they can get.'

Three barricades later, the officer in charge, supported by a machine gun contingent, demanded the equivalent of forty pounds. With his bush-hat worn at a tilt, his dark glasses, bandolier, swagger-stick and flapping boots, he looked exactly like what he was – a pirate. Alan and the official disappeared several times into a tent pitched in the shade of a thorn-tree. The customs man was scandalised at the amount and shared his distress quite openly with us each time he returned to the cab. It was not easy for us either, wedged in our cramped positions.

Alan said it would not help if we got out. The pirate made a great show of directing the rest of the traffic. We felt we were being punished for some obscure crime. Three-quarters of an hour later, a compromise was reached and both sides settled for two pound fifty. Gingerly, Alan eased the lorry past the glaring soldiers and we escaped down the road.

A few minutes later, Alan said we were through the road-blocks because the road no longer ran parallel to the border. Everyone sighed with relief and the official even managed a grin. About forty minutes later, we arrived in Lubumbashi and were dropped off at the Hotel Shaba in pouring rain.

7

Janie. . .
Entering Zaire was like climbing a high wall, in ignorance and
fear of what lay on the other side. But the Hotel Shaba was an
oasis of surprising charm and plenty. It was lunch-time and we
noticed to our delight a restaurant with white linen, a large
gleaming refrigerator and a central table groaning with fruit and
European wines. There was home-made ravioli, fresh vegetable
soup, frogs' legs fried in garlic, a dozen meat and fish dishes,
crêpes flambées and Swiss cheeses. We hadn't eaten so well in
years. Talking to the waiters, I was pleased to find my O-level
French returning. The children giggled when I replaced forgotten
French words with Shona ones.

The hotel cost more than we could afford. We were not
allowed to share one double room and twenty pounds a night
left a hole in our budget. What's more, the plumbing was
thoroughly un-British. We had to wash and brush our teeth in a
communal shower.

Most of the rooms were taken by Americans. Next to us were
four earnest men, engaged on a feasibility study of rural
electrification. What they made of the plumbing I didn't
enquire. One door was labelled 'Health Logistics'. It was open
so I knocked and went in. Jeff Hoover of USAID explained to me
the health policies of Zaire, the programme he was planning
and the problems it involved. So much went missing when aid
was distributed through the Zairean government that the
Americans now channel their health budget into mission
hospitals. We talked about my work in health education in
Zimbabwe and he asked casually if I was interested in a job,
coordinating an immunisation campaign.

'We don't have a very large budget I'm afraid, only $75 million.'

Charles. . .

The United States invests in Zaire to keep at bay the 'communists' who rule its neighbours, Angola and the Congo Republic. Shaba province produces 60% of the world's cobalt, which is used in high-speed aircraft production. Uncle Sam likes to pose as the self-elected defender of freedom and democracy but, here as elsewhere, he pays a heavy price. President Mobutu Sese Seko is one of the world's richest men. His system of government is best described as a kleptocracy – rule by thieves. Amnesty International, in a report made public in 1986, has described the torture of political prisoners in Zaire as routine and endemic. Early in 1987, a young exile committed suicide on the tarmac at Brussels airport, rather than return to Kinshasa under duress.

Janie. . .

That evening, Alan returned with a Zairean business contact who was willing to cash our traveller's cheques.

'This is Laurent and Yvette.'

Laurent was tall and energetic; Yvette, friendly and chic.

'I am so sorry that I am being late,' Laurent said, setting down his walkie-talkie. 'The plane did not arrive with my chicken food. Storms in South Africa. When are there *not* storms in South Africa? Then we have the usual trouble with the customs.'

He smiled round the table and accepted a drink. It struck me as odd that a country as large and fertile as Zaire should need to import chicken food.

'That's normal,' Alan said. 'The Zairois are great traders, but they don't grow or manufacture very much. The vegetables in your soup come from a Chinese co-op outside town.'

'The beer's good,' said Charlie, 'and the bread.'

'The Europeans taught us to import everything we need,' said Laurent. 'All the barley and wheat comes here from America. Now the *Maréchal* tries to keep us happy with beer at Z 20 a pint.'

Yvette picked up her husband's briefcase and asked to see our bedroom. Once there, she locked the door and took out a plastic shopping-bag full of notes. We counted the money together and

I hid it under the mattress. I felt very innocent about becoming a criminal.

'*Méfiez-vous de tout le monde,*' she said. '*Comprenez* – understand?'

I nodded, even though I didn't.

Daisy. . .
Although the hotel was posh, our bed was like a valley. In the morning we had breakfast and went out for a walk. The streets were wide and full of rubbish and pools of water. Only the main street had a tarred surface. It was raining and the buildings looked dirty.

On a corner near the hotel, we found a strange hairdressing salon. It was just a stool and an old box inside a concrete shell. Someone had built a row of shops but they never got finished. Mummy said I could have my hair done. I took my own hairbrush as an Afro comb would have been useless. We looked at a board with pictures of different styles. The Zaire women have plaits which stick out from their heads like tufty spikes. I chose a style called Maya, because that's my middle name. Five women stood around me and plaited my hair in 'cane rows'. They didn't really know how to cope with such long straight hair and laughed a lot about it.

Then we went shopping. Dad said his socks were too hot. We didn't like his smelly feet much either, so we all looked for thin socks for him. When we found some, Mum got excited because they came from a famous shop in Paris. We stopped to buy doughnuts. They were covered in hundreds of bees. The shopkeeper didn't mind. He just put his hand in and picked them up. We saw several disabled men in three-wheeler chairs which they pedalled along with their hands. One stopped to ask us for a cigarette and put it in his sock.

Janie. . .
After lunch, the children led us through the drizzle to Lubumbashi zoo. The gardens were laid out on a grand scale but something was missing. Each tree along the path carried a notice: 'Patrons are requested not to pick the flowers, feed the

animals or take photographs': also pictures of elephant and ibis, camel, cheetah and kudu, with a finger in the corner pointing to where they lived. But where were the animals?

'Many were eaten,' a keeper told us, 'during the crisis of 1978.'

'The crisis of 1978?'

'Yes. An invasion of rebel army from Angola. Many people hungry. We have crocodile! Come with me.'

He grabbed a white egret which was pecking a cigarette end by his feet and took us to see an ancient crocodile, lounging against a dam.

'*Allez Marie Antoinette,*' he said. '*Allez!*'

She opened one eye, saw the egret flapping desperately just out of reach and pounced with alarming swiftness. The egret disappeared, all except for one feather which clung to a warty upper lip. Marie Antoinette went back to sleep.

The keeper showed us a bird resembling a dodo, for which the French name was 'clog-face', and a skinny lioness prowling her island. We met a small boy who said that a mother had rested her baby on the lioness's wall. The baby fell off and, before anyone could act, the lioness ate it. We stared and the lioness stared hungrily back.

We came to a hyena's pen. No hyena was inside but we read the following notice instead:

Hyène. Les sexes sont très difficiles à distinguer car la femelle possède un clitoris très développé en forme de penis.

Next door was a chimp. 'Patrons are requested not to supply the chimpanzee with cigarettes.' Orlando gave it a roasted mealie. This caused the small boy to exclaim in horror, so we gave him one too.

More islands with solitary monkeys who stopped catching flies to wave to us. They got a sandwich and clapped in gratitude, baring their teeth.

The children played for a while with the boy and his mates in an empty monkey-cage. Charlie and I dozed on a bench. The heavy scent of frangipani mingled with lion musk. Goats and peacocks wandered over to take the crumbs of our lunch.

'Oh look!' shouted Joseph. 'A chicken!'

It was a fish eagle, hunched on the floor of a cage with no

room to spread its wings. Then Orlando found some kittens behind bars: he was most indignant. Next door was an obese jaguar who clearly wanted to eat them. We came across a cage full of crows and another of pigeons. A row of perches sported one tatty parrot.

'Over there!' said Charlie. 'It *must* be something good.'

A keeper beckoned us into his dark aquarium. Proudly he showed us the water bubbling through the tanks. There were no fish.

Charles. . .

The next stage on our route to Kinshasa was a train journey to the rail-head at Ilebo. We tried unsuccessfully to make some useful contacts. While Janie was looking for the British honorary consul, I took a taxi to the Anglican bishop. Both were out of town for the week. In the evening, we had a drink with the Americans, who were blasé and unreassuring. If they wanted to travel into the bush, they took a jeep. We watched them loading one with blankets, tins of food, Coke, beer, water, a kerosene cooker, shovels and metal tracks for soft ground. For longer journeys they flew. Although they were too polite to say so, they clearly believed we were mad.

Janie had been to the station and discovered that the weekly *rapide* left for Ilebo the next morning at eight. This was a piece of good luck. The journey was scheduled to take three days. It would cost us £23 for an adult fare in the *première grande classe de luxe*. The distance was roughly the same as from London to Vienna, so this seemed reasonable.

8

Janie. . .

Thursday, February 28th. Left the hotel at seven-thirty a.m. The cart, called a *chariot*, that took our luggage to the station, cost us £2. Charlie, worried about the time, refused to bargain. He had been up since six, going from office to office sorting out the tickets. Our rucksacks are far too heavy! It's ridiculous not being able to walk further than a hundred yards. We shall have to get rid of something, but what? Reducing our possessions from a houseful to four rucksacks seemed enough of a gesture against materialism at the time.

The train was in, painted brown and cream and absolutely filthy. The deluxe carriage looked no different from the others. At first I refused to believe it was ours. Our compartment was the only one with four beds intact. Was this just chance or had we been favoured again? Other people's bunks had lost their plastic covers; the foam rubber had been torn out in chunks or in some cases gone missing altogether. We had no table, the window wouldn't stay up and the shutters were smashed, but still we were lucky. Ordinary first class had no windows at all. Two Zairois women pushed past me in the corridor and when they saw their home for the next three days, disembowelled and thick with grime, they shrieked with laughter and clapped their hands.

Boys are selling empty Johnny Walker bottles to the passengers. They're asking £1 for them. Others are selling candles. We were warned last night that there would be no water or light on the train. Charlie is filling our plastic container from a tap on the platform. I hope it's clean.

Orlando. . .
There was a white man in the same corridor as us. He came from Australia and his name was Bruce. He was very big indeed. He was eating plain spaghetti with a spoon. Daisy told him where to meet the prettiest prostitutes in Africa, at the Castle Hotel in Mombasa. He said he wasn't interested much.

Janie. . .
Eight in the evening, by candlelight. We stopped at Likasi for four hours. This part of Zaire is relatively prosperous and heavily populated but the arrival of a train is still an important event. The guards evicted several people who were travelling without tickets. One man was carried past our window by his arms and legs.

When we get to Kamina, we shall have to buy some more supplies. There is a magnificent kitchen in the next carriage with charcoal stoves behind a long zinc counter but they have run out of food already. Before sunset we had a Lubumbashi picnic: Provençal pâté, cream and herb cheese, sweet bread and French wine. The lights came on for five minutes and then expired. We have cockroaches for company – the flying variety. It is raining hard with flashes of lightning. We have wedged the window up with pencils. Next door is a family with no windows and no candle. They were sitting in the dark with the wind and rain pouring in and all we could see were eight pairs of eyes. We gave them a candle which they stuck in the remains of their *sadza*. Then we gathered round it and sang to each other.

Charles. . .
Our mood has varied wildly. I cannot make up my mind whether to read the book on my lap or look out of the window. Scrub, damp hills, small patches of cultivation, huts the same grey colour as the soil. The sky is grey too. Dizziness and boredom always get the better of me just before something interesting comes along. We passed several copper mines and their housing compounds, the serried rows of tin shacks looking like a Chinese poster of the Good Life. Children wave to us from a clearing. I nearly missed the Zaire river, flowing northwards

roughly 2,500 miles from its estuary and already as wide as the Thames at Richmond.

Cooped up in this small space, we inevitably get to feel claustrophobic and irritated with each other. The Swiss army knife disappeared for a while and caused a general panic. The children's squabbling drives me to distraction. I wonder too about what we're heading towards. Were we right to ignore the warnings? The train's progress is inexorable.

Daisy. . .
Orlando has stuck up a sign.
   This is a privat department. Please nock.
He and Joseph have made lots of other pictures and no smoking notices as well. I have been giving my Cindy doll Zaire-style plaits. We made paper windmills and held them out of the window on the end of a pencil. They went whizzing round like a propeller. It was great fun until Orlando dropped one and got into trouble with Dad. He said it was his best drawing pencil. We shouted to all the children as we passed them. We could be as rude as we liked because we used Shona and no one could understand.

Janie. . .
Kamina station. Mid-morning on March 1st. We have been here for two hours already. Six Belgian sisters have just arrived. They say that the train may leave at midday or perhaps this evening. There are only two beds in their cabin but they don't seem ruffled by this. They wear bright-blue cotton frocks in stripes and flowers. The station looks like an Impressionist painting – faded blue paint on the weatherboards and peeling maroon columns. Soldiers are slumped in the shadows.

Charles. . .
In the night at Tenke, another train drew up alongside us. I was woken from a troubled sleep by squealing brakes and darkened carriages thudding past the window. I thought at first it was carrying copper. Then Janie pointed up the line: women and

children were clambering out of a goods wagon. We heard voices and saw a flicker of candlelight. The train shunted backwards and a dim interior came into view with bodies slumped on wooden benches or laid asleep along the luggage-racks. Their faces were in the last stages of fatigue and resignation, drained of all life. It was like a dream – the cattle-trucks that trundled into Auschwitz and Belsen. A cargo of doomed souls. A man was sitting with his elbow resting on the window-ledge, looking out. I went down onto the track.

'Monsieur, where are you coming from?'

'From Kivu.'

'Where is that?'

'To the north-east.'

'How many days?'

'Four days.'

'Are you well?'

He looked surprised at this.

'*Ah non, c'est l'enfer!* Pure hell.'

'You are American?' asked another man.

'No, English, from Zimbabwe.'

'Zimbabwe? Where is that?'

'In the south. Rhodesia.'

'Rhodesia? You are from there?'

I explained I was a teacher. A quiet voice came out of the gloom.

'We are enchanted to make your acquaintance, monsieur.'

Janie. . .

We have just been to the station yard and bought our lunch. Brown gritty *rapoko sadza* and chewy meat. A row of women sat behind their charcoal fires, water on the boil and the fat sizzling in readiness for the train. The male passengers squat on low benches. The food costs Z 30 a plateful. The sisters say that derailments are common on this line and we should eat plenty while we can.

We have been trying to get the Primus stove alight but without success because we've no meths. Each time it lets out a sheet of flame which threatens to set the compartment on fire. The guard has offered to boil our water for us. He said his stomach was aching, so we gave him some worm mixture in exchange. At least it can't do him any harm.

I took my turn at a concrete wash-tub on the platform and rinsed out our clothes. We have put up a line which zigzags between the upper bunks. Charlie found another tap beside the track at the end of the train. Several families were washing there and the sight of his bare white chest sent a baby girl into squeals of terror.

Orlando has just run along the platform in his bare feet. A boy his own age instantly spotted an opportunity, pulled off his own plastic sandals and offered them for sale.

A drunk is lecturing us from the platform. He must have seen the sisters.

'In France there are philosophers. In Brazil there are philosophers. So why not in Zaire are there also philosophers? In Europe you pray to your God for yourselves, only yourselves. Why do you not pray for Africa? In Zaire, we have our own God.'

Now we are leaving at last. The sisters are leaning out and waving their clean white hankies. In the distance, the steps of a mission hospital are lined with waving nurses.

Charles. . .
Saturday, 2nd March. All day, the train has slowly hauled itself across the savannah. The track keeps to the high ground and often we can see thirty miles or more of rolling hills and tall dry grass. It's Nature, pure and beautiful, untouched and empty.

'No cows, no sheep,' observed Bruce.

'It's like a great big golf course,' said Orlando.

Once or twice an hour humans have appeared, standing on a muddy road which crosses our track. Their presence only increases the sense of isolation. The Belgian sisters tell us that the whole area is infertile and plagued by the tsetse fly. There is very little game. Later, they call us to point out a line of electricity pylons built by the Americans. We stare, not so much because the idea of pylons in this wilderness is eerie and unexpected, but because they looked so reassuringly normal. We are beginning to feel our customary points of reference slipping away. I am struck by a disturbing sense of futility.

What's it all *for*, this empty expanse? Is this the wide heartland of Africa – that poetic void so beloved of philosophers and game-hunters?

Every traveller presumably has to cope with it. We carry out familiar, routine tasks. The businessman looks for clients. The missionary establishes a church, a school and a clinic. The hunter pitches camp. Janie and I have the children and each other to look after.

Janie. . .
In the tiny stations we pass through, hundreds of people appear with food to sell. Plantain bananas two feet long, bright red and orange chillis, avocado pears and insects, Z 1 a handful, both cooked and uncooked. The fried caterpillars taste like fish. The termites have pincers and wriggling feet, so you pinch their heads before putting them in your mouth.

Charles. . .
In the evening, the locomotive broke down so we all climbed out and sat on the grass. Leaving behind the domain of *première grande classe de luxe*, we were frequently asked why we were travelling.

'*Vous êtes touristes?*'

They clearly didn't believe us. What would become of our children?

'Why is it that you ask that?'

They only looked away and shook their heads, smiling.

'Tcha. You travel in Zaire with your infants. *Mais pourquoi?*'

'To look at your country,' said Janie.

'To look?' replied the women. 'There is nothing to look at!' And they shrieked with laughter at the idea, slapping each other's hands in recognition of a good joke.

I met two '*apôtres*', members of the Apostolic Faith, sometimes called the Church of Zion. In Zimbabwe they can be seen under a tree on a Saturday afternoon, dressed in white and red and carrying crooks. The men shave their heads and grow beards. They keep themselves apart from society and there was some resistance to government policy on free education and health care. A song making gentle fun of them was number one in the Zimbabwean hit parade for several months. *Ndinoda tii obvu* – I like thick tea. They were rather proud of this and I passed a vaPostori house with *Tii Obvu* on its gate.

The Zairois *apôtre* was an afflicted man. His friend told me that he had heart disease. We had a long talk about his misfortunes, stretching back to a grim childhood. He was convinced a curse had been put on him. The train had restarted by this time and we prayed together in the corridor while people pushed past us.

The breakdown delayed our arrival at Ilebo to midday on Sunday. Throughout the last morning the train clattered downhill. It grew hotter and hotter and the landscape closed in so that branches thwacked against our window. The guard was standing in the corridor with a Lingala hymn-book, a far-away expression on his face, crooning to himself. Janie locked herself into an empty compartment to dictate a description of the train into a Walkman for BBC radio. If the official had found out, she could have been in trouble, but she wanted the singing as background music.

Every so often, the guard suggested we gather up our belongings, but the heat had made us lethargic. When Ilebo appeared outside, we were still hunting socks and saucepan lids in the muck beneath the benches.

9

Charles. . .

At Ilebo, the background on our Michelin map turned green. To the west the equatorial rain forest of the Congo basin thrust southwards along the rivers Kasai, Loange, Wamba, Kwilu and Kwango. The route to Kinshasa lay across these deep valleys and the high savannah in between. Copper from the mines in Shaba made the journey by barge down the Kasai, a treacherous river with sudden floods and shifting sands. A weekly passenger boat to Kinshasa was supposed to connect with the train.

We passed our belongings in a dozen bits and pieces out of the window onto the platform. We were feeling flustered by the sticky heat. Bruce and I were directed to a small hut in the station yard. It was dark inside, crowded and so hot that the sweat trickled off my chest and blotched the form I was given to fill in.

Name, age, place of birth, nationality, name of spouse, age of spouse, place of birth of spouse, nationality of spouse. When Evelyn Waugh crossed from the Belgian Congo into Northern Rhodesia in 1959, he was asked to supply the sex of his spouse and the details of his six children who were tucked up in bed in England. Zaire has immigration officers at every point of arrival and departure within the country. It appears to be a sinister form of movement control by a police state but the system would long ago have ceased to function were it not also a lucrative pastime.

Bruce was soon involved in an exchange, conducted on his side in a bizarre language I can only call 'Froz', which disconcerted the official by its power of invective. A soldier with an automatic weapon left off lounging against the door jamb.

'Pay him Bruce, for God's sake,' I said.

'How much shall I give the bastard?'

'Try Z 50.'

The official sat at a table which took up a quarter of the hut, wearing dark glasses despite the gloom and a beret pulled down over one ear. He took my passports next and alarmed me by placing them in a drawer. I dug into the belt-purse beneath my trousers and got out the card supplied to us by the Zaire embassy in Harare. A receptionist with an expensive hairdo had pressed it on me.

'Take this. You never know when you might need it.'

'Is tourism dangerous in Zaire then?'

'How should I know, I've never been there.'

'Excuse me for saying so but isn't that a London accent?'

'I'm from Ghana but I used to live in Clapham.'

The card was written in English.

Dear Tourists, Welcome to the Republic of Zaire.

Madam, Sir,

On behalf of the President-Founder of the MPR, President of the Republic, of his Government and of my fellow citizens, it is agreeable for me to wish you a wonderful sojourn in the Republic of Zaire.

In this country, you will discover majestic sites, a luxuriant flora and an exceptional fauna.

The kindness and hospitality of the Zairois people will facilitate your knowledge of their tradition and folklore.

Our young Nation expects much from your suggestions and thanks you for your contribution in helping it to welcome the friends you will send us in a much better way.

Zairois, help our visitors. The friend holding this card is our guest. By helping him, you help our country. Never forget that tourism provides us with returns which allow us to create new jobs, to build schools, hospitals, factories etc.

On the welcome that our guest would have received will depend our touristic future.

The official frowned at it for a long moment before handing it back. He reached for the passports and put them in front of me, except for Bruce's which he waggled at us, saying something in Lingala which made the soldier grin. Bruce swore and grabbed it and I hustled him outside.

Janie. . .

I had been making enquiries about the passenger boat and learnt that it was stuck and not due for four days. I commandeered a hand-cart similar to the one we had used in Lubumbashi. The youth in charge of it piled up our bags and set off at a gentle run up the hill to the town.

'Blimey,' said Bruce, 'he's trying to lose us.'

We toiled after him. The heat was like nothing we had yet experienced. Humidity seemed to enter the brain. It was just possible to think, provided you did it slowly and concentrated on one thing at a time.

We passed a few whites crossing the street or watching us from doorways. I was wondering how much of an unusual event we were. None of them returned my smile. The whole place was strangely silent. There were no cars, only a few lorries parked haphazardly. The road surface was loose sand which muffled our footsteps.

We came to a roundabout. Someone had been working hard, digging holes and setting white-washed boulders in place. It all seemed rather pointless since there was no traffic. In the centre was a large board with a painting of Mobutu in marshal's uniform. His chest was resplendent with medals and beside his figure were these words:

Le President Fondateur n'est pas un magicien. Seul il ne peut rien faire. Mais, avec l'appui de son peuple, il peut tout.

[The Founder-President is not a magician. Alone he can do nothing. But with the support of his people, he is capable of everything.]

We were looking for the Hotel des Palmes and found it a few yards further on. It was an imposing building with two storeys of stucco colonnades. The main façade looked out over the Kasai. People were sitting on the verandah in vests and straw-hats, drinking beer. We went inside and crowded round the reception desk. A sleepy looking girl appeared and told us there was no room. Everything was taken. *Absolument tout.*

'But that's impossible,' I said, 'there must be dozens of rooms!'

'I am desolated, madame. No chambers.'

I felt completely drained. This was all I needed.

'Never mind,' said Charlie, 'let's have a beer.'

Bruce was already sprawled in a chair with a litre of Skol. The children drank a Fanta each and it seemed to have no effect. Joseph was the colour of a beetroot. Orlando's hair was plastered to his scalp. Daisy sat with her eyes closed, fanning her face with her hat. We ordered two, three, four more Fantas. Minutes after the liquid went down our throats, it reappeared again on the surface of the skin.

We waited forty-five minutes for a sandwich and got a little drunk. At the next table a group of Zairois were drinking with a European. It struck me that he was pointedly ignoring us, as if taking our presence for granted. Bruce breezed over and asked where we could find accommodation. In broken English, the white man described a Catholic mission at the end of town and Charlie volunteered to go there and enquire.

Charles. . .

The sun had finally burnt its way through the fume of humidity and it cleared my throbbing head and restored some clarity to my senses. Two boys attached themselves to me and said they would take me to the mission. We came out onto a wide airstrip. Their friends had set up nets and were busy trapping swallows. In the distance was a derelict transport plane. We passed a hospital and a convent and turned through iron gates into a yard where two men were sitting under a tree. Between them was a large bottom drawer full of loose Zaire notes. They looked up from their counting to direct us to the school on the other side of the runway. The boys were becoming a little tiresome by now and with some expense I got rid of them.

Père Henri offered me a room with two iron bedsteads and a concrete floor. I was reasonably satisfied with this but, as I was leaving, I bumped into the European again. Diffidently, he told me that he was master of a petroleum barge departing for Kinshasa the following morning. Warming to his description of pleasant air-conditioned days on the river, I accepted a lift and hurried back to tell the others.

'One thing though,' he called after me, 'you will need permission from the *chef du zone*. Meet me at the docks at seven o'clock in the morning.'

I found Janie and Bruce established in a beautiful room at the hotel!

We had misunderstood the system. There is always a system in Zaire. In this case Janie stumbled on it by accident. The rooms were all let to a commercial company but she had found an employee who was happy to sub-let and move in with a friend. We had a wide double bed, a noisy air-conditioner, a cracked bidet and a very large bath. Bruce camped out on the verandah and upset the manager's sense of propriety by hanging his clothes over the railing.

Janie. . .
For supper, we had omelettes, baguettes and more cold beer. The children romped around until they were shouted at. The hotel had been built for a visit by King Albert before the First War. The lobby had deep leather armchairs and a mahogany staircase which divided into sweeping curves. There were stuffed heads mounted high on the panelled walls and dusty display cases with samples of minerals and faded raffia work. In seventy years only the colour of the clientèle had changed.

Charles. . .
At seven the next morning, Bruce and I met our friend by his barge and walked across to the docks. Gangs of men were hanging around hoping for work and a diesel locomotive shunted back and forth. We had a long wait and I plied the captain with questions to which he gave terse replies.

He was a Polish refugee who had married a Belgian girl. His master's certificate was acquired on the Rhine. They were out in Zaire on a three-year contract which had six months left to run. He was paid US $40,000 a year, plus an allowance for his family apartment in Kinshasa. He only went upriver for a quarter of each year. The rest of the time he had a desk job.

Despite all this, he was far from content. I realised with increasing dismay that his shyness hid a can of worms. The poor fellow was corroded, eaten up inside with racial cynicism.

Nothing worked. They were idle, corrupt, inefficient, stupid, incapable. The country was all washed up. Finished. *Foutu*. But

53

what could you expect? Their fathers were cannibals. They ate monkey. Monkey! It's . . . it's like eating dog! They didn't care, so why should he? If his boat got stuck, if it sank, it was all the same to him.

Not surprisingly, he was pessimistic about the *chef du zone*.

'He will try to rob you. They're all thieves.'

The prospect of five days in his company was appealing to me less and less.

The *chef* finally turned up and we were shown into his office. He said we would have to pay the equivalent of a first-class fare by way of 'insurance'. Since this amounted to over £200, we declined his offer and bade farewell to our Pole.

'You can always go by road,' he said, 'there are lorries. I told you right, *hein*? This country, *c'est un seau de merde*,' and he went off in gloomy satisfaction to run his boat aground.

We met Janie and the children returning from the market with enough food for the boat trip. This included fifteen loaves of bread and two live chickens hung over Daisy's shoulder. We had a good laugh, packed our bags and went down to the ferry landing where the lorries picked up passengers for Kinshasa.

10

Charles. . .

A muddy track had been cut into the hillside. At the bottom the road disappeared into the Kasai, brown, swirling and wide. A drive-on ferry was moored against the bank and women were using its platform to do their washing. One or two fishermen arrived in dugout canoes, skilfully manoeuvring them across the current.

Rain began to fall, a fine spray of moisture which grew imperceptibly stronger, lighter and stronger again. The sky was a pale green and the temperature was still in the nineties. It was like a Turkish bath. I squeezed into a small, crowded hut. The mud had fallen out of the walls and the palm thatch hung awry over the doorway. Inside a cheerful throng was being entertained by the immigration officer from the railway station. His mood had changed entirely. He waved my papers away and began to question me about Europe, though I soon realised he was not that interested in what I might say. After the weather, housing and wages, we got on to sex. Would I like to swap my wife for one of his? He indicated several candidates on the opposite bench. Uncertain about what he had been saying in French, they offered me toothy smiles. On impulse, I agreed and, going to the door, called Janie over. She made everyone laugh by taking control of the bargaining. How much was the bride-price? How old were his wives? Did he wash behind his ears?

Around four o'clock a lorry showed up and a crowd of people immediately surrounded it. Bruce, who had been waiting patiently on his own, lifted his nose out of a tattered paperback and weighed into the scrum. He was head and shoulders above everyone else. Two men who subsequently became known to us as Marto and André set up a booking office on a beer crate and shouted at us to form a queue. Marto was cross and officious, André indolent and charming. Between them, they tried to extract 4,500 Zaires from me.

'Ah, that is too much!'

'It is a long way to Kinshasa.'

'How many days?' Our Pole had been vague.

'Three days.'

'My children are small.'

'But your baggage is many.'

'Everyone has baggage.'

They shrugged. I was wrong actually. Several young men were embarking on the 900 kilometre journey with only the T-shirts on their backs. Eventually, we agreed on half price for the children but they wanted a full down-payment.

'There's no way I'm going to agree to that,' said Bruce. 'Ten per cent now. The rest if we arrive in one piece.'

They were adamant and started to serve the next customer. For the umpteenth time I wiped my specs on my shirt and tried to take André aside. He made as if he couldn't understand me.

'Half now and half when we arrive?'

He shrugged. Marto looked up and waved his finger from side to side. I stuck 2,000 Zaires (£40) into his hand and watched as he counted them and wrote a figure in his exercise-book. It wasn't enough but he appeared to be satisfied.

Janie. . .

We waited without knowing why. Bruce and André went out in a *pirogue*. A crowd gathered and lent raucous support as Bruce teetered inexpertly and dug the long paddle-blade into the water. It takes a lot of skill to stand upright in a hollowed-out tree trunk. Bruce stayed on his knees and mainly travelled backwards or sideways but he survived without mishap until they were once more in the shallows. Then he transferred his weight rather clumsily out of the boat, sending André flying into the water. There was an explosion of laughter from the onlookers which died nervously when he failed to reappear.

Had he struck his head?

Just as our anxiety turned to alarm, he surfaced several yards away, blowing a spume of spray between his grinning teeth. He waded ashore, making a pantomime of wringing out the towel round his neck so that he could use it to dry himself. He went to chase Bruce, changed his mind, shooed away the children and disappeared into the bushes to remove his trousers.

Charles. . .
The ferry's engines started up and five trucks splashed across the logs and up the ramp. As we moved out into midstream, I was summoned to the bridge and introduced by Marto to a man with a clean white shirt and a leather attaché case. It was *le patron*, the owner of the lorry. He gave me a cursory glance and resumed his conversation with the captain.

'He says you must pay the full amount now,' said Marto.

'Tell him I have paid 2,000 Zaires already.'

'He knows that.'

'I will pay 1,150 Zaires when we reach Kinshasa.'

'That is not acceptable.'

'I will give him a promissory note.'

'What?'

I took out my notebook and wrote a handsome letter to the *patron*. It seemed the most direct way to communicate with him. Marto took the paper from me and held it out but the *patron* continued to scan the open expanses of the river.

'It is not acceptable,' said Marto.

'Look, does he believe that I have the money? Does he want me to show it to him?'

The *patron* spoke in Lingala. Marto translated.

'He wants to know why you cannot trust him.'

'I am asking myself why he does not trust me.'

'If you have the money,' said Marto, 'you can give it to him. It is safer in his case.'

'I have the money. It is his. But I will look after it for him. It is safe here too,' and I tapped the bulge below my waist.

Neither spoke. The *patron* seemed to have forgotten my existence. I took this as my cue to retreat and went back down the ladder.

Janie. . .

It took about ten minutes to cross the Kasai. On the far side, Marto called out the names of the passengers from his exercise-book and, one by one, we scrambled up into the lorry. The back was protected by a frame of steel rods welded together. It was not particularly big and contained a quantity of empty bottles in crates at the front and sacks of cassava towards the rear.

Only now did the truth begin to dawn on me. There were an awful lot of us. Young men, mothers, children, grannies and a smart middle-aged woman with a fragile teapot, which she kept in a blue plastic bucket. I counted twenty-nine other people on Marto's list and they installed themselves in all the most comfortable nooks among the cassava sacks. With some difficulty, we found a niche for Joseph behind a drum of diesel. Daisy and Orlando squeezed in next to the blue bucket. The two chickens ended up inside the spare tyre. Bruce was perched above the cage. I found myself squashed beside a young woman clutching a hold-all which she dumped on my legs. I felt envious of Charlie who had a place next to the edge where he could stretch his limbs.

Charles. . .

There was a hubbub of bickering and complaints as people fought to establish rights over their corner. The tension was getting to us and it was not an auspicious start. A boy called to me from the road, smiling and waving his arms like branches in a gale but, before I could interpret his message, the lorry roared into life. With a grinding of gears that filled us with alarm, it moved off very slowly up a steep hill.

Almost at once, we lurched violently against the bank and tore our way through a tangle of thorny creepers. I started back in alarm. My hand could have been snapped off at the wrist, my skin lacerated, my flesh shredded from the bone. The other passengers looked placidly back down the hill. The next moment we swung the other way and I was thrown heavily, trapping my ear between my skull and the iron cage. I smiled grimly. No one took any notice. The lorry continued its patient climb. Every lurch was accompanied by an agitation of sound. The beer bottles clattered, the baby cried, Joseph called out in alarm, the chassis creaked and groaned. Disintegration, capsize, the perishing and destruction of all on board seemed imminent.

At length, we reached the top and a short stretch of firmer road lay ahead. We accelerated to fifteen miles an hour. A gentle breeze ruffled my hair. Someone started to sing and several voices picked up the refrain. Cautiously I raised myself and looked round. André and Marto were sitting up front with their arms on each other's shoulders and their feet resting on the driver's cab. They were exuberant about the open road, singing lustily and holding up André's wet shirt like a pennant. A low tree appeared round a bend and they got down onto the cab roof to avoid it.

'Attention! Attention!'

A moment later there was another, and another. A bough three inches thick caught Janie a clunk across the head and she was forced to grin through a gale of unkind laughter. The children took up the cry.

'Attershaw!'

'Watch out Mum!'

'Attershaw!'

'This is fun!'

Janie. . .

Only an hour of daylight was left when we set off. At dusk we stopped to buy more sacks of cassava. The *patron*, who rode in the cab along with two girl-friends and the driver, struck a bargain with a peasant. He had lugged his crop to the roadside and sat waiting for a buyer. Loading the stuff meant shifting everyone from their jealously guarded territory. It was done by three ragged young men who normally stood on the tailgate. André and Marto watched and commented on their efforts but made no effort to help them. Each sack weighed well over a hundredweight and the hard bony roots protruded through the hessian. When we went back to our places, they were all a little higher and more exposed to the branches.

Charles. . .

The headlights were broken. About two kilometres further

down the road it became too dark to continue. We started to climb off yet again but the *patron* told us to stay put. We waited on the lorry for thirty minutes while the driver, a short friendly man in grubby white overalls, poked unhopefully with a screwdriver. We were plainly going to be here for the night.

An unruly crowd of children taunted Orlando. When matters threatened to get out of hand, a man took off his belt and whipped them away.

Marto and André were talking about hotel accommodation. They were concerned that we should find European beds though it didn't seem very likely to me.

'We will find something for you, *pas de problème.*'

'Madame, there is a mission along the road. Good fathers.'

'Is it far?'

'Two kilometres, maybe four.'

'I don't believe it for one minute. Anyway the children are too tired to walk.'

Janie spotted a painted signboard. *Hôtel Basongo. Pension 30 Z.* Sixty pence a night?

'How about there?' she said and, ignoring their protests, took Daisy off to investigate.

'It must be okay,' I called after her, seeing the *patron's* girls take his luggage in. We were given two rooms with double beds. They were tiny mud-walled cells grouped round a central courtyard.

Bruce was there too.

'Blimey it's dark. Where's the shit-house?'

We were the only passengers able to afford this luxury. The rest slept among their belongings, either on top of the truck or in the road beneath it. We bumped and groped around. The children were very tired after such a long, unpredictable day and they fell asleep almost immediately. We fetched water for the chickens and I tied them to a leg of the bed. Then we put our padlock on the door and went to find a drink.

The villagers were used to moving about freely after dark. The road was crowded with laughing, jostling young men calling to each other in the velvety blackness. Little paraffin lamps were spluttering in the cool dew which brought out goose pimples on our sunburnt arms. There were rickety stalls selling cigarettes and perfume. We found cool beer and dined off three or four of our loaves and some sardines.

The moon was up. The lager fizzed. It was one of those moments when a cigarette tastes like a million dollars. André had lured Bruce into buying a round for his table. No one hassled us. For a rare precious moment, Janie and I were alone.

'Glad we're not on the boat with that Pole?' she said.

'You bet. It's not too bad so far, is it?'

'Not bad at all. I just hope the kids don't get bored and restless. That Mrs Blue Bucket is so bossy! And the *patron*! He obviously thinks we're much less important than his sacks of cassava.'

'We're probably worth less. I wonder what the mark-up is in Kinshasa? We're a lot more trouble, that's for sure.'

'What time are we leaving in the morning?'

'I think André said dawn.'

'Don't let him cadge off you. He's always after something.'

'I know. He's a scoundrel. I love him.'

'I think he fancies me. I keep getting smouldering looks.'

Soon after, we went to bed. The room smelt of old mud and stale sheets. I could hear the occupant of the next room breathing. I lay on my back and wondered – how fragile must a wall be, before it no longer makes one feel secure? The room was like a theatre set; an arm could have been thrust straight through the wattle. Yet for some reason I felt trustful and content. It was bugs within the stained sagging mattress that I dreaded most.

We slept. The bugs slept too, if there were any.

At five-thirty I was jerked awake by a violent outbreak of strangled cries right beneath the bed.

We had bought cockerels who obeyed the call to crow.

61

11

Janie. . .
A chilly start. Mist lay among the trees. People were already hard at work as we passed, hoeing their plots of land. On the lorry, the passengers huddled into their blankets and stared empty-eyed. The *patron* made another stop which lasted over an hour. I counted on fourteen more sacks of cassava. Surely we must be close to overloading?

The road plunged down and up across the river valleys. The bends and high banks were more perilous when descending than climbing out. The lorry slithered sideways in low gear, swaying and creaking. Seldom was the driver able to apply his brakes and he gambled heroically with the slimy surface and deep crevices.

On the bank of the Loange, conditions became even worse. We wallowed through a pit of liquid mud which churned and swilled around the axles. The loaders got filthy, stuffing branches under the rear wheels as the lorry tried to climb out. The air behind us filled with flying mud which spattered into the surrounding bush.

Next we were told to get down and walk. We plodded along in the sapping humidity for about two kilometres. Mrs Blue Bucket took off her shoes and carried them on her head. Joseph rode on Charlie's shoulders. The road was scored with ditches where the rushing water had eaten away the surface. Some were deep enough to conceal a person.

Men overtook us carrying palm wine in a row of calabashes, nestling in long baskets balanced on their heads. We passed through a small settlement. The climate must have destroyed the mud walls almost as soon as they were built. On one solid patch a philosopher had daubed:

OASIS DE PAIX. D'être pauvre n'est pas un crime.
[Oasis of Peace. To be poor is not a crime.]

We were getting hungry. No one had found time for breakfast before we left, so we were grateful when the lorry stopped at another river-crossing. There was a food-stall and I asked them to fill a bottle with tea. It took longer than I had anticipated and I had to leap the gap as the ferry pulled away from the bank. On the far side immigration officers were holding up the traffic and we had plenty of time for more beer, coffee and bread-rolls.

Charles. . .
We climbed aboard once more, but not for long. Two miles into the forest there was a dull crack and the suspension broke. We shouted and the driver pulled over. The loaders jumped down and stood scratching their heads. It was a serious injury. The bit of metal that held the rear leafspring under tension had come away from the chassis. Four bolts had sheered through. We were stuck.

The *patron* took the news calmly. He reached into the cab for his briefcase and strolled off up the road. André and Marto looked at the stricken undercarriage, shook their heads and tutted. The driver took control. A few hundred yards from the river we had passed a dead truck lying on its side in the undergrowth. A few of us walked back to it, armed with a spanner and some bolt-cutters. We prodded around and discussed the design of truck suspensions. The wreck was entirely incompatible and there was nothing doing.

By this time, I was so hot that I decided to return to the river and have a bathe. I found a tree on the bank whose roots provided a seat under the water. The brown water surged past. I ignored the risk of bilharzia and soaped myself from head to foot. Then I got dressed, bought an armful of Cokes and trudged back to the truck.

Janie. . .
The lorry limped along to a small settlement which opened onto the road. The children and I rested with the others under a thatched shelter. Charlie's appearance was most welcome.

'Monsieur Charles has brought us beer,' exclaimed André, making a lunge for the bottles.

'Where is the beer, Monsieur Charles? *Donnez-moi, donnez, donnez.*'

He and Marto were playing with our pocket-set of Chinese chequers. Joseph was sitting as close as he could to their cigarette smoke to gain protection from the small black flies. The Coke soon went but it didn't take our thirst with it.

'What's water, Mum?' asked Daisy.

'*L'eau.* Say *où est l'eau*?'

'Ooay low? Ooay low?'

The villagers pointed listlessly to a path between the huts and went on skinning cassava roots. They were preparing another sack or two for the *patron*. Daisy and Orlando wandered off but soon returned, sweaty and dispirited.

'We can't find it.'

'Well I can't do anything about it, darling.'

'We're thirsty.'

'So are we all.'

'These flies are beastly.'

'I can't breathe.'

'*L'eau, c'est loin*? Far away?' asked Charlie.

Not far, they said. Follow the path down the hill.

'It must be a stream,' I said. 'Come on, we'll all go.'

'What about the lorry?'

'Dad, you go and check with them.'

Charlie. . .

The crew were trying to jack up the rear axle without unloading several tons of cassava first. The jack they had was far too small and each time they got the wheels off the ground it disappeared into the soft sand. Various chunks of bruised timber lay around. Now they had brought along a giant boulder and were digging a hole for it.

The driver was the only one with any French.

'How will you mend it?' I asked.

'With wood, till we reach Idiofa. There are workshops there.'

'Do you know how you will mend it with wood?'

'Not yet.'

'How many hours?'

'Who knows?'

'We are going to the water.'

'Okay.'

I followed the others. The path led between dry mealie stalks where tiny chicks fled cheeping at our approach. Janie had one of the cockerels under her arm.

'Got your knife, Charlie?'

We left the last hut behind and walked downhill into the forest for about a mile. We passed children climbing the other way with full buckets on their heads. The ground was wet from frequent splashing. For the villagers by the road, fetching water must have been a major task.

It was really very beautiful but I was not in a mood to see it. The sun filtered through the canopy and the children ran ahead, whooping and shrieking. Feeling morbid and enervated, I picked my way past greasy roots and over fallen tree trunks, blooming with fungi. I seemed to be entering a damp pit of contagion.

Supposing one of us fell sick here? How would we get out? Jolted by the lorry, exposed to the sun. For how many days? We were still 150 kilometres from Idiofa. The road was marked in red and white dots on the map: *surface liable to disintegration: unpassable during the wet season*. A hundred and fifty kilometres at ten to fifteen miles an hour. That was ten hours – *if* they mended the spring – *if* it held! Surely they must ditch some cassava. But he was buying still more. Perhaps they would ditch *us*? The path went on and on. Where was that bloody water?

'Here Dad, down here!'

'Come and join us, it's lovely.'

'It's really magic, Dad.'

I came upon a shallow stream. Three inches of water flowing clear and cool over silver sand.

'Mummy's naked.'

'There are fish-traps.'

'Come and help us make a dam.'

'Look, I'm Tarzan.'

'Careful Orlando!' I said. 'How do you know it won't break?'

'It's incredible Dad. It must be a hundred feet long.'

'I can't see what is holding it at the top.'

'Charlie, come and help me with this chicken.'

'Ah, poor thing,' said Daisy, 'it's so scrawny.'

'Joseph's doing a poo.'

'Not in the water Joe! Go along the bank a bit.'

'I can't.'

'Why not?'

'There are women washing their clothes.'

Janie. . .

We looked up. The women seemed becalmed in the beauty of the place. I grabbed a *khanga* and wrapped it round myself. We waved and they shouted greetings.

'Perhaps I can do a bit of washing too,' I said.

I went over. I had some shallots in my bag and exchanged them for a bar of soap.

A small girl tried to shoo the children away from her fish-traps among the rocks. They were intricate little baskets, woven out of vine. She removed a small, whiskered fish, wrapped it carefully in a leaf and tucked it into her knickers.

'Ooh, it's cold.'

'Orlando!' shouted Daisy. 'Daddy, Orlando pushed me in!'

'Come on,' Charlie said. 'Let's walk along a bit. She'll never catch any fish if we splash around here.'

'I want to make a dam.'

'Okay, we'll find a good place.'

The next few hours were spent making dams and a wooden bridge. Pirates attacked, led by Joseph in a battleship. A tidal wave destroyed the bridge at the third attempt. The cockerel was plucked and drawn but there was no fire on which to cook it. By four o'clock, we were all feeling hungry and the children were shivering. It was time to leave our idyll and return to the flies, the *patron* and the sickly smell of cassava.

Charles. . .

We found the men still in a huddle around the wheel. It was clear we were there for the night. The children decided to pitch the tent. Janie made a fire with plenty of helpful advice from

André. I climbed up and rummaged for our cooking pot and we put the chicken on to boil with some onions and rice. We were so absorbed by the promise of supper that it came as a complete surprise when the lorry set off without us.

I fought with the tent, losing half the pegs in the process. The children leapt from bush to bush grabbing T-shirts and *khangas* which had been left to dry. Janie ran with the pot full of half-stewed food. It sloshed out under the lid and scalded her fingers. André and Marto reached down to grab us.

'Come on madame, this is not a picnic. *Allez-oop.* Hurry now. *Dépêchez-vous.*'

'Where is Joseph?' asked Daisy.

'You're sitting on top of me.'

'This is too much!' Janie said. 'How far are we going?'

Darkness was falling.

'To a village, madame. Not far.'

'Is there a bar?' I asked.

'Nice bar, monsieur. Cold beer. Cigarettes. You like dancing?'

This time, we all gasped and braced ourselves whenever the lorry swayed. Slowly and painstakingly, it lumbered out of the Loange valley. I watched Bruce as he ladled a tin of sausage and beans into his mouth. We were crossing high ground by moonlight. Twenty minutes later, we entered a village and stopped outside a hut.

'This is the bar.'

I was too sick and tired to move. Janie went inside and came back with two bottles of warm Fanta.

'Where's the beer?'

'There *is* none. This is all the drink in the village.'

'Food?'

'Nothing.'

It was ridiculous. How had I got into this state? I wanted to howl and sob. I began searching feverishly in the dark for the paraffin stove, hurling luggage to left and right. Then I tried to get it going on the sand. We had no methylated spirit. Why, oh why not? Each time I pumped up pressure and released the spray, a sheet of flame roared into the sky. The children were crying. People were milling around and bumping into me. It was coming, I couldn't stop it.

'Aaaaaaagh!' I cried, 'won't some-bo-dy help me!'

Janie. . .

A woman brought me kindling and glowing embers and we soon had a fire going. We ate the rice a while later but the chicken was tougher than old boots. We were shown a room in a hut nearby. The beds were cane pallets and it was very hot, so we decided to sleep outside on the sand. Charlie and the kids dropped off immediately and I went to investigate some drumming further along the road.

A group of schoolchildren were dancing and making whoopee in the moonlight. When I pulled out my tape-recorder, they thought it was a camera and posed in a grinning bunch. I played back their chatter to them and then the singing really took off.

Later I lay down to sleep with the others on the sand. The mosquitoes were whining round my head and I cocooned myself in the sleeping-sheet I had invented. It came right over my head with a gauze window to breathe through. I woke with a red bump where the material had touched my cheek.

12

Charles. . .

'Charlie, come down,' Janie said. 'There's food here.'

'Food?'

'Yes, rice things, and samosas.'

'Vin de palme, Monsieur Bruce,' André called. *'Venez boire avec nous!'*

'Heh, yo! *Monsieur Bruce. Venez, venez.'*

'What're they saying?'

'They've got some palm wine for you.'

'Dad, look at these dear little tins,' said Daisy. 'They're like something out of a dolly's shop.'

'Condensed milk, that's lovely stuff. Full of energy too.'

'Buy some for us, Dad.'

'How much are they?'

'Thirteen zee.'

'How many has he got?'

'. . . nine, ten, eleven tins.'

I peeled two notes off the wad in my pocket.

'Here, buy the lot.'

'Great!'

'Give me one!'

'Can you open it for me, Dad?'

'No, save it for later. Have some of these rice cookies now. Look they're nice.'

'I don't like them.'

'Try one, Joe. They're not spicy. Come on, you must eat.'

'I don't want any.'

'Well have a sardine then.'

'Not sardines again! We had sardines yesterday and the day before.'

'They're good for you. We don't want to get hungry and cross like last night.'

'*You* were the one who got cross.'

'That's why I'm filling myself up now.'

'I can't eat sardines every day.'

'Have some monkey then.'

'Oh yuk!'

We had just watched a monkey being skinned. The Zairois smoke the meat until it is black and tinder-dry. The *patron* bought five small corpses, split like kippers and stretched flat in a cane basket.

We were in the middle of a vast palm plantation interspersed with coffee bushes. My first thought on entering it was, At last the forest is conforming to type! This was real jungle. The palms were outlandish like the illustrations in *Babar the Elephant*. The dew steamed through their careless, top-heavy fronds. The milky sunlight leaked in upon hairy trunks which rose out of a chaotic tangle of undergrowth. Then I realised that I was looking down straight rows. The coffee bushes escaped every now and then from the choking weeds, their branches wandering unpruned, their red fruit unpicked.

We went through many settlements along the road with the same basic dwellings of sticks and mud. When we passed a Belgian planter's villa, alone in a clearing with its roof and walls intact, there was no path trodden to the door.

At Kapia, where the road turns south, we had a second breakdown. The spring was wedged in place with chunks of wood, which were lashed together with vine thong. I had been wrong to doubt the driver's ingenuity. The road continued to be every bit as bad and for five hours the repair had been a remarkable success. However the wedge had slipped and once again the loaders set about lifting several tons of deadweight with the inadequate jack.

We squeezed into a narrow ribbon of shade beneath the eaves of a hut. A young man came up and spoke to us confidently in a language I didn't understand. Daisy asked him politely what he did, listened carefully to his reply and explained to me that he was an English teacher! He offered to show us the *institut* where he worked.

'Is an *institut* a secondary school?' I asked.

'What?'

'I am a secondary school teacher too.'

'Oh, even you? That's good. Is she your daughter?'

'Yes, this is Daisy. How much do you earn?'

'Eh?'

Daisy repeated my question in the African accent she had learnt from her schoolfriends. He seemed to understand it more easily.

'I am being paid 600 Zaires by month.'

The lorry trip had cost us 900 Zaires and, watching the other passengers paying Marto, I made sure we were not being stung. This young man would spend six months' savings on a journey like ours.

The school was empty. The young *maître* said everyone was at a funeral. We walked through a low door into a classroom.

'Here is mine. Here I am teaching English.'

The desks and chairs were fashioned from mud and grew out of the floor. Blackboard paint had been applied to the end wall. We hunted for some chalk and I wrote up a message to the class.

Dear students. I am an English teacher from Zimbabwe, visiting your school. It gives me great pleasure to be in your beautiful country. . .

A bicycle bell was tinkling madly in the distance.

'Dad,' called Daisy from outside. 'Mum's here.'

'Mum?'

I wondered why.

'Yes, she's pedalling like mad.'

Janie stopped when she saw us and began to beckon. Her face was bright red and she was fighting for breath.

'Hurry, hurry – they're going without us!'

'They've mended the lorry,' said Daisy.

A great cheer went up as we came into view.

'*Mondele*, white man, where have you been?'

'We are leaving you behind.'

'Monsieur Charles,' said André, 'this is a business trip. Don't you know that we are businessmen?'

I went to the driver's window and apologised. He was half asleep behind his wheel.

'It's nothing,' he said. 'Today we reach Idiofa – with your permission.'

The *patron* leant forward and growled. The driver let out the clutch and I swung myself up as we gathered speed.

Janie. . .

We did not stop again for seven hours. In the forest we had to be constantly on the alert for low branches. We crowded into the back half of the lorry to get our heads down. It meant we were all on top of each other and Mrs Blue Bucket kept up a constant moan; but at least the road was shaded.

After midday, the lorry climbed a hill and made its way along an undulating ridge. We spread ourselves on top of the tarpaulin. Blissfully, I stretched my limbs and lay back.

There was no shade. The sun beat down through a gentle haze. Around us were the same empty grasslands we had seen from the train. The road had cut deep into the dry sand which lay in clogging drifts. A fine coat of dust settled on us and dried our throats.

Mrs Blue Bucket now showed her class. She produced a glass goblet and a bottle of mineral water, braced herself, poured out a small tot and drained it at a gulp.

Our own water supply was quickly exhausted and we had to turn to Bruce who was very generous with his gallon jar and his jelly babies. The sun burnt with a fierceness that made our limbs stiff and our heads giddy. We tried to shelter from it under makeshift awnings. Bruce's enormous thighs went redder and redder and the ginger hairs curled up and frizzled in the heat.

'Mum,' said Orlando, 'how much longer till we get there?'

'I don't know darling.'

'I need a pee.'

'Oh no.'

I looked around in desperation.

'Use a beer bottle,' said Charlie.

'Dad!'

'Go on. There's plenty of them. No one will notice.'

Joseph had seen us. 'What's Orlando doing?'

'Nothing pet.'

'Mum, how long till we get there?'

'I don't know, Joe.'

The route might have been laid out to exasperate us. On every hilltop was a village and naturally we thought the first and the second and even the third were Idiofa. Then a stretch of road came into view with three more hills on which stood three more villages. When Orlando saw it, he clapped his head in his hands. 'Oh, bloody hell.'

'Never mind son,' said Charlie. 'Perhaps we'll find a drink stall.'

'We haven't seen one so far.'

We drained the last of the water from Bruce's jar. The villages were uniformly drab, dry and poverty-stricken with not even a rusty Coke sign to raise our hopes. We could see a river gleaming in the valley bottom. A baby started to cry. It cried and cried, making a dry rasping sound. Its mother crooned softly and swayed to and fro. Bruce offered her the last of his jelly babies but when the baby spat one out she threw the rest away.

'How much longer, Mum? When will we get there?'

Charles. . .

Somewhere in that long afternoon, we passed a solitary road-worker. He was leaning on the long handle of a shovel which he had used to shift a sand-drift a foot or two. As we drew level, he put his fingers to his lips and sucked. I threw him a cigarette. He shouted and gestured rudely at me. André reached over, pulled the packet out of my fingers and tossed it to him.

And somewhere else we passed an orange-tree. It was growing right beside the road and a branch stretched out into our path with two pieces of fruit on it. We leant over and managed to dislodge one which fell into the road. A loader jumped down and went back for it – we were going very slowly at the time. We had to watch in a mad fit of envy as he ripped off the skin, spat out the pith and sank his teeth into the pale-yellow flesh.

When the sun had lost its burning edge and begun to fall out of the sky, we finally came to a halt. The driver dropped from his cab and stretched wearily. Idiofa was on the horizon. We lowered ourselves stiffly to the ground and went into the bushes. I met Janie and we smiled and licked the salt from our cracked lips. The children were slowly coming alive. Bruce was declaring that in his experience – and he had done South America too – there had never been such a ride. We could feel our spirits reviving. Even the engine perked up. Someone started a song. A wave of conviviality swept the lorry. We were making a triumphal entry.

The outskirts of the town appeared as a dense maze of mud-shacks and banana-trees. The verge was lined with graves encased in concrete steps. Most were falling apart. What were they doing there? Was it sacred ground? Were they the victims of accidents?

Once among the houses, the road divided into a dozen muddy tracks which wove their way at random between the buildings. It was like penetrating a crowd. We made several right-angle turns and splashed through a small pond. The homes grew more solid with small verandahs and tin roofs. We rounded a bend into the main street and went along it to the imposing entrance of the Catholic mission.

The driver parked and went to find the workshop foreman. André came with us to find a father. The man wiped his spectacles on his cassock and looked in astonishment at the children. Then he sat us down in the refectory with several jugs of water and went to enquire about beds. The compound was neatly laid out in areas of sand containing a few struggling flowers, marked off by the usual white-washed stones. There was a hospital and a seminary. The father returned and apologised. They were playing host to a training conference and all the rooms were taken.

'No problem,' André said, 'we take you to hotel. Cool beer, cigarettes, dancing, plenty girls. Here no beer, just sleep. Madame, you belong to André tonight.'

'She's not yours,' said Orlando. 'I'll fight you for her if you like.'

'Come on you ol' bugger,' said Bruce, heaving himself wearily to his feet. 'I'll buy you a drink.'

We went out to the lorry and drove back to a hotel. Trucks were parked here and there like ships at anchor. People were making camp around them, lighting fires and spreading their blankets. We were given two spacious rooms and double beds for a total of £4. I waited an age while a man cleaned a paraffin lamp for us. I was dying of thirst and the beguiling sound of music and laughter was drifting in from the street. He trimmed the wick, filled the tank with fuel, fumbled in the darkness with a crossed thread and dropped the glass and chipped it. Eventually we had light and I fled after the others.

Zairois music is loved throughout Africa but it has to be heard on a tin-pot machine in a wooden shack on a hot night when the sweat stings your skin. The falsetto voices glide and swoop in harmony. The brass makes a crazed entry. The rhythm is rapid and unpredictable, violent and delirious. It thumps you in the groin, then leaves you twirling helplessly in the air.

The bar was full of soldiers and girls. The driver was there beside Daisy, sharing a bottle of Vital-O raspberry. Janie had bought two litres of Skol for me, sticks of bread and a fresh tin of sardines. I opened my parched throat and poured the beer down in an ecstasy of greed. Bruce was on his feet, dancing like a ponderous bear. André joined him, swivelling his hips and flashing his teeth at Janie. Orlando gave a wild demonstration of break-dancing. Joseph sat in a corner, his eyes closed and his head thrown back on the window-ledge.

Much later, I felt my way back to our room, lurching unsteadily across the courtyard. The door next to ours opened and a man stepped out and hurried past me, his head lowered. I opened number sixteen by the light of a match and fumbled out of my clothes. As I sank gratefully into the bed, Janie turned and put her arms around me. Together we slipped gently into oblivion.

13

Daisy. . .

When we arrived at Idiofa, as the lorry went among the houses, there were low hanging branches with hard wood. A man at the front pushed up a branch to save himself and because the lorry was moving it came down crack on my head. It was so hard I didn't cry.

The next day was spent wandering around having a nice time. We had breakfast in the market. The coffee was cold. All down the road there were stalls selling pills, hats and baskets. If you walked behind them, you found even more stalls with clothes and food. Mum bought some fried insects in a cone of paper. We got a smart straw hat each and Joe got a drawstring bag. He spent the rest of the day punching holes in bottle-tops and tying them to the tassles. There were four small girls who belonged to the mother with the baby. We bought them a present of a basket each and some tins of milk.

Dad, Orlando and I walked down the road and found a church. The bricks were arranged with gaps to let the air through. Inside it was amazing. All the walls, pillars and even the crucifix had been painted in brilliant, complicated patterns. The crucifix was very tall and thin. It was at the front of a stage with the chairs all round. The figure was an African. He looked sad. The cross had bar patterns all up it. It was better than the boring varnished ones. We found a short man who was still painting one of the pillars. We took his photo and he gave us a guided tour.

There was a school by the church. It must have been their break at eleven o'clock because many of the pupils were outside. They chased Orlando who got very cross with them. The ground was covered in lots of litter, including many exercise-books.

We went back to the hotel and played 'crazy eight' with some of the passengers. Instead of saying 'card' when they had one left, they touched their noses. The painter from the church arrived. He had a home-made guitar with him. The arm was made of wood and the body was a floor-polish tin. His music was really good and Mum taped it to take home.

Janie. . .

At sunset there was still no sign of the lorry. Charlie and the kids went to look for it. The dusk had a thickness to it, as if you could feel the darkness closing in. The muggy air squeezed itself into a few heavy drops of rain. I couldn't bear the sight of the four little girls, crouching under the truck in the yard. I decided it was time to book into the hotel again and at least get them under cover. I had just obtained three rooms when the driver turned up and said we were leaving.

Charles. . .

The lorry had been repaired and was parked outside a depot. We found a group of passengers unloading the beer-crates. Bruce and I joined in. Everyone worked with a will as the daylight faded.

'What are the plans?' I asked.

'I think we're moving out tonight,' Bruce said.

'Tch, *mondele, aidez-moi.*'

André was standing beside a shoulder-high stack of cassava bags. I tugged feebly at a corner and gave up. Bruce hoisted one above his head and everyone stopped to cheer. Then they used his back as a platform-lift to roll them onto the lorry. The driver tugged my sleeve.

'Your wife needs your help. You must come here quickly with your luggage.'

'We are going now?'

'Yes now.'

'Shall we stay in Kikwit tonight?'

Kikwit was a big town on the Kwilu river. The tarred highway, built by the Americans, started there.

'No, Kikwit tomorrow. Maybe in morning.'

77

I found Janie and we returned with our rucksacks.

'I think we're going to drive through the night,' I said.

'On a normal journey, they must drive non-stop if they manage to do Ilebo to Kinshasa in three days. We can thank the headlights and the spring for our sleep these last few nights.'

It was completely dark and the air was thick with smoke as the citizens of Idiofa prepared their evening meal. Tense and uncertain of what lay ahead, we waited on the lorry until half-past eight. I couldn't find Joseph's rucksack in which we had put the waterproofs.

'It won't rain, will it?'

'No, I'm sure it won't rain.'

One thing cheered us – most of the passengers had gone, so Janie and the mother were able to make the children comfortable.

Janie. . .

We waited and waited. I ran to the bar for some beer. The *patron* came and shouted at the mother that her kids took up too much room. She looked at him in silence, then complained bitterly to the other men and burst into tears, saying it would have been better on the boat. The two older girls also cried. We heard the engine start up. At last we were off.

At the top of the street we stopped outside a hotel. All the other passengers came out and climbed aboard. Mrs Blue Bucket was wearing a new dress. Six more sacks of flour and cassava were dumped on top of us. A sleeping girl was thrown in my lap.

Orlando screamed.

Joseph said, 'This is disgusting!'

The passengers laughed and jostled us.

I yelled at them.

The *patron* shouted at me.

I burst into tears.

The *patron* went round and shouted at Charlie.

I lost my place and ended up sharing the oil-drum next to the tailgate with a man who stared dumbly at me. I had my arm round the child to stop her falling off. My behind kept slipping. Once again we started and this time we kept going.

Charles. . .

Somehow being on the road calmed us down. The lorry gave us a common purpose and a shared helplessness. The powerful headlights lit the way ahead. We were on open ground, under a cloudy sky.

We met several other trucks coming towards us. Our driver, being a good sort, risked his neck each time and pulled onto the soft verge. Finally the moment came when he refused to budge. We were facing a big MAN truck with a roofless cab. There were a large number of people on board. Both sides spent five minutes flashing their lights and shouting angrily at each other. Then individuals went and prodded the sand.

More stone-walling.

Would it come to a pitched battle?

André had an idea and beckoned Bruce to come forward. He told him to stand up on top of the load. Bruce must have looked an awesome sight, towering out of the ring of the headlamps. For good measure, he beat his chest and gave a rugby player's yodel. Within seconds, the opposition had started their engine and were making for the side.

We met no more traffic after that. The moon came out and showed us clouds scurrying past. It grew colder. One or two drops of rain splashed onto our faces.

Janie. . .

I was becoming increasingly numb and desperate. The child lay heavily across my lap. The man was constantly niggling for more space. Charlie called out:

'Are you all right love?'

'Surviving, but I can't move an inch.'

'What about Daisy?'

'I don't know. I don't know where they are.'

'I'm okay,' came a small voice. 'Joseph is asleep in my arms and I'm comfy.'

'It's not too bad up here,' Charlie shouted. 'Come and join us.'

He and Orlando were squeezed into a space between two bars, about eighteen inches wide and five foot long. By pushing and shoving, they had managed to create a nest among the sacks. I slipped into the space next door. I was in the centre of the lorry, with my feet to the front and my head resting on a bag. Someone else's head was there too and the battle went on all night.

We were making a lunging progress downhill, back into the forest. The wind grew stronger all the time. Palm-trees loomed over us and thrashed and rustled in the gathering storm. The moon did a frantic dance.

'Isn't it *fantastic!*' said Charlie.

We rumbled over a narrow iron bridge, the wheels slipping on the wooden planks. It was about one a.m. and the rain came down.

The lorry stopped and the men unrolled the tarpaulin and pulled it down tight at the sides. It had a split in the middle. Charlie and Orlando were under cover but I was exposed from the waist upwards. All I had was a sack of woven plastic which André gave me. He snuggled down on my other side.

'He's got his wish at last,' Charlie chuckled.

André had only a thin cotton shirt and his precious towel. I gave him an end of my sleeping-bag.

Bruce sat bolt upright behind us, his hair matted and the water dripping from his beard.

I thought my legs might stay dry but the tarpaulin collected all the water from round about and poured it through the crack onto me. After an hour, the only dry parts on my body were my feet and armpits. I tried to control the shivering. I had read that it was the body's way of keeping warm, but it frightened me.

Could one die of hypothermia, so close to the equator?

The moon had gone. There was nothing to see for hour after hour. The others slept fitfully around me. It was dark and cold and wet.

Charles. . .

At four-thirty we came out of the forest and there in front of us was a floodlit factory. Moments later, we crossed a long bridge.

The Kwilu river!

Kikwit could not be far away. The *Shoestring* guide said an express bus ran from there to Kinshasa every day. We could leave the lorry and rest for a few hours. There would be a decent hotel; perhaps a chance of a bath and certainly a large mug of hot coffee.

Two hours passed. It began to get light and the rain stopped. I stripped off my jersey and gave it to Janie. When her teeth went on chattering, I gave her my jacket as well. Bruce let out a shout and pointed ahead.

'The tar, the bloody tar!'

The lorry paused, negotiated one last puddle and launched itself onto the blissful smoothness of a two-lane highway. It even had a white line up the middle.

We felt like weeping tears of joy. The town soon appeared on our right, built on the slopes above the river. The buildings looked solid and prosperous. We passed several turnings and began to look for the big one, the main road into the centre.

'Look, a real live signpost!'

'What does it say?'

We stared in dumb astonishment. The name KIKWIT in bold blue lettering had a single red diagonal line through it. We were not going to stop! We were leaving it all behind!

Janie looked as if she would crumple. I put my arm round her and André peered into her face and grinned.

'We stop soon, soon, madame. The driver is tired too.'

'I don't care. I want to stop now. I want to get off. I'm cold, I'm hungry, I'm fed up. Tell him to stop, Charlie. Please!'

I couldn't. We were part of the cargo whether we liked it or not. I shrugged and sat there, feeling spineless. If Janie thought the same of me, she was too kind to say so.

Janie. . .

Thirty minutes later, we halted in a lay-by nowhere near a café or any type of refreshment. They gave us just long enough for a quick leg-stretch. I looked in a bag and found three dry T-shirts, a dress, Joseph's socks and some knickers. Then I climbed down, using the cab window as a foot-rest.

People were walking past on their way to work and here was a white woman undressing at the roadside. I tried to be discreet but I was past caring what they thought. My soggy trousers were putting up a fight when the *patron* called to me.

'*Entrez!*'

Damn him, I thought. He's surely not going to leave now, when I'm only half changed. I laid into him in my best school French, with the trousers round my ankles.

He had no sense of humour at all, nor any honour. He simply repeated his command.

'*Entrez, entrez, madame.*'

Then I realised that he was embarrassed for me. He was trying to say, do you mind going behind the hedge.

Sheepishly, I did as I was told.

The sun came out and our spirits rose. The express bus roared past and we were able to cheer it on its way. We went at a gentle pace and stopped for breakfast at eight o'clock. The little café made of palm leaves was decorated inside with pages from the *New Yorker* magazine. We gulped down coffee and bought fresh bread, tomatoes and condensed milk.

The morning passed slowly amid pungent smells. The damp cassava was the worst. I dozed and read inside a sleeping-bag and felt comforted. At two o'clock, we stopped to bathe in a river. The women led Daisy and me downstream from the bridge. They stripped off and splashed each other with the cool, brown water. Shyly, we hitched up our skirts and washed our legs. The mother was vigorously soaping her four naked little girls. She shouted and gestured at us to get undressed and wash properly. You can't get clean like that, she said. Daisy and I exchanged glances and took the advice.

Charles. . .

Orlando and Joseph were wading naked in the shallows when André and the other men joined us. They were astonished that the boys were uncircumcised and asked if it was the custom in our country.

'How can you be *civilised* if you are like that?' André said.

I had to demonstrate that I at least was civilised before they would let the matter drop.

The driver had been at the wheel for eighteen hours with two short breaks. While we were bathing, he was too tired to get out of his seat and the *patron*, who looked as cool and suave as ever, simply left him there. Our lives were in his hands, so I bought him a large pineapple and began to slice it into rings with my penknife. This so exasperated him that he roused himself and found a *panga* under the seat. He lopped off the sides with three deft blows and gorged himself. Then he went for a wash.

The river we had reached was the Wamba. We still had 166 miles to go. This should have taken three to four hours but our progress during the remainder of the afternoon fell to fifteen miles an hour. The lorry meandered from one side of the road to the other. Whenever another vehicle approached, we practically came to a halt. The driver kept himself awake by changing gear. We would surge ahead, climbing into top; then lose momentum and change all the way down again. The landscape was empty and dry. The drains at the side of the new road were clogged and cracks were already appearing. It was very dreary.

To keep our spirits up, we sang songs we had learnt in Zimbabwe. André protested that we were making a complete nonsense of the music, so Janie asked him to sing.

'What?' he said. 'I know nothing.'

'Sing the national anthem,' she said.

This simple request was greeted with merriment. André made several attempts to get started, but each time he was drowned by laughter and choked on his own giggles. Eventually he sang a few lines to a tune bristling with martial fervour – a first cousin of the Marseillaise.

> *Zairois in the land that has found itself again,*
> *A united people, we are Zairois.*
> *Forward, proud and full of dignity,*
> *Great people, people free for ever*
> *. . . Around a River Majesty.*
> *. . . Tricolore, in the wind refire the ideal*
> *Which binds us to our ancestors, to our children;*
> *Peace, Justice and Work.*

The flag of Zaire shows an arm holding a flaming torch. Joseph thought it was a paint brush.

A group of children waving cassava branches were silhouetted against the sky at a bend on a hillside. The freshly cut leaves are eaten as a green vegetable. We stopped to buy some. The children scurried off down a path and reappeared, their arms full of more. The bundles were light but bulky. Marto arranged them on top of the cab and the lorry acquired a bushy wig.

Just before nightfall, we halted outside a hotel.

Our hopes rose.

The *patron* could not decide what to do. We sat down at either end of a courtyard and had drinks. Janie asked the price of a room. We were ordered back on the lorry but once again nothing happened for a while.

We bought kebabs. Orlando, who was eating one with his fingers, rubbed his face and landed a speck of chilli in his eye. It was very painful and his howls attracted a large crowd of children. We were actually grateful to leave them behind.

Janie. . .

Another night on the lorry lay ahead but we were calmly resigned to it. One can get used to anything!

After dark, we settled the children down between the sacks and they were soon fast asleep. At half-past nine, we stopped in a village and sat round a fire with the driver and the *patron*, drinking coffee and chewing bread. I asked for a latrine and one of the men, seeing I was barefoot, removed his shoes and insisted that I wear them. An old man led me through the huts in the dark to a padlocked privy. He hadn't got a key so he lifted the door off. A small pig tried to come in after me but I shooed it away. Moonlight shone through the chinks in the bamboo walls and I could just make out where the hole was.

Near midnight, the wind got up and it started to rain again. This time the men were more ruthless. André, Charlie and the children were ordered to the back and the tarpaulin was refolded to cover the split. I liked my niche and somehow managed to stay put. A person climbed on top of me and felt my head. I heard him say, '*C'est un pacquet,*' and then they lashed the tarpaulin down. I was afraid I would suffocate or something might be dumped on top of me. After a tense few minutes, we started again and the draught made breathing easy, though the rain brought back the bitter, rancid smell of the cassava. Snores came from nearby, so I knew I was not alone.

Charles. . .

The rest of the night was unpleasant. There was a great crowd of us under the tarpaulin and the rain dripped through in a dozen places. It was stifling and smelly – impossible to sleep.

I began in a twisted, half-reclining position midway up the pile of sacks. I had someone's head on my shoulder, an elbow in my abdomen and a back against my legs. After an hour of this, I grew so cramped and claustrophobic that I braved their curses and wriggled down until I was sitting on the tailgate, my feet dangling over the road.

Joseph and Daisy were in the corner beside me. Joseph was exhausted. He twisted and moaned on my lap, unable to get comfortable. Daisy was so deeply asleep that nothing seemed to wake her. I was extremely envious but I couldn't shut my eyes or Joe and I would have tumbled into the road.

The surface blurred past between my feet. We were wandering from one ditch to the other, slowing, accelerating, slowing. Would he kill us all? How many hours now? Twenty-five, thirty? Somewhere in the darkness behind me, the mother began to pray. She murmured passionately and we all became caught up in it, muttering and grunting in agreement as she paused for breath.

Three hours or so after midnight, the patter of rain stopped and I thrust my head outside the tarpaulin. There was a thin drizzle. The moon lit the earth through the cloud cover. We were passing parked lorries, masses of them. There were voices from the cab. We were coming to a halt. Bruce jumped down ahead of me.

'Look Charlie!'

I rubbed my eyes and gave a whoop of joy. The Congo flood-plain lay before us. Kinshasa, Brazzaville, five million people! The horizon was a blaze of light from end to end.

My first thought was to thank the driver. I went to the cab window and held up a packet of cigarettes.

'*Pour toi,*' I said. '*Bravo. Merci beaucoup.*'

The form behind the glass did not stir. Instead the *patron*'s head appeared. He wound down the window.

'*Qu'est-ce que vous voulez messieurs?*' he said. '*Nous sommes arrivés, hein. Votre argent alors,* your money, *donnez le moi, s'il vous plaît!*'

We waited for dawn before covering the last fifteen miles, past the airport and university and through half a dozen road-blocks. I watched a portion of our fare slipping to Mobutu's police. Although it was still drizzling, we cast off the tarpaulin and gratefully breathed in the reek of a third-world slum.

The city was grey, muddy and impersonal. It felt enormous. As we penetrated to its heart, the inhabitants awoke and took to the streets in ever greater numbers. Around the monument to Patrice Lumumba, a great jam of honking buses, cars and taxis had formed. We pulled into a quiet side-street and the *patron* beckoned us down.

'*Vite, vite!* Quick *monsieur, 'dame!*'

Nothing we ever did for this man was free from pressure.

Our belongings were scattered all over the lorry. The passengers removed the shirts and jumpers we had lent them to keep warm. A shoe had fallen down between the sacks and could not be reached. At the last minute, someone discovered our surviving chicken in the spare tyre.

The women, including Mrs Blue Bucket, were waving and shouting goodbye. Daisy kissed the baby. Janie gave André a peck on the cheek and he recoiled in embarrassment.

The *patron* hailed a taxi. We crammed the rucksacks into the boot and sat back on the soft, torn seats. I turned for a last view of the lorry as we drove away. The *patron* had disappeared. Sacks of cassava were being dumped in the road. The passengers waited meekly. The driver leant against the cab and sucked deeply on a cigarette.

'Hotel Yaki,' said Janie, her nose deep in *Africa on a Shoestring*. '*Hôtel Yaki, Av de Stade de 20 Mai.*'

'Has it got a bath?' said Bruce. 'What do you say to a hot tub and a few hours' kip, followed by a steak the size of your arm? Then I think it's a plane ride for Bruce. I've had my fill of this dump. I rather fancy the Swiss Alps.'

There was no room in the Hotel Yaki. The Hotel Monarque had disappeared. The Mini-International had moved up-market. We owed the taxi-driver a small fortune.

'I take you to CAP,' he said.

We drove into a residential area and entered a yard surrounded by small chalets. A sensible-looking woman came out to greet us.

'Hello. My name's Ruth, Ruth Clinch. I'm sort of hon sec round here. You've come a bit early. There's no one in the office as yet. I expect they can find room for you.

'Do you need a bath? Come into my house. There's plenty of water. Goodness gracious, look at those children.

'Have you eaten? Breakfast is in half an hour. Tea or coffee? I will have to pop over and order for you.

'Oh, by the way, where are you from?'

We told her.

'Hm. You don't look like any Anglicans I've ever met.'

14

Janie. . .

We were safe. The *Centre d'Accueil Protestant* (CAP) was a hostel for doctors, teachers and evangelists from up-country missions. We sat down to a breakfast of scrambled eggs and coffee and conversation went on quietly around us: no one made demands on our tired senses. I was next to a soft-spoken, middle-aged man who listened to the children and enquired where we were heading.

'Up the river by boat to Kisangani and then east through the Ituri forest.'

'Then you must certainly come to stay with us: but be quick because we fly back to Europe in mid-April.' He held out his hand. 'Pierre-Etienne Pfister. We are stationed at Mandima Mission in the Ituri. Do you know Pat Nickson at Boga?'

'No.'

'She's in town until this afternoon. I will arrange for you to meet her.'

'We seem to have landed in the right place.'

'You will get to know everybody if you stay long enough.'

Ruth reappeared with the secretary and we were taken to a room with three single beds, a shower and toilet in working order and a small verandah opening onto the compound. It cost £12.50 a night.

'Do you want your children to go to the British school while you're here?' Ruth asked.

'What a marvellous idea. Where is it?'

'Through those gates, next to the church.'

'Oh Mummy, *must* we?' Daisy exclaimed.

'It would give us a chance to sort out the money and visas,' Charlie said.

'Is it air-conditioned?' asked Orlando.

'Yes,' said Ruth.

'I'd like to go to school,' Joe said unexpectedly.

'Well okay,' Daisy said. 'As long as it's not for more than a week.'

So that was decided.

'There's an international fête this afternoon,' Ruth said, 'at the American High School. The whole town is going.'

'That sounds fun. We'll be there if we manage to wake up.'

We collapsed onto our beds and it was three in the afternoon before I surfaced. The children were standing under the cold shower, shrieking with delight. Charlie was sneezing in the heat.

'We need to find a fan.'

'Leave it till later. Let's go to the fête.'

'How are we going to get there?'

Two doors away, an Arab sat darning a hole in his sock.

'Ask him,' I said.

The Arab was doleful but anxious to please. 'You wanna go place. Fazal take you. I have car.'

We piled into a battered Renault 4 and set off down a long road beside the river. The Congo or Zaire river is a mile wide at this point. The sunlight on its glassy surface hurt our eyes. On the other side, Brazzaville, the capital of the Congo Republic, appeared as a faint blur. Fishermen poled their dugouts in the shallows and clumps of weed drifted past on the current. Surprisingly Kinshasa turns its back on the waterfront: there are no hotels or promenades and, apart from a half mile of embassies, the shoreline is overgrown and untidy.

It took us thirty minutes to reach the American School on a hill beyond the Presidential palace. We entered a street jammed with Mercedes and Peugeot limousines. Fazal left the car and we followed the sound of a steel band through the gate and under the trees. The crowd was largely European, pushing baby buggies and nonchalantly greeting one another. Their T-shirts were printed with aid agency slogans in a dozen languages. The children queued to buy pistachio ice-creams, helium balloons and paper-hats. Germans called us to sample Bratwurst and cold beer, Danes stood behind a table groaning with cheese, Greeks were deep-frying doughnuts and the Italians baked pizza.

'Where are the British?'

'I haven't found them yet.'

A pale young man called James sat in a tent on the far side of the gymnastics display, offering a tepid cuppa beneath a photograph of a Bailey bridge.

We sat and watched the bronzed teenagers from the school in bright cotton slacks and open shirts, laughing and teasing each other, passing round cigarettes and Cokes. The boys wore pigtails and the girls had tangled perms. A few African youths swaggered past with dreadlocks, a gold earring or snakeskin boots over tight jeans. Not one ragged figure was to be seen.

'What a contrast with yesterday!' Charlie remarked.

James was explaining about the mail from England.

'It generally takes two to three weeks, but it's not terribly reliable I'm afraid. Poste restante is not to be recommended.'

'We were given a language teacher as a forwarding address. Lawrence Morgenstern: perhaps you know him?'

'Know *of* him. Married a local girl, didn't he?'

Fazal appeared at Charlie's elbow. He was slightly tipsy and his face had grown more mournful than ever.

'Plice arrest Fazal's car. We gotta go.'

'Kids, Fazal wants to go now,' Charlie shouted.

'But I haven't seen the model railway.'

'Joe is queueing for the trampoline.'

'Five minutes, Fazal. We'll meet you by the gate.'

'You be there.'

Charlie turned back to me.

'We'll go and look for Lawrence in the morning.'

Charles. . .

I was growing anxious to know the result of my selection board for the Anglican ministry. A long time had passed since I drove away from Bristol in the February snow.

'You're flying out on Sunday, aren't you?' the clergyman had said. 'Don't worry, I'm sure it will be okay. I'll give you a ring before the end of the week.'

I felt satisfied that I had got on well with everyone, but the phone call never came.

*　*　*

Lawrence lived a few streets from CAP in an apartment block. He was fast asleep when we knocked on the door, but once we had established who we were, he invited us in, opened a bottle of Primus and asked his wife Georgette to cook us all some lunch. The children were soon glued to a TV.

'You see some funny things on the box out here,' Lawrence said. 'A few weeks ago, the head of ONATRA – the state-run transport syndicate – was asked to report to the studios. He was a Belgian who had been given the job of sorting out the latest mess they had got into. When he arrived, he found Mobutu waiting for him and he was sacked, live on the air, during the evening news. They gave him twenty-four hours to be out of the country.'

'Don't you ever feel scared it might happen to you?'

He laughed. 'I'm not important at all. Anarchy can be fun, as long as you know the rules.'

On Sunday evening we went across the yard to the International Protestant church. It was an American service and the music was as lush and sentimental as any Country 'n' Western fan could wish. Monty Nelson, the pastor, spoke with a soft, southern twang and his humour was gentle and self-deprecating.

'I'm sure I ain't gonna have to ask you folks what I once asked my congregation back in Georgia. I asked them if they had read their Bible study for the week. I mentioned a passage, Mark, chapter seventeen, verses one to seven. About eight persons raised their hands and said, "Yes, we've read it." Good Christian people who read their Bibles. Only trouble was, there ain't no Mark, chapter seventeen.'

When he'd finished preaching, Monty invited all the visitors to make themselves known. We stood up and introduced ourselves and after the service several people asked us to their homes for a meal.

On Monday evening, Lawrence came round to CAP with our letters. None were post-marked Hereford where the Bishop lived. I opened an aerogramme from Janie's mother.

1st March 1985
Darling Janie, our thoughts are for you all. When will Charlie

know? Presumably not yet, as his Mum says he hasn't rung in yet. It will be such a shock to start with, though I know he will be able to call on all that inner strength. Everybody here who loves you and cares is amazed and mostly enraged.

The Bishop rang on Friday evening to say he had the results. 'Hurray' I said but he replied 'I'm afraid it's not hurray', to which I gasped 'I can't believe it'. Well of course he couldn't tell me the reason for their decision, but we did talk for quite a long time. He said, 'Once Charles has settled down again in England, we can see how he's coping with the very different ways here.' I said Westcott College accepted him most warmly, but he said, 'Oh well, they want the money!' which at least was honest.

There were also letters from my father and Janie's younger sister.

Dear son,
You will no doubt have heard the sad news by now. Your mother and I find it incomprehensible. You are just the sort of person that the Church so badly needs. The Bishop writes that he would like to meet you and Janie as soon as possible. Do you not think it would be wise to come home and sort things out now?

Hi folks, this is Alex.
Happy Birthday Janie. I hope it's a happy one. We read your letter from Chingola. It sounds great fun. Dear Charlie, we are all very sorry on your behalf viz those silly old bishops. In the circumstances this postcard of Job Centres is in rather bad taste! I wonder when you'll get home? Relatives have talked of your stopping the trip and high-tailing it home to sort out those bishops. My advice is carry on and enjoy the outing.

Janie wrote our first reply.

Kinshasa, 12th March

Dearest Mummy,
Your letter of 1st March arrived yesterday – the first indication of ACCM's decision. It came with a friend who had invited us out for a drink. When Charlie opened it and I realised what had happened, I simply continued putting the children to bed and insisted that the drink came before any thinking or important discussion. I hope my priorities were right.

Charlie is strong in heart and mind. We both look at whatever

André and the children beside the river Kasai

Washing facilities at Kamina station

Preparing the meal at Kamina station

Road conditions in the forest

Arrival. Note the cattle compartment behind the cab

Kinshasa, Boulevard du 30 Juin

Zairean haute couture, *Kinshasa*

Monkey skull for curing bronchitis on sale in Kinshasa market

In the Kinshasa cité

Western medicine by the jarful

Vévé and the children

Embarkation at the gare fluviale

The corridor outside our cabin on Mukongo

The convoy seen from a tethered dugout

Madame Janie with sputnik coiffure

God throws at us as a good thing, even if it appears in disguise. It was very comforting to have our life neatly mapped out for years in advance, but the best laid plans are always the ones that dissolve before your eyes.

That night, I could not sleep and climbed over the gate into the churchyard. A male-voice choir was practising late in the empty school hall.

'Ah Jezebel, Jezebel, dat bad ol' woman, Jezebel!'

The church was locked so I wandered round the grounds. The Baptists had built a brick water-tank in which to immerse the human sheep. It was home to a family of frogs who filled the night with sighs and belches. I felt stunned, angry, betrayed. How dare they turn me down! How dare they! Not knowing why was the worst of it. My mind raced back and forwards over the interviews. Was I guilty of some deep, unrecognised failing? Was it a mistake?

If only I had known then what I do now: that God was beckoning to me in Zimbabwe to know His love and share it, that putting on a dog-collar was a false lead, an attempt at cancelling past betrayals and that the pain of that night was a preparation for wider horizons and brighter hopes.

Janie was awake when I returned to the room and we talked. We agreed that giving up the journey would be admitting defeat. It was important to carry on, at least as far as the East Coast. July would be time enough to fly home and look for a job.

Three nights later, we were dining with two members of Monty's congregation who had been in Zaire for twenty-five years. Orlando said:

'Daddy's sad because he's just heard the Anglicans won't have him for a priest.'

'Why be sad?' our host replied. 'In the Baptist Church we have no priests, Charlie. We believe that every baptised Christian is his own priest: there can be no intermediaries between man and God. You say God is calling you; then He is, have no doubt about it. God is active in changing all our lives for the better; that's how He works.'

'My faith is still strong.'

'I have found that faith is not confidence in God's will, so much as obedience to it. Will you have some more pie?'

93

Our most pressing problem was obtaining more money. We had left Zimbabwe with the little we were allowed and about £80 remained. Kinshasa, so Lawrence assured us, was a lot dearer than London. We were armed with a letter of credit and an American Express card. A clerk in Barclay's looked doubtfully at them both and disappeared into a back room.

I got to know that office well over the next fortnight. The clerks scribbled and filed in much the same way as bank clerks do anywhere, but the men's jackets were collarless and florid in the extreme: one had gold cockatoos on a green background. This, I learnt, was the *abacos*, a garment which President Mobutu made mandatory in his campaign for African *authenticité*.

The official returned. 'Please to see Mr Maguire.'

The manager was solidly English and his jacket knew no pedigree other than Savile Row.

'What is all this, Mr Hampton?' he said, waving the letter of credit at me. 'I can't give you anything on the strength of this.'

'Why not?'

'Because they don't specify an amount, a credit limit. How much do you want, anyway?'

'A thousand, maybe two,' I said. 'What about American Express?'

He smiled. 'There are no facilities for Amex in Zaire. I shall have to telex London on your behalf. It will cost you twenty pounds.'

'How long will it take?'

'It's hard to tell. Maybe a week.'

'But surely a telex is quicker than that.'

'It will depend on how fast your bank replies – and we have to go through the post office.'

'Couldn't we telephone?'

Mr Maguire smiled again. 'No international calls have been accepted from Zaire since before Christmas.'

'Why not?'

'They haven't paid their bills.'

I looked at him in despair.

'I take it you would like me to telex then?' he said. 'How much shall I ask for?'

'Better make it three thousand pounds. That should see us home. Could you let me have a small advance?'

'One hundred, no more.'

I made out a cheque which he handed to his assistant. We rose and shook hands.

'Are you planning to stay long in Zaire?' Mr Maguire asked.

'We thought we might spend a few days on the coast and then go upriver to Kisangani.'

'You will find the hotels at Muanda are dirty and expensive. The beach is nice but don't get sunburnt. It can be foggy too. On no account allow your wife and children to go out by themselves after dark.'

Janie. . .

It took a fortnight for the money to come through, a frustrating wait when we wanted to be on the move. Getting visas involved foot-slogging several times round the embassies. We discovered we couldn't go to the Congo Republic, so tantalisingly close, because our Zairean visa would not allow us back in again until three months had elapsed.

On one of our daily visits to the bank, we found the street sealed off by armed police. Music blared out of loudspeakers. In the road, a troupe of dancers in T-shirts saying *Ballet Coca Cola* were swinging their hips. There was a brass band sitting on the pavement who scrambled to their feet and managed a ragged tattoo when a black official Mercedes finally appeared. The VIP dabbed his brow impatiently with a silk handkerchief and then escaped into his office.

Walking around was much safer than it had been. A year ago, Lawrence told us, Mobutu decided to stop paying his police and they responded by arresting citizens and robbing them. Since then there had been an election. Bill-boards still proclaimed, *Le Peuple dit oui au Maréchal* and *Mobutu a 100%*

'The voting system was like a referendum,' Lawrence explained. 'You picked up either one of two cards and put it in a box. Red, I don't like Mobutu, green I do. The only trouble was, they printed very few red cards and some polling stations got none at all.'

It was still a city of nerve-racking unpredictability. The taxis, for example, crammed in fresh customers all the time and you could find yourself diverted miles off your route. Returning one evening, our taxi stopped abruptly and the driver scrambled to his feet, hauling himself up through the sun-roof. We were bewildered by this. The car was alone in the middle of the road. An armed soldier stood under the trees, but his gaze did not rest on us. What could be happening? After a short pause the driver sat down again and jerked his thumb towards a gate in a high wall. As we drew level we looked into the courtyard of a military barracks where the *tricolore* had just been lowered.

'You have to show respect,' the driver explained. 'If not. . . .' He drew his finger across his throat.

Daisy. . .
Our room at CAP was very hot and stuffy, even though Ruth had lent us a fan. The only time it was easy to breathe was during thunderstorms. We still had the chicken from Ilebo living with us. He was so scrawny that we hadn't the heart to eat him. At night we tied him to a chair outside our door. One morning, the chicken was there but the chair had gone.

Our school was just like one in Britain. Joseph did a project about William the Conqueror. At the weekend, Orlando and I helped with a jumble sale in aid of Oxfam. Mum gave away more of our belongings and Joseph won a dot-to-dot book in the bran-tub.

Janie. . .
Shopping was a tantalising experience with our limited funds. The price of imported goods at an *épicerie* – a pound for a pot of yoghurt – put them way beyond our reach. The cost of a European lifestyle was twenty times that of a local inhabitant's. We ate rice and vegetables from the market and the fresh bread, kebabs and roasted corn that were sold on street corners.

The central market in Kinshasa must be one of the largest in the world. Thirty thousand people buy and sell there each week day. Making our way carefully along an alleyway of tins, we stopped to smile at a toddler perched on a stall clutching a tub of Blue Band margarine, surrounded by high-rise stacks of Ideal Milk, tomato purée, pilchards and lavatory paper. The awnings were made of a patchwork of American flour-bags.

One large section was devoted to Zairean fabrics, which are wax-printed, boldly patterned and brightly coloured. They were sold in standard five metre lengths: two for the blouse and three for the skirt. The *couture authentique* for women was a tight-waisted bodice with a low neckline and accentuated shoulders. As a style, it graced diplomatic receptions but looked decidedly odd lined up on a sandy pavement.

In another corner, we found an employment exchange. The men had set out symbols of their trade – a tap connected to a piece of pipe, a light bulb on the end of a wire, a saw and a paintbrush. When I asked if I could take a photograph, they rushed at me with their hands out. *Non, non, non.*

We passed a line of dozing barbers and a fortune-teller.

Discover your truth with Doctor Salomon
Tariff: Secrets in public Z 15
       Personal secrets Z 20
       Washing of the body Z 150

I sat down and gave him Z 15. He held my palm and ran his fingers over the lines.

'You will become a Catholic, have eight children, marry your boss and live to be eighty-five.'

Was this what he thought I *wanted* to hear!

'Because I've said so much,' he went on, 'you must pay me another Z 85.'

Coming out of church at the end of the first week, someone pressed an invitation into my hand.

Brunch with the Christian Women's Club. Thursday, 9.30,
Intercontinental Hotel, cost Z 160. Music by Mark Tanquist
and Nancy Graber. Speaker, Bunny Wiles.

It was my birthday so I ironed my dress and went along. When I entered the ballroom, the duo were performing at a grand piano. Fifty American women in pale linen suits sat eating scrambled eggs and croissants. The talk was of the fête, who was there and how much had been raised. We said a prayer and then someone organised a parlour game about romance and vegetables. Another prayer and the chairwoman asked for attention. Everyone knew Bunny and her wonderful way with gardens. In her twenty-five years in Zaire, she had moved house twenty-three times!

'There's so much greenery in Kin at the moment,' Bunny said, 'but don't despair! Grow some Busy Lizzie, but do watch out! Zaireans love to water, especially if it's already raining. Try not to let your gardener overdo it.

'A healthy hibiscus needs a horse. Go to the stables with your manioc sack and watch the little man who fills it very carefully. Give him a rubber glove and make sure he only picks up the droppings and not the wood shavings. The droppings are full of the wonderful bacteria which our soil needs. Don't let your gardener burn your leaves either. They love to sweep them into the street and make a fire. I get my man to go and collect other people's leaves.

'You'll have instant non-success with cucumbers unless you kill off the bugs first. Next time you go home, could someone bring some hormone rooting powder?'

Surrounded by women with homes to go to and husbands in work, the strain of the last few weeks abruptly caught up with me. As soon as Bunny Wiles sat down, I rushed to the bar and ordered a double whisky.

'What's the matter dear?' someone said.

'It's my birthday,' I replied and burst into tears.

Charles. . .

The main entertainment at the weekend was a cricket match; the British diplomats versus the Indians. It was terribly hot and the players hung about looking limp. Last man out was Paul Simon, the Oxfam field director.

'Come over to the embassy club with us,' he said. 'It's so snobbish, it's about to disappear up its own backside: but they've got one of the few decent pools in town.'

We already knew how difficult it was to have a swim. A hotel had tried to charge us five pounds per person for a dip.

A children's party was in full swing when we arrived. Wrapping paper was scattered under the chairs and Joseph's eyes bulged at the expensive Tonka toys. The guests were playing with balloons in the water. Our children were suddenly struck with shyness.

'Have some cake,' said an amiable voice.

'That's our brand new ambassador,' Paul murmured.

Her Majesty's representative put a few slices on a plate and brought them over.

'Hello,' he said. 'Can I buy you all a drink?'

'I'm afraid not sir,' Paul said. 'You see, you're not yet a member of the club.'

He laughed. 'I suppose I'd better join then,' and turned to Paul's wife. 'Will you propose me?'

'I'm afraid I can't,' Pat said. 'I'm not a member either. They told Paul that the list was closed.'

'There's been a feud,' Paul said. 'The place is bleeding to death. I suppose I'd better get a round. What's it to be?' He stopped, remembering something, and grinned sheepishly. 'It'll have to be soft drinks though.'

'Why's that?'

'Another rule: guests can't be served alcohol.'

Paul and Pat lived in a beautiful wooden house, shipped out in bits fifty years ago and sited on the river bank. We went there each evening to play snooker and drink Scotch.

Paul had travelled all over Zaire and was full of stories. Some of the best were about a Dutch Catholic priest called Jacques Sier.

'I wanted to get an urban programme going in the *cité*, but I had no time myself. Someone suggested I go and talk to this ancient monsignor, about a hundred and fifty and batty as a coot, and he put me onto Père Jacques. I trundled out to the suburbs and found him living in a small compound with three Zairois: a carpenter, a teacher and a textile worker. We talked about my project and two weeks later he turned up at my office in town and said, I'll do it. He had already started a two-year sabbatical from the priesthood. He was working down at the airport, but the Bishop got wind that his employer was a gangster and he had to leave.

'Jacques is angry with the Church in Zaire. He says it went wrong from the start. The clergy live behind bloody great walls and don't see people until it suits them – when they've finished dinner and their afternoon nap. He wants to work from below not above: from the bottom upwards. So now he's running a health programme for us.'

'Jacques has been out here nearly twenty years,' Pat continued, 'and, as a result of the paludrin you have to take to ward off malaria, he has lost his sense of smell. Once he was conducting a funeral for a man who had been dead almost a week. His body was pretty high. Jacques couldn't understand why the congregation were all sitting at the back by the door. He stood in his normal position by the coffin and conducted the service. Afterwards people treated him with even greater respect.'

'You must meet him,' Paul said. 'We'll take the Land-Rover over there tomorrow.'

There was fresh rain overnight and we needed four-wheel drive to churn along the dirt roads of the *cité*. This great urban sprawl stretched for twelve miles south of the city centre, uniformly grey and featureless. Jacques met us at the start of his district and took the wheel. He was a sandy-haired, suntanned man in his early forties, gentle in answering the children's questions, alert and competent in dealing with the mud and the traffic. When we got out at a market, he was greeted on every side.

'Salut, Père Jacques!'

Our first call was a hospital run by the Kimbanguists. This Zairean Protestant sect was founded by a prophet, Simon Kimbangui, who died in a Belgian prison after twenty years in captivity. It is one of Africa's largest and most important indigenous churches. The hospital was enormous – a long range of single-storey buildings in a dusty compound. It had a catchment area of ten thousand people, there were sixty new patients each day and it was fortunate enough to have a doctor.

On the edge of town, we fell in behind a funeral procession of several lorries, the relatives shuffling silently in their wake.

'Three years ago,' Jacques said, 'this was virgin bush. Now the cemetery stretches for five kilometres. One thousand six hundred metres of bodies each year and still they come to live here. The population will grow a million by the year two thousand.

'Next we will visit a maternity clinic.'

Home deliveries have been illegal in Kinshasa since Belgian times. The clinic coped with ten births a day. We watched a nurse trying to transfuse blood from a young man to his sister who was jaundiced and lying unconscious. The tubes were not clean and kept blocking as the blood coagulated. On the wall was a poster about the prevention of diarrhoea – *pulu pulu* in Lingala.

The day was hot and sticky and the children were wilting. We went to Jacques' compound and sat in the shade of a mango-tree drinking tea. The yard was neat and swept clean. A few chickens scratched in the dirt. Jacques proudly showed off his new well, which was lined with oil-drums.

'Sadly, I have discovered that I must boil all the water. The ground is polluted to a great depth because there is no sanitation.'

He took us into the tiny chapel where he said mass each morning. There was a sign over the door:

The religious life is the Christian life lived at high tension.

The teacher who belonged to his community took me to visit his school nearby. It had been built by the parents, who could not afford doors or windows. We saw them at work on a new toilet-block. I was taken into a classroom where sixty assorted children sat quietly on their benches, copying words from the blackboard.

'Is this your class?' I asked.

'Oh no.'

'Where is the teacher?'

'He is at work.'

'But isn't this his work?'

'He drives a taxi,' the man explained. 'We do not get paid for being here.'

'Not at all?'

'Sometimes – if we are lucky.'

We found the others in a bar. Paul was describing the livelihood of a *pousse-pousse* man.

'He doesn't own his *chariot*, even though it may be in the last stages of disintegration – broken axle and flat tyres. Like everything else in Zaire, the market is controlled by entre-preneurs who lease them at Z 150 per day. He can only operate in one area and he must join up with others to defend it against infiltration by rival gangs. The work is very spasmodic. He can expect to be idle for much of the time. On a good day, he may take home Z 400. Life is tough in Kinshasa.'

When the money finally came through – the telex had been waiting at the post office for four days – we decided to abandon the trip to the coast and push on up the river. On our last evening, Paul and Pat took us to a night-club in the *cité*.

Orlando. . .
Before we went dancing, we decided to eat a roast chicken. We stopped beside the road and sat at a table next to an open drain. The waiter brought half a chicken each, which we ate with our fingers. Another man was trying to sell us a tray of eggs. The waiter told him to go away and when he refused they had a fight. The tray flew in the air and the eggs fell on Mum.

'It's a good job they're boiled,' Joe said.

Daisy. . .
At *Le Faubourg*, soft drinks cost a pound. It was open to the sky and there were sunshades over the tables which seemed odd considering it was a night-club. For two hours or so, we were the only people there. The band started off with four instruments and grew as the evening went on. Around midnight, Tabu Ley, the most famous star in Zaire, appeared and lots of rich people in beautiful clothes turned up to hear him. He had a strange high voice. Orlando and I danced with the rich people. They rubbed their hips against each other, rolling their fat bottoms very slowly in time to the music.

15

Charles. . .

The *gare fluviale* was only ten minutes walk from CAP. It was deserted at eight a.m. on Sunday morning and the gates were locked. I shouted through the bars and a uniformed official appeared.

'I thought the boat was leaving today. I've come to buy tickets.'

'You come tomorrow. The boat leaves on Tuesday.

The next morning I was shown to a small room off the entrance hall. The narrow space was jammed with people, competing for the attention of an official who sat behind a thick glass partition. He worked indifferently at his own pace and, since he couldn't hear a word, people scribbled their requirements on a scrap of paper and pushed them through the crack wrapped in a small bribe. I squeezed in, keeping an anxious hold on the £500 beneath my belt. It was every man for himself and, if the face didn't fit, you were simply ignored. When my turn came, the official took the wad of notes, counted them rapidly and tossed them into a box at his feet. I acquired a ticket for a second-class cabin with four bunks and a meal a day for Z 206,126 – about £400.

'Second class passengers have the right to 40 kg or three items of luggage in their cabins without charge. The cases must be of a dimension that allows them to slide under the bed.

ONATRA wishes you *bon voyage.*'

I went out onto the quay. Two cranes emblazoned 'Made in Bath' stood idle on my left. Several passenger barges were alongside and the largest, most rusty and decrepit was named *Mukongo*. A glance at the ticket confirmed my worst fears: this was our home for the next fortnight. I decided to look around and climbed over a twisted rail onto the deck. Hammering came from the bilges and a sailor walked past with a bunch of padlocks. Otherwise the corridors were deserted, an unyielding world of rotting iron and dirty green paint. The stairs and corridors were narrow, slippery and uneven. In places the railings were missing, as if torn away by a giant hand. The cabins ran across the barge from one side to another. I peered in one before the sailor locked it and saw a narrow cell, about eight feet by six, containing two double bunks placed at right angles. The cabins next to the outer decks had some light and air: those situated amidships were pitch dark and presumably airless. Ours was one of these. I could see nothing through the small grill but it smelt dry and slightly foetid. There was a strong padlock already in place.

'*Mondele, rendez-vous ici de bonne heure,*' the sailor said. 'Come with your own lock, white man. Otherwise someone else takes your room.'

Janie. . .
On Tuesday we got up extra early but the road leading to the station was already full. Bread and vegetable-sellers were doing a brisk trade and we stocked up with fresh food. Other passengers came by, keeping a watchful eye on their belongings piled high in a *chariot*. They clearly meant to be comfortable – cane chairs, a mattress and a pot-plant were wedged among the cases. Four or five soldiers were making a nuisance of themselves asking for money, but we got through on a wave and a smile.

Outside the station gates, the crowd grew thicker. Our *pousse-pousse* abandoned us and Charlie pushed through to a burly policeman who told him to report to the immigration office. The kids and I went upstairs to a gallery in the hope of taking some photographs. The scene on the dockside was complete mayhem. A boat had just come in and hundreds of people were disembarking and stacking up their produce – fish, monkeys, goats, even crocodiles – while hundreds more battled to get on board. Below us were half a dozen live turtles, tethered by their hind legs. Their owner had chopped one into pieces and was stewing it on a charcoal-burner. He looked up when he heard the children's voices and beckoned to us to try some. The texture of the flesh was rather soft and jelly-like but it tasted delicious.

Charlie reappeared and said we could go on board. *Colonel Ebeya*, the boat which contained the engines and first-class accommodation, was tied up at the quay. The barges floated a few yards out and the only way to reach them was via her foredeck.

'Follow me,' I said.

Dozens of other people were trying the same thing, scrambling round tables and chairs and over trunks, bed-rolls and bundles of clothes. An officer in white uniform put his elbow in my face: he was too busy shouting instructions to notice or apologise. A whistle blew in my ear and a porter shoved me aside, hands on hips, straining furiously under the sack balanced across his shoulders. Something wet and cold was raining on us from above. I looked up to see a frozen gazelle being hoisted from the cold store. A woman stared down at me from the bridge, a baby suckling her breast.

'My God!' said Charlie, 'we've joined a Hollywood epic.'

'Where's Orlando and Daisy?'

'They went on ahead.'

'And Joe?'

'I'm here.'

'I must get to that cabin, before anyone else does.'

Orlando. . .

We got on the boat and Dad had a row with an ONATRA man who had put his padlock on our cabin and refused to budge. Dad sent Mummy to fetch the captain and told me to cry as loud as I could but I felt too embarrassed. He tried pinching me but it didn't work. A man called Noel joined in the argument on our side and we won before Mum came back. She told us we were lucky because the captain had said company agents could take people's cabins if they wanted. Dad gave Noel a present and he promised to help us again.

Daisy. . .

It was very hot so Joseph and I went to sit on the roof of a barge. We had a nice view of the river and the sunset. Suddenly Joseph shouted, 'We're moving!'

I looked round at the shore and it was a long way off. Our barge had drifted out into the river. We could see Dad standing on another roof waving his arms, but there was nothing we could do.

'There's other people downstairs,' Joe said. 'I should think it's all right.'

Eventually, a motor-boat came to push us back. The captain was getting his convoy into the right order.

When we were ready to set off, *Mukongo* was in the middle. They put a flat barge loaded with containers in front and two smaller passenger barges on either side. There were two other flat barges carrying new Toyota lorries. That made six, all tied together and pushed from behind by the *Colonel Ebeya*. It was like a floating town. You would never have thought it could steer straight against the current, but it did.

Joseph. . .

Our cabin had a hole in the floor where the rats could creep in. Orlando found some men mending the boat. They agreed to come and patch the hole. We could hear rats walking about on the ceiling too but they couldn't get in that way. Sometimes I saw their eyes, peeping through the wire.

Charles. . .

Noel told us no boat had been able to leave Kinshasa for four weeks because the river was too low: *Ebeya* was pushing three barges more than usual. Despite this, the convoy was so crowded that many people were forced to live on deck. Several families camped in the corridor outside our cabin. Within a yard of our door, a mother was cooking her evening meal on a portable charcoal stove while granny sat on a three-legged stool and four children spat in the dust and drew with their fingers. They used the same grubby hands to play at turning their eyelids inside out. A stack of cassava had blocked our window

106

so we kept the door open and hung a *khanga* over it for privacy. A toddler peered in from time to time and sniffed our supper. Janie was boiling the cockerel, whose career as our alarm clock had finally come to an end. Cooking in that tiny, airless space required a conscious effort of will. We were groping around by candlelight. Although two live wires hung from the ceiling, no one had warned us we would need our own light socket. Somehow, being able to see would have made everything else bearable. The other cabins were all brightly lit, though without any switches, I wondered how they had made the connection.

Noel looked in to check we were all right. Bravo, he would find us a light! Or so he promised.

Janie. . .

The convoy finally left Kinshasa around ten at night. The children were asleep, despite the continuous racket. Noel said mattresses would be distributed but none came till the following day. The metal slats on our bunks were excruciating, so I took my sleeping-bag outside and lay down on a bench. The deck was deserted: there was a light breeze and I supposed that no one else had blankets. I woke to the sting of rain hitting my face. At first, I tried slipping deeper into my bag but a gust of wind drenched me with spray and forced me back to the cabin to change. *Mukongo* was moored to the bank to sit out the storm. Wind groaned down the corridor. Ragged bundles lay hunched up at my feet. I saw a light burning in the purser's office and decided I would console myself with a book. I rummaged among our belongings for a treat I had picked up at the school jumble sale and made a dash along the slippery deck.

My watch said two a.m. The purser was still working, dressed in underpants and a vest. The naked light-bulb swung gently to and fro and drips ran down the wire and sizzled as they hit the hot glass. Behind him, a door opened onto a bed, piled high with trunks and bales of material. A woman lay asleep on the floor, her baby nestled in her arms.

The purser ran his finger down a list and scratched his head with the end of a pencil. I sat down on the floor, opened *The Diary of a Provincial Lady* and tried to imagine myself in a Home Counties drawing-room. The outer door clanged open and a

107

worker stepped over the threshold, swearing violently. He dumped a dripping bag of salt onto a pile and went off for more. The Provincial Lady was having trouble with the servants: cook wished to hand in her notice. Her adored husband made no effort to sympathise with her complaints or even listen to them. He just sat in his chair behind a copy of *The Times* and grunted. I could see how wonderfully sane and predictable he was.

The ship shuddered in the wind and I looked up. What I had taken to be a pile of clothes was another woman. The worker was prodding her with his toe. He growled and kicked the woman until she stirred. I saw with alarm that he had a knife between his teeth. Was I about to witness a murder? The purser was unconcernedly totting up the pile of bags. The woman sat up and began searching in the bundle she used for a pillow. He pointed with his knife.

'There, there!'

You stupid woman, I thought, do what he wants! She held out a loaf of bread. My murderer cut off a thick slice, sprinkled it with flakes of salt and went out, slamming the door.

Charles. . .

The next morning, we set out to have a wash. Orlando, Joseph and I joined the men on the rear deck of *Ebeya*. Beyond the roar and vibration of the engine-room, we stripped naked, lathered ourselves from head to toe and threw buckets of water at each other. The deck was covered in diesel grease and it was difficult to stay upright or clean.

Janie and Daisy had to use the *cabinets* on *Mukongo* which were both washrooms and lavatories. There were eight between several hundred people but the better ones were kept padlocked. The walls were crumbling with rust and a bang on the door encouraged the rats to leave. The stench of ammonia made your eyes smart.

Breakfast was porridge oats, milk powder and river water, boiled in a saucepan. We used a large tin on the end of a washing-line to collect the water. It took me a while to acquire the knack of making the tin dig into the waves: as always, people were generous with their advice. Once or twice, the bucket tipped as I hauled it up, splashing heads below.

Orlando. . .

There was an American lady called Mrs Brown travelling in first class with her daughters. Mum and Mrs Brown were pleased to meet because they had read each other's books on health. They talked about diseases and toilets. Mrs Brown's room was like a hotel and the decks outside were wide and uncrowded. I didn't like walking around *Mukongo* because people pinched me or grabbed my arm and asked me things I couldn't understand. Noel said that if I fell in, the boat would stop while the captain radioed Kinshasa to ask what to do next. They had no lifeboats or anything like that.

Dad was giving us lessons each day, mainly sums and writing stories with pictures. When we had finished, there was nowhere for us to play. The benches along the deck were full of men reading their Bibles and brushing their teeth. We tried sitting there while Dad read to us but it was useless. People kept pushing past and interrupting. I said we should go to first class. We asked Mrs Brown who said we could play outside her cabin. In fact no one tried to stop us going there.

We met two French people called Eric and Veronique. Eric had a ginger beard and Veronique was very pretty. They were travelling round Africa like us. Their last job was washing up at the seaside in Congo Republic. They said they were very tired and needed somewhere to sleep. Their cabin on *Bambala* barge had four beds and seven people. It was next to a bar with loud music all night long. Mrs Brown let them have a wash and a rest.

Daisy. . .

Above Kinshasa the river becomes a lake which is called Stanley Pool after the famous explorer, Henry Morton Stanley. He came here in 1877. Mrs Brown showed us the book of his journey and we saw the cliffs where he met four kings for breakfast.

The first day we spent tied to an island. We had only gone a few miles but they said we had to wait for the engine to be repaired. At five o'clock we started again and at seven we stopped near a village called Bolobo. We went along to the front of the boat and ran down a plank onto the sand. It felt lovely, squidging through my toes.

109

Mum and I talked to some women who were washing their clothes. They thought that France was next to Zaire. It was the only other country they had heard of, apart from Congo across the river.

Orlando and Joseph pushed Dad into the river. We all had a swim. The surface was as smooth as velvet and the water was really warm. Fireflies were winking in the air and one settled on my head.

'What about crocodiles?' I said.

'Don't worry,' Dad said. 'All the noise will have frightened them away.'

Music was coming from the nearest barge. People were singing and shouting in a party mood. Mum and Dad had a kiss. The boat looked pretty with a string of lights along the deck.

Charles. . .

The note on our ticket said personal luggage should not exceed three bags or forty kilos. The couple in the cabin opposite us could hardly move. Plugged into their electricity supply were two light-bulbs, a small fridge, a cooker, an electric fan, an iron and two ghetto-blasters. We lay in the darkness listening to a strenuous voice singing a lover's complaint. It was played over and over again in broken snatches without rhyme or reason. For a few hours after midnight, some fitful sleep came our way and it was blissfully cool. Then the noise restarted at dawn: a dozen other radios, the children stirring and crying on the floor outside, male voices in animated conversation, a coffee-seller tinkling his bell, a football rattle announcing a church service, drums and singing from a distant roof-top, a bugle call on *Ebeya* as they raised the flag.

Janie. . .

Veronique and I were sitting on the roof of *Bambala* barge, sharing a beer. A Zairean joined us.

'Are you sisters?' he asked.

'No, we don't know each other.'

'Then why are you sitting together?'

It was a straightforward question but I was lost for words. I

110

did not want to answer, Because we are the only whites in second class. We had no idea whether we liked each other: we didn't even share a language. All we had in common was being strangers and feeling confused.

'Because France is next to Britain,' I answered feebly.

The daily meal was served some time between two and five: arrive too soon and you had to queue for a couple of hours, too late and it had all gone. The kitchen was a large dark room with giant cooking pots resting on the rims of lorry wheels, filled with glowing charcoal. I waited in line, not wanting to receive preferential treatment, but two men motioned me to the front. I handed our bowls to a woman at the hatch who shouted *'Cinq!'* A few minutes later they reappeared at another door, generously piled with rice and fish-heads: the larger the bowl, the more you got.

'Who eats the fish's bodies?' Joe asked.

'I don't know darling: obviously not us.'

Sometimes we found a shrimp stuck between their teeth.

We shared our food with two soldiers who had cornered Charlie, claiming to be hard up. They came every day and became more demanding until finally I lost my temper. I told them they couldn't just barge into our cabin and harass us. The children in the corridor needed feeding just as much. This put them into a sulk and they didn't reappear. Later Noel said they had been arrested for deserting from the army: it took six ONATRA policemen to wrestle them to the deck.

Daisy. . .

A Congolese boat overtook us. It was smaller and smarter than ours and we wished we were on it. When the people on *Ebeya* saw what was happening, they stood round the flagpole and sang the national anthem. Policemen came along the decks of *Mukongo*, blowing their whistles and telling us to join in. The Congolese sounded their siren and we all whooped and cheered when our captain replied with a mighty blast on his foghorn.

'Did you notice the whistles were striped ones out of Christmas crackers?' Orlando said.

111

Orlando. . .
In places the river was ten kilometres wide. You could never tell whether you were looking at the shore or an island. Some had people living on them but not for long because the mosquitoes were bad and their homes got washed away. The boat often steered close to the islands which had big white arrows to show the way.

As we went along, the gaps between the barges filled up with rubbish and weeds. There was a dead baby pig in one place. The weeds were water hyacinths. A hundred years ago, a Belgian lady brought them for her garden but they grew like mad in the hot climate and now they are a terrific nuisance.

Janie. . .
Canoes were coming alongside with fruit, fish and monkey for sale and we now discovered why there was so much luggage on board. During the second morning the whole convoy was dramatically transformed into a market. Tarpaulins were stretched between the containers and the passenger decks on either side. Sheets of plastic were laid out on the floor. Second-hand clothes, rubber shoes, lengths of wax-printed cloth, bags of salt and flour and piles of bread were spread out for sale. The clothes were clean and well pressed. Noel said they were imported by the ton from West Germany and the United States.

'We are the contact between the river people and the outside world,' he said. 'Everything they possess, they buy from us. Bring your children, I want them to have a present. Joe, come with me, you are my special friend.'

The lower decks were even narrower than before, congested now with stalls selling cigarettes, watches, trinkets, sweets, fish-hooks, ironmongery, perfume and 'Clere' skin lightening cream – 'as used in smart American society'. Someone offered us a copy of *Jane's Defence Weekly* and *The Merseyside Chamber of Commerce, Annual Report for 1979*. Noel brushed him aside. There were certain stalls he wanted us to visit where he didn't have to part with money.

'Why do you think I am called Noel?' he asked.

Charlie translated.

'I dunno,' said Joseph.

'Because I was born on Christmas Day, that's why.'

'What's Noel's job, Mum?' Orlando asked.

I got no direct answer when I relayed this question. He seemed to be a shop steward among the traders.

'We have an association to look after everybody's interests. It used to be a very risky business. Our goods were seized, thieves came aboard in the night and robbed us of our takings. Now the ONATRA police give us protection and every trader must buy a licence. We are all friends.'

The most disturbing aspect of the floating market was the dealers in medicine. We watched four young men, gathered round a trunk, filling plastic tubes with colourful patterns and sealing the ends in a candle flame. The contents looked as attractive as ·sweets and had as much effect: one aspirin, one tetracycline, a vitamin tablet and a contraceptive pill. The twentieth century to the rescue. Some dealers offered to inject antibiotics and vitamins for an extra Z 50, with a syringe of questionable sterility. One told me that he had taken a test to obtain his medical licence: he believed that antibiotics were cures for colds and diarrhoea.

Noel chose Joseph a pale-green gingham suit with 'Beatles' embroidered on the pocket. I thought it looked ghastly and the trousers didn't stay up, but Joseph was thrilled. A shift was run up for Daisy on a treadle machine. Orlando set his heart on a pair of long corduroy trousers, which appeared so comforting and familiar that he couldn't accept they were utterly impractical. He wore them for thirty minutes and then complained of prickly heat.

Charles. . .

Our neighbour and night-time tormentor introduced himself; a handsome, confident man with a neat moustache, open-necked shirt, neatly ironed trousers and Gucci shoes with gold buckles. His name was Aimé and he ran a shoe-stall. The ghetto-blaster kept him company and pirated tapes were his latest sideline.

Titi, his wife, was pregnant and so radiantly beautiful and self-possessed that I couldn't take my eyes off her. Her face was arabic rather than negro, with strong cheek-bones and a delicate nose. During the day she wore her hair braided and wound,

Medusa-like, around her head. She was pounding steamed plantains in an ebony mortar and slicing the yellow dough with a piece of cotton held between her teeth. When she squatted on her haunches, the printed image of President Mobutu nodded on her behind. In the evening she put on a silver kaftan, its embroidery rough and rich against her skin.

Aimé introduced me to his friend Tonton and we shared a bottle of Primus in his cabin. Tonton was hiding a girl without a ticket. She climbed into a corner of the bunk and crouched behind a blanket.

'Why the emergency?' I asked.

Tonton nodded to the doorway where a boy kept watch.

'The purser is coming round.'

'What will happen if she is caught?'

'She will be beaten and put off at Mbandaka.'

The boy looked in and muttered:

'He's coming!'

Moments later the captain put his head round the door. Tonton rose and greeted him like an old friend. We all shook hands. The purser joined us.

'Everything okay, Tonton?'

'Just fine chief.'

'We dock at Mbandaka tomorrow morning. Two hours only. No time for Suzanna, Tonton.'

'You must be joking!'

The captain never stopped smiling but his eyes darted here and there. The girl was breathing quietly just behind me and I sat tight until they left.

Before each trip, Tonton bought ammunition in Brazzaville. As the boat travelled upstream, he traded it for beans. He sold the beans in Kisangani and with the proceeds bought fish and game on the return journey. The mark-up in Kinshasa could be three or four hundred per cent. Tonton had started three years ago with capital of Z 15,000 – £300 – and reckoned that by the year's end he would have enough to leave the river. Aimé could not understand why he should want to. On a boat the risks were so much less; no soldiers, no gangsters demanding protection.

'But who buys the ammunition?' I asked.

'After Mbandaka, hunters will come.'

'How many traders are there?'

114

'On this boat? Maybe two thousand. It's not usually such a big one. The last trip was bad.' Tonton shook his head. 'We were forty days on the water instead of twelve. Imagine what that means! Many times we got stuck. We sat on a sand-bar for one whole week. The food ran out. Ten people died. We suspect the captain was hiding fish in the cold store. Those bastards would do anything for a profit. The ONATRA police cut up rough and threw a thief overboard.'

'But how many passengers are there – people like us, just travelling to Kisangani?'

'Hardly any. Why should people put up with this when there is a plane?'

Janie. . .
'Come and have a drink,' said Noel. He had been looking rather bleary-eyed of late. Whenever I visited his cabin in the hope of getting a light socket, I found a different woman combing her hair or cooking a meal. Noel said they were his sisters.

There were five bars scattered round the convoy. The lager tasted vile if it was not ice cold. Twice a day, the beer-sellers gathered outside the cold store: each man kept his own giant padlock on the doors so that no one could cheat.

Noel took me to the lower deck of *Bambala*, only two feet above the glassy water. Upturned beer crates were scattered round a chest freezer and music pounded from an oil-drum. A dozen *pirogues* were moored up to the side and more joined us all the time. The slender craft tipped sideways across the current and the men stood to dig their long blades into the water with swift sharp strokes. A canoe hurtled towards us and its owner leapt onto the rails, grasping the bark rope in one hand and bracing himself to take the weight. His chest read:

My Mom and Dad went to Canada and all they brought me was this lousy T-shirt.

His wives passed up bunches of plantains and then clambered out. Their faces were split by blue scars from the forehead to the tip of the nose. The canoe had been carved from a single trunk, about twenty foot long. It was patched with clay and beaten-out tins. A trussed and bleating goat lay in the bottom.

'Is the goat for sale?' I asked.

The man explained that he was hitching a lift upstream. The goat was a wedding gift.

We bought two bottles of Primus and Noel asked me what I thought of Aimé.

'He must be a wealthy man,' I said. 'I think he's very handsome too.'

'He will like to know you said that.'

'Noel. You mustn't tell him!'

Another man sat down beside me. Noel introduced him as the nurse from the *infirmerie*. He began to shout above the music, glancing at me in an intimate way.

'He says he loves you,' Noel said.

'Me?'

Life was growing complicated.

'Well, not just you,' Noel admitted. 'He loves all white women. If Charlie won't let you go, can he marry Daisy?'

'But she's only eleven years old.'

The nurse looked rather puzzled when this was explained to him.

'He wants to know how much she costs,' said Noel.

'Z 250,000.'

'He will pay in instalments.'

'She won't be ready for ten years.'

The nurse listened as Noel translated and protested loudly. Now it was Noel's turn to look puzzled. They began to argue.

'What's the matter?' I asked.

Noel turned to me rather shyly, cupping his hands to his chest. 'He says she is a big girl.'

'Not Daisy,' I replied and burst into laughter. 'He is thinking of Veronique! Tell him she's not my daughter.'

The nurse grumbled and took a long pull on his bottle.

That night, I was jerked awake by my head banging against the wall. It was pitch dark. The sound of lapping water had stopped.

'Charlie?' I whispered. 'What's happened?'

'We've run aground,' Charlie said.

'Are you sure? Shall we wake the children?'

'Not yet. Let's take a look first.'

116

No one else had stirred. We picked our way between the bodies in the corridor and looked down from the rail, straight into the water. The barge which had been there was adrift at right angles, about two hundred yards away. One end was tilted úp very slightly and for an awful moment I thought it was sinking. We heard shouts and saw men leaping over the side.

'What are they doing?' Charlie said. He'd come without his glasses and all the lights were out.

'Abandoning ship. No, wait a minute. They're standing in the water. It's only up to their knees.'

'Poor buggers,' Charlie said.

'What about us?'

Charlie tried to see as far as a moonlit island.

'Take a fix on the shore. You should be able to tell if we're moving.'

'We're still afloat,' I said presently. 'Drifting backwards.'

When we woke in the morning, the convoy was under way once more. The impact had torn out the bollards and peeled open the deck plating like a tin of sardines. More railings had disappeared and we banned the children from using that side.

Charles. . .
Friday, our fourth night, was another bad one. Orlando came and found us in the bar at nine o'clock, complaining of a sore throat: he was running a temperature. Joe and I shared a bunk, which meant little sleep for either of us. Aimé worked on his tapes till half-past midnight. In the small hours, someone took a long time to smash a padlock with a sledge-hammer; deafening blows that woke the whole barge. Two women had an angry shouting match. The police arrested a man and beat him until he screamed.

In the morning, Janie said, 'We can't go on with this.'

'I know.'

'Orlando's as white as a ghost. I'm worried he may get asthma.'

'Do you want to get off at Mbandaka? '

'I don't want to be stuck on the equator. How much money have we got?'

'You're thinking of first class? I'll go and see.'

117

The purser sent me to the captain. On the way to the bridge, I passed the victim of the police, handcuffed to the railings. They had made a crude job of shaving his hair in two narrow swathes.

A cabin with two beds was available. We did our sums and decided we could afford it. By continuing to use our present cabin to sleep in, we would have a bed each, a shared bathroom and toilet, two more meals a day and plenty of deck space. We could survive.

Janie. . .

Orlando and I paid a visit to the *infirmerie*. The male nurse was unable to help us.

'Your son has a hangover. Go to the drug dealers: they will give you a *pilule*.'

'But he hasn't been drinking! He's only ten years old.'

The nurse shrugged.

'Here we only deliver babies.'

'How much do you charge for a baby?'

'Z 300 or Z 450 for twins.'

'Have there been babies on this trip?'

'Yes. Two so far.'

'What do you do if a mother is too poor?'

'If she cannot pay, then I cannot help her.'

The first-class bar was a relatively calm and civilised place. The beer cost Z 10 more but there were tables and chairs. I was writing my diary there when Aimé found me. He had a look in his eye.

'I hear from Noel that you have been saying things about me.'

'Well, yes, I suppose so.'

'You think I am wealthy.'

'Yes, I did say that.'

'You are a polite woman.' He held out his hand. 'Please take this.' He put Z 40 into my palm.

Charles. . .

March 31st was Palm Sunday. The stairwell outside the kitchen was decorated with branches. A bit of lace made a pile of trunks into an altar and over a hundred people crammed the benches in front of it. The choir wore T-shirts printed with *Zaire Catholique Ebeya*. An island appeared like an incongruous back projection behind them. It was an occasion I would normally have enjoyed: singing in rough and cheerful harmony and being part of a shared feeling that transcended language and race. But, somehow, this service lacked conviction. Everyone was drained by the heat. I stood on the edge of the congregation and remembered Bokkie's words in Chingola.

'Up the Congo? What do you want to go there for? It's such a nasty place!'

There was a sudden commotion as a hatch-cover gave way and people scrambled to safety.

My pocket Bible was open at Ecclesiastes.

Every river flows into the sea, but the sea is not yet full. The water returns to where the rivers began, and starts all over again. Everything leads to weariness – a weariness too great for words.

Later that same morning the convoy docked at Mbandaka, a town of tin and crumbling stucco, swooning in fierce, sticky heat at zero degrees latitude. The smell of the land was sweet and tempting. The children said they preferred to stay in the new cabin so Janie and I went ashore and took our first free steps for five days, skipping and swinging our arms wide under the shady trees. A market was there to greet us and we bought bread, boiled eggs, mangoes and pawpaw. Janie suggested a walk and we were sitting with a drink at the other end of the town, when a stranger stopped and told us to return quickly to the boat. As he spoke, *Ebeya*'s horn sounded in the distance. We hurried to the quay and found the market deserted and most people back on board. The children were relieved to see us.

'There you are!'

'We nearly went without you.'

'What would you have done?' I asked.

'Drunk fifty Cokes a day.'

'Did you see Eric and Veronique?' said Daisy.

'No,' said Janie, 'why?'

'They wanted you to go with them to the Botanical Gardens.'

'Heavens, that's ten kilometres away. Charlie, go and check they're back.'

119

It took me ten minutes to reach *Bambala*.

'*Où sont les Français?*' I asked.

The Zairois family looked up from their lunch.

'Not here, not here,' they said. 'They leave their cases, cameras, everything.' They held them up to show me.

I took a deep breath and raced back to the bridge. The captain was giving the orders to cast off.

'*Les jeunes Français ne sont pas revenus encore,*' I gasped.

'*Tant pis. Je ne peux pas attendre.*'

'*Mais vous partez avec leur passeports.*'

He shrugged and smiled disarmingly. Their predicament offered some mild amusement.

'I said to them, *Une heure.* They must have thought I meant one o'clock. I have orders to obey. I cannot wait.'

Defeated, I returned downstairs.

'Poor Veronique,' said Daisy, staring at the shoreline, her eyes full of tears. 'It's her twenty-first birthday next Tuesday.'

'What will happen to them, Dad?' said Orlando.

'I don't know darling. I hate to think.'

Suddenly, Janie let out an excited shriek.

'There they are!'

She was pointing at two figures scrambling down the bank.

'What are they doing?'

'Looking for a canoe perhaps?'

'No one can paddle fast enough.'

'We *must* tell the captain to wait.'

'No look, they've found one – with an outboard!'

A long *pirogue* was heading out from the shore, leaving a creamy wake behind it. Eric and Veronique squatted amidships, clasping the sides. The children waved and cheered. The convoy was completing a slow manoeuvre that took it down the channel and out into deep water. The captain's face appeared momentarily at a window and the engines turned to full ahead.

We could hear the buzz of the outboard by now. The canoe was planing perilously over the waves.

'Come on Veronique!' shouted Daisy.

They caught up and came alongside. I saw the man from *Bambala* take the rope and begin at once to argue with the boat-owner. Some time later, Eric and Veronique came to find us, grinning sheepishly.

'May we borrow the bath?'

'We're so hot after the excitement.'

'Daddy tried to make them wait for you.'

'Did it cost you much?'

'He was asking for Z 1,000, but the people from our cabin came to rescue us. He took some cigarettes and a little money.'

Janie. . .

The afternoon was sticky and humid. Orlando was breathing heavily and we sat on the roof to find fresh air. A bank of navy blue cloud promised rain soon. An island village slid by. Children were splashing in the shallows and poling their own toy-sized dugouts. The nets drying on the bushes looked like joke spaghetti: it was April 1st.

We were making pictures with felt-tips and water-colours. A small crowd had gathered round us, among them a soldier who was squatting next to Joseph.

'*Donnes-moi ton cahier de dessin,*' the soldier said.

Joe got out his dot-to-dot book and passed it to him. We all stared.

'This is Sammy,' Joe explained. 'He's very good. He doesn't miss a dot. He did two this morning.'

Sammy opened the book on the deck, chose a felt-tip and concentrated fiercely until the picture was finished. He held it up for us to admire; an elephant balancing on a ball.

'Why don't you colour it in?' Joe said, but Sammy got to his feet, lit a cigarette and strolled away.

Charles. . .

The chief occupation of the first-class passengers was watching the river people coming and going. They arrived at all times of the day and night. Some canoes could hold twelve or fifteen people: quite a few had an outboard motor. Occasionally they made a mess of their approach. They found they couldn't paddle fast enough or scrabbled unsuccessfully for a hand-hold. The convoy left them bobbing in its wake and the chance to buy and sell was lost for another fortnight. I felt desperately sorry for them.

121

The bottom deck was always crowded with traders, shouting against each other, holding out wads of money and pointing to what they wanted. At their feet, pinioned and tethered turtles strained pathetically towards the water. Some of the fish in the *pirogues* were fifty-pound monsters which had to be sold to the captain because he controlled the cold store. Since he could not leave the bridge, the fish had to be dragged up three flights of stairs for his inspection. Angry disputes broke out and the fishermen seldom looked happy on their way back down.

They arrived with empty crates and went on a concerted binge as the boat took them further from home. Filled with beer, they made a quick round of the stalls, buying nails, hooks and line, cigarettes and bread. The bread was mouldy and green by now but they paid the same price as in Kinshasa: perhaps they had never seen or tasted a fresh loaf in their lives.

Getting away from the convoy was not easy either. The canoe might have disappeared beneath fifty others. It had to be found, righted and bailed out, while the owner balanced with legs astride the adjoining craft. Sometimes a party got aboard minus a member and became impatient to leave. They would cast off and drop astern, calling to their friends to go into the bar and dig him out. The young man would appear at an upper rail and throw himself into the river with an exuberant cry, holding one arm up to keep his cigarettes dry. We would watch his head bobbing in the soupy water until his friends hauled him over the side. Then the frail pencil of wood, its slender figures bending to their blades, fell away into the great silent expanse, heading for a faint smudge of shoreline.

Orlando. . .
April 10th, in a week's time, was going to be my birthday and Mum bought me a real live crocodile for £2. There were lots to choose from, tied to the railings where the canoes landed. Some were ten foot long. Mine was small enough to hold in my arms and I called him Oscar. He was very quiet.

'Are you sure he's all right?' Mum asked the fisherman.

'Yes, he's just tired. He has had a long journey.'

Oscar had a cut on his tail and I put some sticking plaster on it. Joseph and I had a bath with him. He had a bit of wood between his teeth and some rope round his jaws so that he couldn't bite. He made the water even more muddy than usual. Unfortunately the next day we found Oscar was dead. Dad said the fisherman must have bashed him too hard but Mum reckoned he had drowned in the bath because he couldn't close his mouth. We gave the body to the cook and he skinned it. He ate the meat and we kept the skin.

Me, Joe and Daisy had water fights in the bathroom. We filled up the bath, shut the door, took all our clothes off and splashed each other with cups. Then we had to mop up. Dad didn't mind because the bath always emptied onto the floor if you took the plug out. The only way to avoid a flood was to bale the bath-water into the lavatory.

Janie. . .
Into the eighth day, wrote Graham Greene in his *Congo Journal* in 1959, *and I really feel I've had enough. I'd like to be transported to a bathroom in the Ritz and then to a dry Martini in the bar.*

I was fed up with the grime and sweat too and longed for a crisp white cotton frock. Our second week on the river lacked the excitement of the first. The hot, breathless days passed in a sluggish, aimless way; reading, eating, dozing, playing games with the children and watching the fishermen.

A man with a Polaroid persuaded four teenagers to pose. One had on a black lace petticoat over his jeans: they all wore green eye-shades advertising Mercedes Benz. When everything was ready, the photographer lifted his eye from the camera and upped his price to Z 400. The boys protested and dragged in a fifth to share expenses. He insisted on borrowing the photographer's wristwatch. Again they froze. Then someone came up the stairs, hauling a giant fish by a cord passed through its gills. The blue eyes swivelled and its gills flapped in terminal gasps: rust, mud and bottle-tops clung to its gleaming red scales. While its owner's back was turned, the camera flashed and the young men roared with delight. The captain came out, named his price and sent the fish flumping back down the stairs. The photograph was handed round for all to admire. The boys stood at a drunken angle, inert and bleached; the fish was in darkness.

The captain's family lived round the corner from us. They had a garden of potted plants with bamboo chairs, mats and a gaily filled washing-line. The captain used to skip there to keep himself fit. Orlando presented him with a picture of his boat, which made him very pleased. He taught the children three new knots in return. The captain's mother, an enormous woman, sat in the garden all day long, making sure her grandchildren didn't stray too close to the rails. Her water-melon breasts rested in her lap and her behind spilt over the chair. She fascinated Joseph, who would play with the children just to have an excuse to stare at her. He had never met a human being so stationary and immovable.

'Do you think the crane lifted her on at Kinshasa?' he asked me.

I made friends with a young woman called Veve who traded in plastic shoes. Her French was not much better than mine and we laughed with each other without a care for grammar. She had been on the river with her husband Kofi for four years. Their two children stayed with her mother-in-law.

'Don't you miss them?' I asked.

'Not a lot. I would worry too much if they were here.'

Veve plaited my hair in the Zaire sputnik style. It was too straight and slippery to grip the thread for long and my white scalp showed through the many partings. I thought people would laugh at me but instead they clapped and smiled.

'Très bien! Une vraie Zairoise!'

Daisy. . .

We had a friend called Eliki who slept outside our first-class cabin. When the men hosed down the deck and scrubbed it in the night, Eliki came in with us. He had a strong chest and big muscles on his arms but polio had withered his legs when he was a boy. If Eliki wanted to move quickly, he walked upside-down on his hands. He had been to Kinshasa to find a new part for his wheelchair. I think ONATRA let him travel free because he had no money. We got plenty of food, so there was always enough to share with him.

Charles. . .

On Thursday, 4th April, we stopped at Lisala, a trading centre built on the first hill we had seen in five hundred miles. President Mobutu was born here and we scrambled up the hill to see the official bungalow. The building was empty and decayed.

It was wonderful to be out of range of the stench of drying fish and to look down on the chamber of horrors from a distance. The far bank of the river was just visible. The Zaire flowed due west at this point and, for the first time in days, we could pinpoint ourselves on the map. The hyacinths were very dense but there was plenty of water and Noel said we would reach Kisangani on Sunday, only a day late. It was not a moment too soon because we had very little money left. Getting some more might prove difficult too: Noel was doubtful if the banks had even heard of traveller's cheques. I tried not to think about it.

A blast from *Ebeya*'s horn sent us hurrying back. I bought mangoes and oranges and watched a harassed white woman counting her beer-crates on the quay. A young European paddled into view in a dugout. How I wished we could get away for a week's fishing – alone in that emptiness, between the water and the sky. Instead we were imprisoned with hundreds of others, surrounded by majestic space we could see but never enjoy.

Daisy. . .

It was Easter Day! They held another long service in the morning: even Dad got bored after a while. There were no cool drinks left in the bars and the kitchen had stopped serving food. Everyone was tired of being on the boat and it made them cross and grumpy.

Eliki was behaving very strangely, talking to himself, sticking food all over his hair and dancing from one arm to the other.

Orlando. . .

Where was Kisangani? Dad said we must be close because they were killing the goats. There was a horrid smell of burning hair.

125

Kofi said he wanted to give Mum an Easter present.

'Would you like a goat or a lizard?' he asked.

Mum said a lizard would be better. It was bright green and three feet long.

'Whatever shall I do with it?' she exclaimed. 'It'll never fit in my rucksack.'

Kofi cut it up and Veve cooked it in *piri piri* sauce. It tasted like chicken only nicer.

On Easter afternoon, there was a crowd round a radio on the roof of *Bambala* listening to a football match between Zaire and the Congo. At first they were cheering and shouting: then they became gloomy. The Congo had won.

Janie. . .
Joseph was sitting with us in the bar. It was hot and clammy. Noel, Tonton, Kofi, Aimé and the nurse lounged about, laughing at everything Joe said, while Charlie acted as interpreter. Joseph, usually so shy, was intoxicated by their attention and beamed.

'Why does he smile like that?' Aimé asked. 'He smiles all the time. In the end, I ask you my friends, what is there to smile about?'

'Smiling keeps me cool,' Joe replied.

16

Janie. . .

The boat arrived within a few miles of Kisangani just after dark. The port was closed, so the captain moored to an island. It rained heavily and hungry mosquitoes took shelter in our cabin, biting our ankles and the tips of our ears. The noise of frogs replaced the all-night bars.

At five-thirty we were on the move again in a bleak, grey dawn. Kisangani was in sight when a horn boomed over the water from downstream and we were overtaken by another ONATRA boat, pushing just one barge. The traders looked on angrily as it swept past and raced into the quayside. There was only room for one of us. A rumour quickly circulated that we might be kept waiting another day.

A flotilla of canoes came alongside. We haggled briefly over the price and piled into one with our luggage. The dugout was very unstable. The river was flowing rapidly, the surface was choppy and there were only three or four inches to spare. We squatted, not daring to move, until the bow nosed into the reeds. We had landed downstream of the quay, which thankfully meant missing the immigration officials. The ferryman tried to double the fare but at the sight of paths, trees and city streets, we were filled with new confidence and Charlie swept his protests aside.

We found our way into town and hired a room at the Hotel des Chutes, overlooking the river. It had a lumpy double bed, as usual the loo didn't flush and the bath was rough with rust. I boiled up a pan of water and stripped off. It was such a luxury to be cool, private and unhurried. I scrubbed myself hard all over, then fell into bed. The kids played marbles in the courtyard and Charlie went to find a bank that would change our traveller's cheques.

Charles. . .

I returned two hours later in an excellent mood.

'Did you get some money, Dad?' asked Daisy.

I tapped the fresh bulge on my waist.

'No trouble at all,' I said. 'A long wait but no problem. Eric and Veronique are outside. They've found somewhere nice to eat. Wake up Mum and we'll have a real blow-out.'

'What's a blow-out?' asked Joe.

'I'm going to blow up your stomach with chips.'

'Chips!'

'And burgers.'

'Burgers!! With tomato ketchup?'

'Wait and see.'

Eric led us to a Greek restaurant, light and clean, serving home-made soup, veal and chips, water ices and imported wines. We ate until we could eat no more. Janie sat back and sighed. Veronique raised her glass.

'To life after the river,' she said.

Kisangani has had a troubled history. V.S. Naipaul set his book, *A Bend in the River*, here. An Asian trader, born on the Kenyan coast, moves up-country in the hope of making a quick profit during the first years of independence. There is no direct allusion in his narrative to the violent episodes of that period – the civil war in Katanga, the murder of Patrice Lumumba or the Simba Rebellion of 1963: but the book portrays Kisangani as a fearful town on the verge of collapse. The campaign for *authenticité* provided an excuse for the Zairean authorities to confiscate the businesses of Greek, Italian and Asian *marchands*. The hero becomes entangled in blackmail, corruption and sexual intrigue. There is no neat ending.

Reading the book in its setting was a strange experience. It explained the bullet-scarred walls and the atmosphere of stymied lethargy. And what had changed? Not the daily grind of existence, as we were to discover.

Andy Gandon was a young Anglican clergyman, working on the staff of the Bishop of Haut Zaire. With his wife Margaret and son James, he made up half the British community of Kisangani. Within an hour of making contact, Andy arrived in his pick-up and took us away from the Hotel des Chutes to his cool, peaceful home. The Bishop came round for a glass of Vital-O and introduced us to the ordinands and trainee lay workers at the nearby *institut*. Later, we sat cutting dog-collars out of used Vim bottles while Andy answered my questions. How, I wanted to know, did the Anglican Church come to be working in francophone Zaire?

'The first Anglicans into the Congo were from Uganda. They were mostly Africans: the most outstanding was called Apolo Kivebulaya. He was a really remarkable person. Will you be going to see Pat Nickson at Boga?'

'Yes, we met her in Kinshasa. It was Pat who gave us your name.'

'Well, Boga was Apolo's base: Pat can tell you all about him. It's a beautiful spot, right on the edge of the Rift Valley. They have built a new church there now and dedicated it to him.

'Until the 1960s, the pattern which Apolo had known survived. There was no diocesan organisation in Zaire, only missionaries: but the clergy and lay councils were African and this made the Anglicans popular. The Baptists preferred to give authority to their American and European missionaries and they lost converts as a result. Naturally they resented this and I'm afraid the two Churches refused to co-operate.

'Then Mobutu issued an edict restricting the burgeoning number of Christian sects in the country. His government recognised only three bodies – the Catholics, the Kimbanguists and the *Conseil Protestant*. To belong to the latter, a church had to be of a certain size, measured crudely in terms of its financial turnover. As a result, many small, indigenous churches found their way into the Anglican fold and our membership doubled overnight. It has created enormous problems because they don't know what being Anglican means. We are dwarfed by the funds and personnel available to the Catholics, our attempts at a diocesan establishment alienate the Protestants and we meet with a standard objection from the Zairois that we're neither one thing nor t'other.'

Next door to the office was a petrol garage, a rare sight in Zaire. I noticed that Andy was keeping a watchful eye through the window.

'Do they ever have fuel?' I asked.

'Once in a while.'

'How do you manage to run your pick-up?'

'I don't very often. I use a trail-bike for long trips. Petrol and diesel are rationed by allocations, which have to be registered with a ministry in Kinshasa: the list is closed. To get hold of fuel, you therefore have to bribe someone whose allocation is greater than their requirements. Such people are not hard to find but you end up paying for the petrol twice – and that's not the end of the story. Armed with your allocation, you keep a careful watch on your garage. Whenever fuel reaches the depot, the news is all round town inside an hour but you can never be sure how much has arrived. A day or two later, when it is distributed, you have to be ready with your own oil-drums. There's a long queue. Sometimes the supply from Kinshasa is insufficient, or part of the consignment has been pilfered along the way. If you are lucky, you get what you are entitled to. Within an hour or two, it's all gone and the back of the queue goes away empty-handed.'

'Is that it?'

'Then you have to find a secure place to store it. I lost twenty gallons last month. Stolen.'

Janie. . .

Margaret Gandon spent a lot of time inside her house, trapped there by heat, culture and motherhood. Baby James, aged eight months, had been born in the local mission hospital with a cleft palate. They had flown him back to Britain for an operation and now he could eat and drink using a special cup.

Before he was born, Margaret had begun to train primary health workers, but it had not been a great success. People were not interested in preventative health care when so many curative drugs and medicines were available in the market. Her trainees used their qualification to set up as private practitioners, issuing prescriptions rather than teaching people about hygiene and nutrition. There was fierce competition between the Churches, each of which ran its own health programme. An effort to combine forces with the Catholics had been quashed. It was a disheartening struggle.

On Orlando's tenth birthday, Margaret lent us her push-bike to go into town and collect the mail.

'Letters?' said Andy. 'You're expecting some?'

'We gave this poste restante as an address where we could be reached.'

'Well I hope you're lucky.'

'I hope we're lucky too,' said Margeret. 'We haven't had a thing for three weeks.'

'It gets like this sometimes. The government has no money. There was the affair of the parcels . . .'

'Oh!' said Margeret. 'The parcels! Andy received a note to say he had a parcel from England. He went down to collect it and they told him that he had to pay a surcharge on all the parcels he had received over the last six months before they would release it!'

'Then they put the telephone charges up.'

'They went up by three hundred per cent. People just couldn't afford it. We wrote in and told them to cut us off.'

'Did they?'

'No, it's still here. It was a silly idea because with fewer subscribers, the system was even less efficient than it had been.'

The outside walls of the central post office were lined with green private boxes. The Gandons' was empty. There was nothing for us in poste restante either.

'Where to now?' Orlando asked.

'Let's explore.'

We passed brightly painted stores and a burnt-out apartment block.

'Hello Orlando, Janie!'

Aimé and Titi were trying to wave from the pavement, their arms full of parcels.

We followed a rutted track between untidy rows of mud-houses. Children stood round a tap at each intersection and skinny dogs scavenged among the rubbish piles. By the time the track turned into a path, we had a gang of boys following us.

'Are you sure you know where we're going?' Orlando said.

'Of course I do,' I said in a 'Mummy-knows-best' way.

People turned to stare but I waved confidently and carried on. The path took a sudden dive downhill into long grass. The boys sat and waited. We waded through the grass and came to a stream with impenetrable bush on the far bank. Some girls were

131

having a wash. The boys behind us giggled. I greeted the girls as if we had come all this way especially to meet them, while Orlando turned the bike round in the mud.

We took the road back through the slums and finally emerged behind a mosque, right beside the river. The setting sun and glimmering water were mirrored on the underside of its magnificent golden dome. A man with a cold box was washing his feet from the bank.

'You like ice-cream?'

'Just what we need!'

We bought the last two, just before they melted. The President's residence was near by, a large white building with closed shutters and a bare flag-pole. We stood on the crossbar of our bike to peer over the wall. Concrete paths snaked between the rosebeds: they were painted with dotted lines and halt signs.

'Do you think he drives around his garden in a pedal car?' Orlando said.

We took a small lane up the side of the house. A soldier came out and pointed his rifle at my chest.

'This road is out of bounds,' he said. 'Can't you read? Go back immediately or you will be arrested.'

This is ridiculous, I thought. Mobutu is probably a thousand miles away. I opened my mouth to argue and the soldier stepped forward and motioned us into the compound. We marched across to a garage littered with empty bottles where a sergeant reclined on a camp-bed. I spotted an outside tap by the garage door.

'Ah, there it is!' I said to Orlando. *'Wash your face!'* I whispered. Enthusiastically we washed our faces and hands and thanked the sergeant for his kindness. Orlando offered him the remains of his ice-cream and we hurried away without looking back.

Daisy. . .

One afternoon we went to the Wagenia fisheries. Stanley came here on January 26th, 1877. He wrote:

The Wenya catch an enormous amount of fish by means of poles and conical baskets, attached to long canes. . . The force of the current is

terrific as it rushes through the narrows to the grand breadth below
Wenya island.

It was still just the same. The river poured over the rocks and
the tall poles sent up sheets of spray. Men were clambering all
over the scaffolding, leaping from rock to rock, climbing up the
poles and hanging from the cross-pieces. It looked very
dangerous. The fish-traps were about six feet across at their
mouth and looked very frail, as if the current would smash them
to bits. After heavy rain, Andy said, they were swept away and
the fishermen had to start all over again.

Orlando. . . .
We took Andy and Margaret out to an old European club for a
meal. There was an open-air squash court at the bottom of the
garden, all overgrown with creepers. Mum asked for Soup of
the Day. We waited a little and then the waiter came back with
three packets.
'Which one would you like?' he said.

Charles. . .
There was a French cultural centre at Kisangani. I took the
children to see a video of cowboys rescuing black slaves on a
palm-fringed beach. A power failure put paid to the entertainment after twenty minutes. A day or two later I went along to
see Jacques Tati's *Trafic*. The auditorium was full of mosquitoes
and before long we were behaving just like the characters on the
screen: slapping our legs, trying to sit on our bare feet, pulling
on cardigans despite the heat and puffing out clouds of cigarette
smoke. I looked around at the irritated faces and giggled
helplessly.

Leaving Kisangani to the east entailed a lorry ride along the
Trans-African Highway, a rutted, single-lane dirt road through
the Ituri forest. Our next task was to find a lorry. Eric and
Veronique had gone to stay at the Olympia Hotel, a favourite
stopover for European travellers. We found Eric stretched out in
bed with a fever.

'Can we help at all?'

'It's nothing. I have it every month since the Congo.'

'Do you have medicine?'

'Yes.'

The yard outside was a makeshift camp-site for the overland safaris, operated by travel companies from London. Bedford trucks were parked under the trees and blue jeans hung out to dry.

'Joe,' said Orlando. 'Let's go and stare at the whites.'

They were a mixed bunch of surprisingly varied ages, disoriented by the Sahara crossing and strained after four weeks in each other's company. The young women were brown and bra-less, the men unshaven and smeared with grease. No one sat still. Legs stuck out from under axles, heads met over rocker valves. The women folded sleeping-bags, unfolded maps, walked twenty yards with a tea-bag and came back for water. It was midday but no one shared a meal. No one bothered to greet us.

Travel in these lorries was very different from our own experience. The back had a hard top and canvas sides which could be lowered if it rained. Aircraft seats had been bolted to the deck in tight rows. Here they sat watching the world pass by for twelve hours at a stretch. Whenever they reached a village, it was as twenty Europeans all arriving together: as such no doubt they were received. The overland companies all followed much the same route. We listened to stories of border confiscations, of papers not in order and of couriers who turned out not to speak French or Spanish. Behind the stories I saw bored officials, puzzled by the traffic in First World consciousness-raising, grabbing a few bucks or sticking a spanner in the works just for the hell of it. The stain of tourism trickled through desert and jungle. We were back among our own kind.

'Do you want to take a lift with them, Janie?'

'No thanks.'

They refused to take us anyway.

'It is company policy not to give anyone a lift.'

'See you in Goma then.'

'Bon voyage.'

The Olympia stood in a thriving part of town. Children begged in the mean, sandy streets but behind the battered façades, merchant fleets of Toyota, MAN and Mercedes Benz were being loaded with coffee, palm-oil and grain for the long haul east to Bunia, Beni, Butembo, Goma and Bukavu. I made the rounds but found nothing leaving that day.

'Go out to the airport,' someone said. 'There's a stopping place near there.'

Back at the Olympia, Janie was talking to the Greek proprietress. News had just come through of a coup in Sudan.

'It sounds bad. Juba is cut off. They are firing at planes leaving the airport.'

Which way should we go home? When we planned the trip in Zimbabwe, we considered heading south to Bujumbura at the northern end of Lake Tanganyika, taking a boat from there to Kigoma and crossing Tanzania by train. After that, our route lay northwards through Kenya and up the Nile into Egypt. The coup was not the only incentive to reconsider our plans. Janie's ears were infected. We had all lost weight. Cairo seemed a long way away. We decided to push on through the forest and review Uganda when we got closer to it.

Janie. . .
The next morning we got out on the airport road around nine. It was a dull day and a dull spot to be waiting in. We sat there till four o'clock, looking at mud shacks, banana fronds, a baby goat bleating for its mother and children bowling a bicycle rim. Ten minutes went by between each vehicle: most of the traffic was on foot. Old women tottered past, bent double under bundles of firewood, sheaves of roofing grass or baskets of charcoal. Young mothers strode into town, smart shoes balanced on their head, the baby on their back snuggled inside a towel which knotted over their bosom. The men had home-made barrows piled with plantains, tomatoes or cane furniture.

It began to drizzle and we took shelter beneath a grass awning where a soldier dozed, his feet up on a box. I sketched him while his children played with Orlando and Joe. A youth sat near us with a wooden tray, selling single cigarettes and sticks of chewing-gum.

The trucks became more frequent after midday. They slowed

down to look at us but accelerated again when they saw the soldier. Then a lorry stopped abruptly and a group of soldiers in the back called loudly to their colleague to join them.

'They must have highjacked it,' Charlie said.

'They looked very drunk.'

It began to rain more heavily. At half-past four, three brand-new Toyotas emerged from the mist. Orlando shouted with delight. They were the very ones from the river boat! The first two roared past but the third slowed enough to give Charlie an opportunity to leap onto the footplate and shout through the window. The glass came down an inch or two. Charlie named a price, the driver revved his engine, Charlie improved his offer and improved it again. To our great relief the truck came to a stop, the engine died and the driver got down from his cab.

'All aboard the Skylark!' Charlie shouted. The men eased the tarpaulin off. It was a wooden frame, only half full with bales of hessian and some beer-crates. There was one other male passenger who greeted us cheerfully. It was too good to be true.

'Next stop Mandima!' said Charlie.

'How much did it cost?'

He did a quick sum.

'Sixteen quid each for us and another sixteen for the children. It's about five hundred and fifty kilometres and will take us two days. The road is bad after Epulu.'

The rain got heavier and the driver invited Daisy and me to join him in his cab. Kisangani disappeared into the clouds. Tall trees loomed up on either side: forest trees eighty, one hundred feet high. The road carved a straight track between them, rising and falling gently. No other road went in this direction for hundreds of miles on either side. Ahead lay virgin forest, rain-clouds and the pygmies.

17

Charles. . .

Twenty years ago, Colin Turnbull, a British anthropologist, wrote several books about the Ituri forest and the *baMbuti* pygmies who live there. *The Forest People* is still in print and justifiably so: it's a clear-headed and sympathetic account of pygmy culture and reading it made us look forward to this stage of our journey with enthusiasm. Another lesser known work, *The Lonely African*, was also in my rucksack.

Turnbull was a severe critic of the economic and administrative injustice of Belgian rule. He also described the damage caused by white missionaries when they tried to impose their own values on a society whose order and health they were too prejudiced to perceive. He was scathing about their hypocrisy, their self-righteousness and their ignorance.

It is when the African judges the religion of the white man by the behaviour of its professional exponents, that he loses faith in Christianity. The African respects truth, but he sees no truth in the lives of many of the missionaries. How can they talk about brotherhood when they fight among each other, call each other unbelievers, and even refuse to enter each other's churches?

Turnbull believed he understood the root cause of this behaviour.

The missionaries said that only by clearing away the savagery and fear and superstition of the tribal African could they prepare that people for conversion to Christianity. But much of the savagery was in their own minds, in their own violently narrow way of looking at a strange new world, in their own inability and unwillingness to understand. The fear was THEIR fear, a fear of the unknown.

The result, said Turnbull was the unleashing of a 'spiritual holocaust' in which they destroyed:

not only the spiritual life of the Africans, but even the deep foundations in which it had its roots. With the majority of missions the work of teaching had to begin with destruction: the total destruction of all old beliefs. It is small wonder that in the place of the traditional beliefs, there grew up a pitiful imitation of the belief of the missionary, a belief that the ways and thoughts of foreigners are savage and superstitious. The African, thus taught, applied the same theory to Europeans.

Turnbull gives an example of this reciprocal mistrust. The Ituri people believed that:

the large and excellent hospital at Bunia was in fact a slaughter house where African undesirables were eliminated by the doctors. They injected the healthy individual with a powerful medicine that made him grow fat. When he was sufficiently succulent he was carved up and eaten. This, coupled with the cannibalistic Christian ritual of eating flesh and drinking the blood of their ancestor, made the white man look even more sinister and evil.

Often, the motives that led to a personal disaster were well meaning but short-sighted. A young man named Ibrahimo was made into an outcast when he was hygienically circumcised under general anaesthetic on the instructions of a European missionary. Without the opportunity to take part in the initiation ceremony and withstand the pain, he could not live with the other men of his village. The Europeans were unable at that stage to offer him a permanent alternative. He was condemned to a life between cultures.

If it appears at first that the spread of our 'civilisation' was an unmitigated disaster for the forest people, it will come as a relief to learn that missionaries were not wholly bad. There was another with –

a very different outlook, who refused to convert, because the Africans did not as yet know what evil was. He preferred, he said, to live among them, trying to understand their world, finding the good in it, and building on that by his own example.

Janie. . .

The lorry stopped after nightfall at a rattan hut. A woman stood in the doorway holding a candle. Her tattooed face frightened the children but she smiled when she saw the driver and made us all welcome. Supper was beer, antelope steaks and *fufu* (cassava porridge). Its texture was dense and tacky.

'My teeth are stuck together,' mumbled Joseph, before gagging on a lump.

Charlie and the boys slept on the truck while Daisy and I paid Z 40 for a room each with a palm-leaf mattress and clean sheets. The driver woke us at dawn and we set off soon afterwards.

It was bliss to know that the truck could not possibly break down. The road surface was in good repair and we went so fast that my cotton hat blew off.

'Hey, *conducteur, arretez!*'

'He can't hear you above the engine,' said Charlie. 'We'll buy you a straw hat.'

'I was fond of that one.'

At least the damp weather meant we were not smothered in dust. The trees and bushes along the verge were a ghostly grey. Fluttering clouds of blue and cream butterflies rose up from the earth and caught in our hair. Orlando pressed one between the pages of his diary.

Our fellow passenger was called Alphonse. He was a beer trader and rented space in lorries for his crates. Around nine, we stopped at his parents' home to unload and drink some tea. The clearing was like all the others we had passed; an untidy patch of cultivation hacked from the forest. Bananas, maize and cassava were planted at random amongst the tangle of fallen trunks, dying branches and straggling creepers. The hut, roofed with banana leaves, was fragile and crumbling.

Alphonse's father called the children over and showed us a pair of eggs about three inches long. One was cracked and we could hear something tapping away inside.

'What do you think it is, Mum?' Daisy asked.

'I expect it's a vulture,' said Orlando, 'or an eagle.'

The old man put his finger to his nose and made a hook with it. The hook went upwards instead of down.

'I don't think it is an eagle,' I said and at that moment the egg split open and out crawled a perfectly formed little crocodile.

139

The children squealed with delight. Orlando began telling Alphonse all about Oscar but then his voice trailed away.

'Look Mum!' he shouted.

Coming down the road on the head of a palm-wine carrier was my hat! Charlie explained to the driver, who went over and tactfully exchanged it for some cigarettes.

Alphonse's parents were not hunters: they scratched a living from charcoal burning. The interior of the forest was unknown to them and appeared so infinite they felt no need to preserve it. Later that day, we passed major clearance schemes, where thousands of acres of prime hardwood had been felled for export. The charred stumps were tombstones of a dying world.

At dusk we came to the top of a long slippery hill and found it blocked by a queue because a truck had overturned. The drivers sat round a crackling fire. Fireflies meandered among the dark trees. We ate sardines and condensed milk and went to sleep on the tarpaulin under a blanket of stars.

Orlando. . .

Alphonse can rip the lid off a tin of sardines with his teeth.

We passed the lorry in the morning, lying on its side in deep mud. It was carrying furniture and the men had decided to make themselves comfortable. They had arranged a double bed and a wardrobe under the trees. As we went past, one was lying back on the pillows having a smoke and listening to a radio, while another was combing his hair in a mirror.

Daisy. . .

People in Kisangani stared at us in a way that made me feel uncomfortable. But in the forest, the women and children smiled and waved to us with both hands.

Janie. . .

Jungle towns are hardly towns at all. Bafwaboli, Bafwabalinga and Bafwasende passed without our being aware. Nia Nia at the Isiro junction was a little bigger – a row of wooden buildings on either side of the dusty road. We arrived at midday, when it was so hot and still that even the shadows had melted away.

'I can smell bread,' said Daisy. 'Lovely fresh bread.'

'I'm thirsty!'

'Let's try in here.'

The bar was dark and empty.

'I think there's someone out the back.'

I pushed open a door and found myself in a dappled courtyard. Pigeons cooed and fluttered under a broad-leafed tree. Two girls were kneading dough on a flat stone. Their mother came up the yard from the well, balancing a clay pot on her head.

'Bonjour. Est-ce que nous pouvons manger quelque chose?'

Her daughters looked up and smiled. Their mother gave orders and the younger one brought us a tray of Cokes and *baguettes*.

'What lovely girls,' Charlie said.

They were beautiful: teak-coloured skin, long silky hair and dark, flashing eyes; they wore bright fabric, wrapped Muslim-style around their waists and over their heads. Their ancestors might have been the Arab slavers who came along this route from the east.

Charles. . .

That evening we reached Epulu, famous in colonial times as a centre for hunting Okapi and the base for Turnbull's field studies. The government had set up an exhibition village for tourists – an outcome he could hardly have intended.

A group of overlanders sat together in a small bar on the main street. They had just been to see the pygmies and were boasting to each other about their illicit photographs and petty victories over bartered goods. This truckload had come up from the south and their language was peppered with the crude and hurtful slang of Johannesburg: *kaffir, munt* and *Af.*

'Dirty. They lived like pigs.'

'With pigs.'

'Chris bought one!'

Laughter.

'He did. Chris, what happened to your piglet?'

'Chris never bought a piglet. They tried to sell him a piglet. He wanted the hunting spear. How much did he ask you for it Chris?'

'Two hundred Marlboro. I told him where he could put it.'

'What is it Ali? Not yet man.'

'Hans, it's your round.'

'Have you people come through Bangui?'

'No, up the river,' Janie said.

'Which river is that?'

'The Zaire of course.'

'I tell you, Nairobi was a bloody shambles.'

'I wonder what happened to Karen.'

'Huh, Karen found herself a *hott* man I shouldn't wonder.'

'Karen went to Mombasa on sex safari.'

'She'll clean up the coast.'

'I can just see the look on their faces in Bloemfontein when she turns up with a *piccanin*'.'

'You people come from Rhodesia, isn't it? Chris! Someone from your country here. Where is your vehicle?'

'How long have you been travelling?'

'Were you born there?'

'I taught economics.'

'In Salisbury?'

'No, a mission school.'

'You have to be born there to understand the problems of Rhodesia, isn't that right Chris?'

'As far as I am concerned,' Chris said, 'it will always be open season on *munts*.'

'They killed his brother.'

'I'm sorry to hear that.'

'The Church should stay out of politics. Look at the bloody mess they've made.'

'Wait Ali. We're not ready yet.'

'These your kids? How do they cope with travelling?'

'Okay. Did you know each other before you started?' Janie asked.

'No.'

'What's it like being in each other's company for so long?'

'We all speak English except Hans.'

'Karen couldn't stick it.'

142

'We'll be in London in a month, hey?'
'Where's Chris gone?'
'Chris is throwing up again.'
'Okay, Ali. I'll pay you, dammit.'

We reached Mandima several hours later after a bumpy ride. The mission was a few miles further on and we decided to leave it till morning. The driver had a girl-friend in the town and left us parked outside her house. Once again, we climbed into our bags on top of the lorry and stretched out under the stars.

The pygmies worship the forest as their sustaining divinity. So far we had been like the *baNgwana*, the negro tribe to which Alphonse belonged, afraid to stray far from the road, sticking carefully to what we knew. I closed my eyes. Titania, who was clearly queen in the forest, served me a breakfast of boiled crocodile eggs. I was afraid to tap the shell for fear of what might come out. Her face was fiercely tattooed – or was it the bars of sunlight seeping through the roof of her hut? Outside, Chris wrestled on the floor with a screaming piglet, but jealous Oberon would not part with his spear. I looked at the canopy of trees and a light shone in my eyes. I woke up. It was the driver and his girl.

'You see,' he told her, 'I was telling the truth: there is a white family on my truck.'

'With three *watoto*? It's incredible!'

'They have come from Lubumbashi. They say they *like* Zaire!'

'Wait till I tell Madi about this. She will never believe me.'

18

Janie. . .

'*Mandima Mission*', said the notice board. A large mango tree stood by the road. Beyond it was a long green clearing, bounded by a brick church and thatched classrooms on the right and a cluster of huts on the left: the European houses were situated on rising ground at the far end. A school bell clanged and children in bright blue uniform ran indoors. We followed the path across the cropped grass. Something in me relaxed at the sight of the tidy, manicured space.

'*Où est Monsieur Pfister?*'

'*Il est chez lui. Là bas.*'

The bungalow was modern and functional. We knocked and Pierre-Etienne came to the door, looking rather harassed.

'Janie, Charles, hello, welcome! We are in chaos here, packing up the home. We are leaving in four days' time. Come in, please. Have you had breakfast? This is Anne-Marie.'

'*Bonjour.*'

We shook hands and Anne-Marie seated us round a table still laid with the remnants of their meal. There was fresh honey and home-made bread.

'Would you like some tea?' she asked.

'Yes please.'

'This bread is delicious.'

'Lillian makes it with mealie flour. You will meet her, I expect. Ah, here are the children.'

Jean-Luc and Charlotte were introduced and stood shyly watching us eat.

'Do you know how long you would like to stay?' Pierre-Etienne asked.

144

'Could it possibly be till the end of the week? We're feeling very tired.'

'They can have the Barnes' house, Pierre.'

'Yes, I was thinking the same. We have a teacher away on leave. There are plenty of beds for you.'

'That's wonderful.'

The Barnes' house was attractively old-fashioned, with wooden floors and bright African rugs. There were evangelical posters on the walls: a verse to complement the snow-clad Rockies or footprints in the desert. The shelves contained Bibles, a religious encyclopaedia in twelve volumes and several yards of *National Geographic Magazine*.

'These people are real missionaries!' Daisy said.

All the cooking was done on a wood stove. There was no electricity and water was collected in drums from the roof. The bath was made of brick and cement and painted to look like an enamel one.

Lillian came round, an attractive woman in her late twenties. She sighed at the fire Charlie had lit beneath the oven and put a parcel on the kitchen table.

'This house is so old, it's falling down,' she said. 'Norma and Donald will move out when they return. I have brought you some flour and yeast. Do you need help?'

'We've made bread before. I think we can manage.'

'Perhaps you will come to lunch with us tomorrow?'

'That would be lovely.'

The children and I spent the afternoon stoking the oven and kneading dough. We produced a pile of rock-solid buns covered in ash. They tasted better when we soaked them in powdered milk.

'You did very well,' said Anne-Marie. 'Norma is always complaining about that oven.'

'Does she teach domestic science?'

'No, Donald is the teacher. She runs the home: she's the most marvellous pastry cook.'

'And Lillian?'

'Lillian worked here as a nurse before she met her husband. He's our engineer. Both of them are engaged in full-time evangelism. Lillian has assisted in educating Jean-Luc and Charlotte since their governess went home.'

'While we are here,' Charlie said, 'we would like to visit the pygmies. Is that possible?'

'I expect so. Ndumbe, our medical assistant, can arrange it for you,' Anne-Marie replied. 'I think they have a small camp on the edge of the forest.'

The next day, Lillian cooked us a quiche and salad that were a *tour de force* with the limited ingredients available. Afterwards she took me to a clinic for under-five-year-olds. The staff gave immunisations free of charge but other medicines had to be paid for. The babies were placed in the sling of a weighing scale hanging from a tree and their measurement was entered on a Road-to-Health card. The pygmy babies were no smaller for their age than the others. Lillian explained that their birthweight is normal but they grow more slowly. Their mothers have especially wide pelvises.

I was surprised at how few mothers and children turned up.

'Oh, the other missions take them,' Lillian said. 'The Catholics are always stealing our patients.'

Ndumbe was introduced as a pygmy chief. He squirted my ears out and agreed to take us to meet his relations. When I asked if they would like a present, he suggested soap and salt.

The following afternoon, he led us along a winding path into the fringes of the forest. It was cool and dark beneath the canopy. Butterflies danced in attendance, ants fell off the bushes down our necks and a bird clattered among the branches high above our heads. The undergrowth was slippery beneath our feet.

'What a squeaky jungle,' Joseph said.

Jean-Luc was with us.

'Do you know this family well?' I asked.

'No, it is the first time I have visited the pygmies.'

He proudly showed me his camera.

The path branched several times.

'I'll put a stick on the ground,' said Orlando. 'Then we'll be able to find our way home.'

'You don't need to,' said Daisy. 'Look, someone has already done it.' Charlie picked some giant leaves and showed the children how to make them into hats, with a twig as a pin. We stuck leaves, flowers and moss all over ourselves. Festooned in this jungle fancy dress, we reached a clearing which contained what looked like compost heaps, about three feet high.

The children stood and stared as people emerged from these bender homes. The adults were no bigger than Daisy and Orlando. I thought I was looking at a girl of eight, until she started breast-feeding a toddler. The men wore ragged nylon shirts and trousers and the women wrapped a cloth around their middles. Their features were neat and rounded; a mouth that smiled easily, button eyes and brows that lifted in surprise at our curious appearance.

There were only two men present. Ndumbe explained that most of the group had gone further into the forest in search of wild fruit, mushrooms, honey and game. He showed us their bows and arrows and a long nylon hunting net and explained to Orlando how they hung the net in a wide arc and then drove the *sondo*, a small antelope, out of its hiding place.

'Shall I give them their presents, Mum?' asked Daisy.

The men were mortified when they saw the salt and soap. Ndumbe pushed his baseball cap back on his head and spread his arms in mock dismay.

'They say they don't want this. Have you brought them money?'

'We haven't got any money with us.'

'They will accept cigarettes or beer.'

We had neither but Orlando presented a brown rag doll to a baby. It took one look and screamed but the mother was thrilled and laughed at the doll's floppy limbs. The men were still making a show of being cross but the women decided we were all right and allowed us to photograph them with the children. I was given a spotty baby to hold, who cooed and gurgled at me, then peed down my skirt. More women came into the clearing, suckling their babies as they walked. One was carrying fire on a piece of tree bark, wrapped in leaves. We sat around and laughed a lot; it was our only method of communication. Then Ndumbe said it was time to go.

I felt vaguely disappointed as we walked home, though I'm not sure what I really expected. Did we naïvely assume that because we had read Colin Turnbull's book and felt we knew Kenge and Moke, Cephu and Ekianga, we would somehow know these pygmies too? Their shyness made us feel like voyeurs.

On the road back to the mission, several people stopped to greet us and ask Charlie if he was an anthropologist.

Daisy. . .

Jean-Luc was very handsome but a bit shy. Loads of children came to play with us each day when school was over and we had a big game of grandmother's footsteps. Orlando swapped his whistle for a balsa-wood Land-Rover which a boy had made. It had headlights and seats and a clicking engine noise when the axle turned round. Unfortunately, it was very delicate and he soon broke it.

Pierre-Etienne took us out in his Toyota. We went to the market and visited a mud church with paintings on the walls and a mosque with a beautiful tower made of sticks.

Charles. . .

'Mandima Mission is an outpost,' said Pierre-Etienne, craning his neck to shout above the roar of the Landcruiser. 'We like it that way. We Brethren keep to ourselves. All our supplies come by aeroplane from Nyankunde. It's a big mission headquarters about one hundred kilometres east of here. The pygmies helped us to cut an airstrip out of the forest. Now the *baNgwana* respect it and their cattle keep the grass down. The only real trouble we've had was from some Europeans in a truck. They asked for permission to camp here and dug a latrine trench right across the take-off path. They also got very drunk. I was not pleased.'

'Tell me about the pygmies.'

'They're unpredictable: it's hard to form a lasting relationship with them. Some hang around the mission for a year or two: they usually work as servants in a village along the road.'

'Do they inter-marry with the villagers?'

'No, never. They come to the clinic. Their children attend school. You think you're getting along fine. Then one day, pouf, they disappear back into the forest. We haven't had much success in evangelising them. Until quite recently the *baNgwana* believed that pygmies could be owned. When we were clearing

148

the airstrip, I was asked to pay compensation for the vegetables stolen by *my* pygmies. Now the government has designated them as "first citizens" and you can be prosecuted for insulting behaviour, which includes taking their photograph.'

Two pygmies appeared at the side of the road. They were naked and pot-bellied. One carried a sheaf of arrows which he waved at us in greeting. He had an impish smile full of broken teeth.

'Do you go into the forest, Pierre, when you are evangelising?'

'No. We do not find the environment there is conducive to Christianity.'

'Could I go there for a few days?' I asked. 'I would like to join a hunt.'

Pierre-Etienne laughed. 'I doubt it very much, unless you have a lot of money. The *commissar de police* would not allow it. There is an official policy of separate development.'

'Do the police make life difficult for evangelists too?'

'From time to time, yes.'

We arrived at the market-place in Mandima and I went off to buy some avocadoes. A villager walked past with a *baraza* – the wooden frame of a roof – on his head.

'Where are you going, Damari?' someone called.

Damari grumbled. *BaMbuti* had stolen all the plants from his garden. His patience was at an end. He was returning to his family. An inscrutable face, sprouting a frizzy grey beard, watched him go. This pygmy possessed that odd dignity, that air of separateness and superiority which the villagers and missionaries found so infuriating. They could not understand it because they denied themselves an experience of its source. What was Mandima anyway but a small clearing in the forest? What did the dusty street and the few buildings really amount to? It was deep under the trees that a powerful reassurance was to be found. I remembered Turnbull's description of a pygmy hunt. How swiftly they had moved through the undergrowth, how his height became a handicap, ensnaring him in the branches: how well they had worked together, driving the animals into the nets, spearing them and sharing out the spoils. If the pygmy culture was so harmonious, so successful, did they need the Gospel? Perhaps the essential message had already reached them, long long ago.

On Friday afternoon, a small Cessna from MAF (Mission Aviation Fellowship) at Nyankunde landed on the grass-strip and everyone turned out to wave the Pfisters goodbye: the schoolchildren in their royal blue uniforms, the nursing staff in white, the pygmies in dun-coloured rags. The luggage was piled into the tail of the aircraft, the children were strapped to their seats and the pilot waited while Pierre-Etienne turned to address the crowd.

He thanked them for the privilege of living among them and sharing their joys and their griefs.

'We rejoice that we are leaving behind us so many good Christian families to continue the Lord's work and we grieve that we must be parted from our friends. Remember what I have worked so hard to teach you: that personal salvation is found only through the saving blood of our Lord, Jesus Christ!'

Some time ago, the fable goes, a white man appeared out of the sky in a roaring bird. He spoke about *Bwana Iesu* who was killed by men but still lived above the clouds. The white man built himself a large house of brick and ate food out of metal boxes. He knew how to make children better when they were sick but he also taught them to disobey their parents. After several years had passed, he returned to the sky again.

Pierre-Etienne ducked under the wing of the plane, dapper in his going-away clothes. The pilot closed the door, the crowd drew back and the engine coughed into life. We watched them taxi along the runway, turn and take off, a parting dip of the wings showing Anne-Marie still madly waving. Then the plane diminished into the smoky blue sky until it was a tiny dot, no bigger than a bird. Finally it disappeared. The fable was completed.

Daisy, Orlando and Joe zoomed around with their arms spread wide.

'I'm flying back to England.'

'I'm a flying doctor service.'

'Attack, attack!'

'Don't be silly, you can't attack me!'

'Yes I can.'

'You can't attack a doctor!'

'Like to bet? Pan-pan. Uhuh uhuh uhuh uhuh!'

150

19

Janie. . .

Madge was an American woman in her sixties. She had come to
Mandima from Nyankunde to run a short course for teachers of
French and was finding it hard going.

'It's the prepositions they can't get hold of. They panic and
then they don't use them at all. I asked one young man what his
father did. His reply was – he works at kitchen; he cooks
missionaries.'

Madge said there was a guest-house at Nyankunde and they
would make us welcome there. She wrote a letter to her maid,
asking her to feed us and another introducing us to the family of
the pilot who had called for the Pfisters.

At six a.m. on the Saturday, we left Mandima on another
truck.

'*Vous allez à Bunia?*' I asked. '*Nous voulons descendre à
Nyankunde.*'

The driver looked blank. 'I'm sorry,' he said. 'I only speak
English.'

'You're Ugandan?'

'Yes. You want to come?'

An hour down the road, we had a puncture. There was no
spare tyre, and the glue pot was empty. The Ugandan cut a
patch from an old inner tube and built a small fire to melt it on.
The repair took an hour to complete and lasted only a further
thirty minutes.

We were in a small settlement in the forest. Daisy pulled a
branch off a palm tree and sat down to weave a mat. Joseph tied
the spare leaves to a stick and made himself a fly whisk.
Watching us was a man who had been stunted and crippled by
bone disease. It was hard to tell his age or even whether he was

151

a pygmy. His emaciated legs were twisted under his body and he hauled himself round on arms which were as flat as a piece of driftwood. He extended a thin, delicate hand in welcome.

'Janie,' Orlando said, pointing at me. 'Orlando.'

'Pelo,' the man replied with a grin.

I scratched a noughts and crosses board in the sand and Orlando found sticks and stones to use as counters. After a while we grew bored of playing by the rules and I tried extending the board to four across. Pelo's lines became flexible, my sticks snaked round his pebbles and the whole thing threatened to slip into anarchy.

'I can tell who's won a game,' Orlando said. 'He always laughs loudest when he loses.'

Then Pelo taught me his version, where each player is limited to three pieces and moves them to block the opponent: this was far harder and he won every time.

'We learnt that game in Zimbabwe,' Orlando said.

Pelo's mother came out of a house and nodded approvingly at Daisy's weaving. She took us into her living-room where she was making the cylindrical baskets which are used for selling charcoal. I wondered why they had to be so long and thin. Pelo's mother loaded a full one onto Daisy's back and placed the grass thong over her forehead. She held up four fingers.

'Four at a time?' I said. 'You carry four like that?'

'Right,' said Charlie, 'now walk to Bunia market, Daisy. We'll see you there on Wednesday.'

'Daddy! My head would fall off after a hundred yards!'

The small house had few possessions: a pair of blackened saucepans rested on three fire-stones, a chair with a leg missing hung from the ceiling; in the corner was a strong bamboo bed without blankets. Charlie was admiring a wooden wheel. Pelo found the other bits and put together a home-made tricycle for us. It had a solid, hardwood frame and an ingenious suspension system. There were no screws or nails; the whole thing was held together by gravity and notches.

'Can I have a go?' Joseph asked.

Pelo nodded and Orlando pushed him round the clearing.

'It's brilliant! So much better than a wheelchair.'

'Pelo would never get into a wheelchair by himself.'

'And he can do his own repairs.'

In the hottest part of the day, we found ourselves sitting in a bar eating rice and black beans, while the Ugandan fought a losing battle with his tyre. The sun had been bearable as long as we kept moving. We were very thirsty but the only drink was a trickle of muddy water from a broken china filter. Joseph noticed a single bottle of Coke sitting in a glass-fronted cupboard. It became supremely important to him to drink it but we couldn't make the waitress understand. Was it an exhibition piece? The last Coke in the forest?

Another lorry pulled up outside.

'Quick!' said Charlie. 'This is our chance!'

He dashed into the road and bargained for a fresh lift. We gave the Ugandan a packet of cigarettes and wished him luck. Ten minutes later, we were on our way again.

Something extraordinary happened next. We left the forest. Somehow I had expected it to happen gradually. Fifteen hundred miles of trees can't just stop. The road had been climbing gently all day and at the end of a long stretch we came out onto green rolling hills. The houses changed from the wattle and palm leaf of the forest to sticks and grass thatch. We saw cattle again. The sky was bright with clouds and a wind cooled our faces.

Charlie scanned the horizon and whistled cheerfully.

'I feel a new man,' he said.

Nyankunde Mission was three miles off the main road. A Range Rover driven by a young Asian stopped to pick up the children and the luggage. He spoke English too.

'Shall I take you as well? Plenty of room.'

'No thanks,' I said. 'It's such a lovely evening, we'd like to stretch our legs.'

They disappeared in a cloud of dust.

'Do you think we'll ever see them again?'

We'd become so trustful of strangers, it was hard to imagine anything going wrong.

'They'll be okay,' Charlie replied.

We discussed our route as we walked along. A short cut through Uganda would get us back to civilisation much quicker.

'We're tired, there's no denying it,' Charlie said. 'We can have a holiday on the Kenyan coast and then fly home.'

153

'My Mum's friend Katie will put us up in Nairobi.'
'But first we must do a hike. These hills are glorious.'
'I want to see Pat Nickson's hospital at Boga.'
'Boga? That was Apolo's home. I'd like to go there.'
'Perhaps we could walk to Boga.'
Charlie beamed at me.
'Would you mind?'
'Not as long as you carry everything.'
'We'll dump some more stuff.'
He cut a bamboo from a hedge and shouted a cheery greeting to the owner of the garden.
'Jambo!'
'Jambo sana.'
We caught up with the children in a busy shopping street, swigging Fantas on the bonnet of the Range Rover. The mission was the biggest we had ever seen – a whole town with a big hospital, a nursing college, two schools and a small airport.

The Asian lived in Kigali, Rwanda, but he was born in Kampala and assured us that he drove to Uganda frequently. His families owned shops.
'What is the situation like there?'
'Very quiet at the moment.'
'Are the roads safe?'
'I should say so, yes. If you're quick.'

Charles. . .
'You lived on a mission in Zimbabwe?' said Pam disbelievingly. 'Is that country open to The Word?'
'There have been Christians there for a hundred years.'
'Mom, can I have some more pumpkin pie?'
'Wait dear. Let's ask our guests if they'd like some first.'
'I couldn't manage any more thanks.'
'It was delicious.'
'Marshall, you'll find some ice-cream in the top of the freezer.'
We were eleven to dinner in the pilot's house, sitting round a cedarwood table in an open-plan lounge.
'Does your church provide you with the furniture?' Janie asked.
'No, it's our own.'

154

'They fly it out here for you?'

'That's right.'

Pam passed round the ice-cream.

'Where do you get this from?' Orlando asked.

'I just call up the stores,' Pam replied.

'Is there a telephone then?'

'No, we use short-wave radios. Marshall, can you arrange for these guys to visit the stores?'

'Sure, I don't see why not. You'll find everything there you ever wanted. You got some American dollars?'

Nyankunde was more than just a mission: it was an outpost of the American way of life. Waffles, blueberries, toothpaste and diet Coke, cookies, ryebread, hamburgers and sweet corn were flown in from Nairobi and Johannesburg. No alcohol though. The community was independent. (It needed to be because the state provided almost no infrastructure in that remote area.) It had all the means necessary to twentieth-century living: vehicle repair workshops, a printing press, a swimming-pool and film shows.

The radio crackled into life.

'That'll be Gary.'

Pam's brother-in-law was over on a three-month contract to supervise the completion of a hangar. The job was behind schedule.

Pam spoke into the microphone. 'How are you doing Gary, over?'

'Put it in the oven for me, Pam. I can't leave here yet.'

'Roger and out. Gary's been working so hard, it's such a shame. Those fellows are driving him mad.'

'Is he training Zaireans on the job?'

'He was,' Marshall said. 'He's discovered now that it's easier to use unskilled labour.'

'The fellows round here can be very cheeky if you're not firm with them. Lorraine, if you want to leave the table, will you please ask your father first.'

Janie changed the subject. 'Do Craig and Lorraine go to school here?'

'No. We have an international school in the north east.'

'Do you learn French there, Craig, or Swahili?'

'Nope.'

155

'They follow an American curriculum. We don't want them to be behind when we get back home.'

'Will that be soon?'

'Next July,' Craig said.

The meal was over. We bowed our heads while Marshall said a prayer and made our way back to the guest-house. The path wound uphill under dark evergreens. The mission was laid out like a campus, with single-storey dwellings set among the schools, the hospital and the church.

'Pam gave me this to read,' Janie sighed. 'It's the annual report. I find it so difficult to make up my mind about these places. Why does life have to be such a muddle? How do you sort out the good from the bad?'

Centre Medical Evangelique, Nyankunde, Annual Report 1984.

The centre was founded in 1965 and immediately began serving an area of 50,000 square miles with only 17 medical personnel. Since that time the Centre has seen expansion in many areas, creating a training, reference and supply centre for 11 church hospitals and some 50 dispensaries in the NE Zaire region.

The centre is a 220 bed general hospital operated by 5 communities of the Church of Christ in Zaire. At present it employs some 189 nationals and 16 expatriates donate their services. Charges are made for in-patient and out-patient care, from which 100% of the running costs of the hospital have to be found. The current charge for a bed in the hospital is Z 6 [30 pence] per day and Z 400 [£20] for a hernia operation.

from: *Diary of the Year.*

Thursday the 16th February was a sad day as one of our missionaries passed into the presence of the Lord after childbirth. We need to remember the Moret family as they readjust.

Unfortunately there were a number of minor thefts of hospital equipment. Our system of controls enables us to see what is missing but the discipline committee had a difficult time deciding what to do about it.

It was an encouragement to us all to see 48 people being baptised in the church on Sunday 1st July.

The hospital was very busy in July with some cases of cholera.

156

28th July was the presidential election. Everything was done very smoothly and efficiently.

It is always great to hear of conversions through the efforts of the evangelists. A young fellow with leukaemia gave up his fetish of cow hide with a bone and a Z 5 note inside. This was later burnt in a morning service in the out-patient department.

You would be surprised at the prefabricated hangar that a team of MAF short-termers put up in just a week. Fortunately they had the help of a mobile crane that was in Bunia; unfortunately the corrugated cladding that goes on the outside seems to have got lost en route, but it should not be too big a job to add it when it comes.

Ken Brown started work on a whole new row of toilets.

The nursing school reopened on October 1st with the largest enrolment ever. There were 36 students who appeared for the jury exam for admission to first year. It was so difficult to weed out the best that all were accepted to start.

A close relative of Idi Amin, and a Muslim, was with us for several weeks, having come for a leg amputation because of gangrene. He initially did very well, his daughter received Christ and his eyes were being opened to receive new life spiritually. Unfortunately he died later after being transferred to Oicha.

As you may all know we have a small mosque 4 km from Nyankunde. The Imam was in hospital here and Emad Guirguis, a medical student who speaks Arabic, spent a lot of time talking to him. The Imam reads his Bible and so we pray there might be fruit.

The school hired a road grader to level the football field; it was a big job but the students very much appreciate it.

The day after the Finance Office ran out of cheques, a new cheque book arrived that had been delayed since August because of insufficient postage. A very small affair but typical of the way the Lord has looked after us through the year.

Several conversions in the hospital on Christmas Eve and a large open air service with about 2,000 present outside the chapel on Christmas Day brought the year to a happy conclusion.

Janie. . .

On Sunday we went to church. It was a large building and full, right to the back. Women and children sat on the left and men on the right. The few white women had lace cloths on their heads and looked like people sheltering from the sun beneath a handkerchief. The windows were gothic, the walls were painted in the Zaire colours, green and yellow, and there was no cross or altar, only a Zaire flag on a pole. A brass band was playing 'John Brown's Body' as we came in: then three choirs took it in turns to sing. The best was accompanied by a band of African harps called *ndungu*, which made a gentle, peaceful sound. The sermon was given in Swahili by an American who used a large flow-chart to illustrate the way to heaven (*Paradizi*) and hell (*Hadezi*). His talk went on for over an hour and I felt cross and tired long before we finally escaped into the sunshine. The preacher was there to shake our hands, his chart rolled up under his arm. When everyone had been greeted, he tied it to the back of his motorbike and sped off to another engagement.

We spent the afternoon in the swimming-pool. It was behind a fence among the European houses and only white children were allowed in. The local kids taunted us through gaps in the fence. Charlie was reading a book and twiddling his toes in the water. Orlando swam up to him.

'Weird mission,' he said.

'What do you mean?' Charlie replied.

'You're meant to know about Jesus, Dad. Explain to me why these missionaries are racists.'

'They're not as bad as all that,' Charlie said. 'They're doing their best.'

'They're not setting a very good example.'

'It looks that way I know, but they're working hard to help the Africans. They teach and train them and make them healthy.'

I was sitting with an English mother called Joy. She was married to the mission's only Zairean doctor and they had two children. She laughed at Orlando's remarks but I could see she had her doubts too.

'It's my children who are caught in a dilemma,' she said. 'I send my boy to the International School but he learns nothing there about his father's culture: they don't even teach his language. My daughter is still at home. I run a playgroup in our living-room.'

I started to tell her about our playgroup in Zimbabwe: how it filled a need for Joseph, the other mission children and also the infants who belonged to miners and peasants in the neighbourhood.

'The black teachers didn't like their kids to mix with the peasants at first, despite all their socialist rhetoric. But they came to see that it posed no threat and the primary school noticed a big improvement in the intake class.'

Sue looked at me.

'How many did you have to cope with?'

'About twenty-four. We employed a helper.'

She shook her head sadly.

'We could never do that here.'

On Monday morning, I went to the clinic about my painful ear. The hospital was organised in three classes. First-class patients saw a doctor the minute they arrived: each in-patient was given a bedroom with a bath and a kitchen where their family could cook for them. Second class shared a two-bed room and third were put in large wards, where their relations slept under the beds and cooked in a shelter outside. The system was more egalitarian than it looked because the wealthy subsidised the others.

I started on a bench in the third-class clinic, a large open-sided building filled with mothers and children, but I was soon spotted and steered to a British doctor who prescribed tablets to open up my eustachian tubes. He led me on a brief tour. We saw nurses in training, a well equipped operating theatre and a workshop where two handicapped Zairois were learning to grind spectacle lenses.

The next day, we sat discussing how to get to Boga.

'I want to walk there,' Charlie said.

'I don't,' said Orlando. 'I want to fly.'

'We haven't got any shoes,' said Daisy.

'I'll buy you some.'

'Why can't we fly?' Orlando insisted.

'For one,' I joined in, 'it's too expensive.'

'How much?'

'About two hundred dollars.'

'And for another,' Charlie added, 'they've run out of fuel.'

'Dad, you're making it up.'

'No, honest. Marshall told me. The tanker from Nairobi is five

159

weeks late. They've got enough left for essential flights only.'

'How far is it to Boga?' Orlando asked.

'The people I've spoken to say it's two days' walk,' Charlie replied. 'We can probably do it in three.'

'How will we find the way?' asked Daisy.

'We'll hire a guide. Pam will find us someone.'

'How can we walk that far with our rucksacks?'

Charlie produced his trump card. 'We can send everything we don't need to Nairobi in an MAF plane. They go every week.'

This was a brilliant idea.

'We can get rid of the books,' I said, 'my jeans, the cooker.'

'No, we need the cooker.'

'Well you can carry it.'

'I want some plastic shoes,' said Daisy, 'like the ones Mum got on the boat. They're really cool.'

'They're the only kind available.'

Orlando tried one more time. 'Can't we fly. I hate walking.'

'It'll be fun,' I said, 'and maybe the fuel will come while we're at Boga. We can always fly on from there.'

20

Charles. . .

I was woken by a knock at the door. Daisy let in a boy of about seventeen, wearing a torn shirt and boxer-shorts.

'*Bonjour.*'

'My name is Michel.'

'You can show us the way to Boga?'

He nodded. 'I will return in thirty minutes.'

The children cut some sandwiches and boiled a panful of eggs while Janie and I packed the rucksacks. We were just about ready when Michel reappeared. He led us across the mission to his house and kept us waiting there for an hour while he ate breakfast and said goodbye to his family. Janie got rather cross.

'All this time we've been at the beck and call of lorry drivers,' she said, 'and just for once, I thought *we* were going to be in control. After all, we're paying him to accompany us.'

'We wouldn't get far without him,' I said. 'We'll just have to be patient.'

It was Michel, as it turned out, who needed patience over the next three days.

Daisy. . .

In my rucksack were my clothes, a sleeping-bag and some food. It didn't feel too bad. I had the straw trilby hat we had bought in Idiofa. My hair was done in African plaits: it itched a bit but I dreaded undoing it because of the tangle. I wore a T-shirt and a sleeveless jacket, which Mum had made, with big pockets and padded shoulders. The boys had safari jackets too. Mum had made Joe a new 'David Livingstone' cap out of a torn pair of trousers. He had embroidered his name in red on the front.

161

Janie. . .

The morning was misty and the thick squidgy mud stuck to our shoes. Michel's had a broken strap and he took them off and carried them on his head. His equipment for the journey was a tracksuit top and a toothbrush in his shirt pocket. I suggested the boys go barefoot as well but they were too proud of their new plastic sandals and stubbornly plodded on, their feet getting heavier and heavier. After five hundred yards, they went on strike.

'I'm not walking a step further: this whole idea is stupid!'

People walking into the mission turned and stared at the pitiable *wazungu*, arguing furiously in the road.

'My rucksack is far too heavy for standing around,' Charlie said. 'Either you come now or I leave you behind.'

Michel clearly thought we were mad, but he found us a path up the hillside and walking became easier.

The landscape was like a crumpled garment. Torrential rain had turned the hills into a higgledy-piggledy assortment of spurs and unexpected valleys which were densely populated. The crops were growing well – ground-nuts, beans, maize and pumpkins. Whenever we came to the space round a hut, marked off with a white stone or a flower-bed, we shouted greetings and asked for permission to enter.

'*Safari wapi wazungu?*' they asked. 'Where are you going, white people?'

'Did you see that woman?' Joe whispered. 'Her bosom was hanging out of a hole in her dress!'

After fifty minutes, we stopped by a bridge.

'Time for a rest,' said Charlie, dumping his rucksack on the ground.

Orlando had a large blister on his heel.

'Perhaps you'll take your shoes off now,' I said.

We could see a long way back over the Ituri forest. The sun was out and burnt fiercely when not behind a cloud. Charlie went down to the river, wet his hanky and squeezed it over Joe's face, which was very red.

'Can I have a go?' Daisy said. She reached up and realised she'd lost her hat.

'Oh no! I've dropped my hat, my beautiful hat!'

We searched everywhere. Charlie went a mile back down the path but he couldn't find it.

'You must have some protection against the sun,' he said and gave her his swimming-trunks to wear. 'Come on, now. We've wasted enough time already.'

Orlando. . .
Daisy kept bursting into tears. I got completely fed up. My rucksack was much heavier than hers because I was carrying the water. When I pointed this out, she took the bottle and emptied it on the ground. How stupid can you get? As usual, no one understood me. *Poor* Daisy. She'd have been better off staying in England and having ballet lessons like normal girls. I was the only one strong enough to carry a rucksack in the end: Mum carried Daisy's and Joe's and Michel took Mum's.

Daisy. . .
Dad and Michel were a long way ahead. We rested every half hour, but by the time we caught up, Dad was ready to go again. I felt well and truly knackered. To encourage us, Mum described terrible hard journeys she had read about in the *National Geographic*. An Australian girl learnt how to look after camels and got lost in the baking-hot desert. The men climbing Everest had to wait for several minutes to get their breath back between every step. My favourite story was about a couple who walked right across America and had lots of adventures. When they reached the ocean, they walked straight in with all their clothes on.

At midday, we reached the top of the hill and stopped to eat the sandwiches under a tree. There were no huts any more. I made a chain of wild-flowers, Dad fell asleep and Michel sat and chewed a piece of grass.

Charles. . .
It was a glorious view to our European eyes. Green hump-backed hills rolled into the distance, a patchwork of moving

163

shadow under a blue heaven and brilliant puffballs of cloud. For once the grass was soft and inviting rather than dry and spiky: only the threat of ticks and snakes prevented us from rolling in it.

In the early afternoon we scrambled down a narrow path and followed a river-course into the valley. I was convinced we were all alone and the sudden clamour of voices came as a surprise. Round a corner we encountered several dozen near-naked men, their dark skin smeared with clay, digging a tunnel in the bank. They worked energetically, scraping at the earth with shovels, broken buckets and even their bare hands. There were no props holding up the roof. They stopped when they saw us. Someone made a joke and they laughed and jostled each other.

'What is it?' the children asked. 'What are they doing?'

'Mining,' Janie said. 'Let's see what for.'

In the shallow river, other men were concentrating fiercely over wide metal pans. Orlando went to watch.

Orlando. . .

The miner dipped the pan in the river and swilled the water round and round so that it melted the clay. Then he carefully tipped the dirty water out and got some more. He did this several times until most of the clay had gone and only gravel was left behind.

'Look!' he said, pointing at some tiny yellow specks. It was gold!

Janie. . .

Some of the miners spoke French.

'Where do you come from?' I asked.

'Chiyekele.'

'Is that far?'

'No we come here each day.'

'Is there beer there?' Charlie asked. 'We've been staying on dry missions for almost as long as I can remember.'

'Plenty beer, don't worry.'

They enjoyed showing off to the children who explored the tunnel, much to my anxiety, and got so dirty that we told them to strip off and bathe. The water was the colour of milky coffee and their pale bodies looked like dollops of cream. The river-course had been diverted into old workings and I found a private corner where I could cool down too.

The path was perilous for the next few hundred yards. We nearly fell into a vertical shaft hidden in the undergrowth: it was so deep that the bottom was in darkness. They were everywhere and we had to thread our way between them. We walked into an open space shaded by tall gum-trees, where the miners' wives were cooking dinner on a dozen fires. They shrieked with laughter when they saw Joseph and he turned redder than ever.

'I think it's because I'm carrying my coat on the end of a stick.'

'They've just never seen a white boy out here before.'

'Are we staying in Chiyekele tonight?' Charlie asked. 'How far is it?'

About ten kilometres, Michel thought. He was a little vague on distances.

'We'll never walk that,' I exclaimed.

'We'll just have to try.'

As Charlie said this, the sun disappeared behind a dark cloud, a strong wind blew through the glade and it started to rain. The miners' wives were caught unawares and leapt to their feet, shrieking with dismay. The gum-trees provided only the flimsiest shelter: there was nothing for it but to press on. As the valley disappeared behind a grey curtain, Charlie rummaged for our kagoules. I had made them myself out of sail material and this was their first serious test. When we left the trees and the rain came down really hard, roaring in my ears and trickling down my back, I quickly realised that they weren't going to work.

Walking was easier at first because it was cool and the rain made us want to hurry. But before long the path became a red stream joined by other black streams gushing down the hillside and the water got deeper until it covered our ankles. A frog floated past. The light was fading: it was slippery underfoot and hard to see. Charlie and Michel were waiting for us at the bottom of the hill. Charlie had fallen over and sat rubbing his leg. There was a shout and a splash and Joe fell over too.

'Ouch! Mummy! I want to go home!'

'Come here, darling. Don't cry. You're wet enough as it is!'

We heard strange panting cries approaching us from behind. 'Watch out,' Charlie shouted. 'Here they come!'

The miners jogged past in single file, holding their pans over their heads. They were singing in time with their splashing feet and their grins raised our spirits. The tail-ender stopped and offered to carry a rucksack. Charlie gratefully handed his over and swung Joseph onto his back instead.

'We've got to go faster,' he shouted. 'We've got to hurry before it gets dark.'

Orlando. . .

This time Daisy was in front. We heard her shout, 'Oh no, it's too deep!' And Mum saying, 'Don't be silly.'

We caught up with them and saw a river blocking our way. The miner with our rucksack was wading across and the others waited on the far bank. Dad went first with Joe. He had to hold on to some reeds to stop himself being swept away. A miner carried me while Dad went back for Daisy. Mum came last.

'Face into the current!' Dad shouted.

Just before she reached the bank, Mum disappeared up to her neck. The miners reached out and pulled her to safety. Mum was laughing but we were all very cold now.

'Come on,' Dad said. 'We can't stay here.'

We carried on and then we met the miners coming back. Another river was flooded ahead. The current looked very fast and strong.

'It's too dangerous,' Dad said.

Two miners dashed past us and leapt in, shouting:
'*Viva Zaire! Viva Zaire!*'

It was too dark to see if they made it.

'It's no good, we'll have to turn back,' Dad said.

'Where can we go?'

He didn't reply.

Daisy. . .

We followed the miners to a hut. It wasn't a very big one but the owner kindly allowed about twenty people to get warm by her fire. Mum wanted us to take our wet clothes off but I felt much too tired. Michel appeared and said he had found somewhere for us to stay. It was horrid going out in the rain again, but Dad carried me part of the way. We saw a light ahead and found a larger house where the family made us welcome. We hung up our clothes to dry. Dad got the cooker going and made hot soup for everyone. Michel borrowed Mum's T-shirt and a skirt: he looked very funny. Then we felt our way in the dark to a clinic where we could sleep. It smelt of disinfectant.

'Funny health care they have round here,' Dad said. 'The sink is full of bran!'

We had to lie on the concrete floor. One sleeping-bag was too wet to use so Dad offered to share his with Orlando.

'I don't want to share,' Orlando said.

Dad picked up a pair of giant tongs to threaten him.

'I'll have your guts for garters,' he joked.

'Those are castrators,' Mum said. 'I know where we are. This is a clinic for animals!'

Sure enough, we were woken in the morning by cattle mooing outside, waiting to have an injection.

Charles. . .
Before we left, our hosts put on their best clothes and posed for a photograph. Despite the warmth, the baby was dressed up in a woollen suit, bootees and a hat; her mother held a wild lily.

The ground was still wet and slippery but the sunshine sparkled on the leaves. We found the river had gone back down. A narrow plank was visible which had been a foot under water: we would never have made it. Orlando wanted to search downstream for the miners' bodies.

We walked for a couple of hours and breakfasted on stubby bananas in a village called Kone. A *ndungu* band was rehearsing and Janie got out her tape-recorder. The musicians, whose names were Nestor, Bakama, Yakobo and Martes, smiled with pleasure and performed two fishermen's songs for us. *Ndungu* are played like harps but they have a sound-box covered in hide: the strings are woven from nylon fishing-line: the bass is so big and solid that the player can sit on it.

Michel wanted to get on with the journey. We struggled up a

long hill and stopped to rest in a cool thatched church with a mud altar. The pew I sat on was a simple log, resting on forks in the floor: it had been worn smooth by long use.

'Where are we?' I asked Michel.

'Chiyekele,' he said.

Janie. . .

We reached the centre of the village and I sank to the ground feeling exhausted and ravenous. Orlando went off to forage.

'The only food they sell is sugar and cigarettes,' he said. 'You can buy glasses, pencil sharpeners, air-mail envelopes and nylon socks.'

'Where's the beer?' asked Charlie.

'I can't find any.'

The store-keeper came out to greet us.

'He wants to give you a meal,' Michel explained.

'That's wonderful!'

We followed the old man into a square hut with a tin roof. On the walls were a calendar, a family snapshot and a verse from the Bible, made out of tinfoil and coloured sweet papers. We sat round the table on schoolroom chairs and watched through the doorway as his grand-daughter kindled a fire in the kitchen across the yard. Ten minutes later, she brought us cups and saucers and a pot of sweet milky tea. Charlie clapped his hands and smiled.

'*Asante sana.* Thank you.'

'*Karibuni bwana.* You are welcome here.'

'Are we going to carry on?' Orlando asked.

'I want to stay,' said Joseph.

'So do I,' said Daisy.

Michel thought we should stay too. He pointed to the sky: dark clouds were already beginning to mass on the horizon.

'Okay,' Charlie said. 'We'll have the afternoon off.'

The dinner arrived, omelettes and sweet potatoes served on new enamel plates brought over from the shop. Afterwards we spread our wet clothes on a hedge round the front door and told the children to watch the cattle didn't eat them.

Orlando made friends with some children and joined in a game of *tzoro*, moving pebbles between four rows of holes in

168

the sand. As in backgammon, the rules are simple but there are complex strategies which depend on luck and skill.

Jean, the store-keeper's grandson, put on his best trousers and invited Charlie and me for a stroll. Chiyekele was a picture-postcard village. The walls of the squat houses were painted in cream, black and ochre bands. The thatch hung low over the front doors. Bordering the sandy street were hibiscus hedges and beds full of golden marigolds. A jacaranda avenue led from the clinic to the school.

We visited the homes of the village elders: the pastor, the medical orderly, the headmaster and the churchwarden. With great courtesy, we were made welcome in each home and offered tea. Charlie or Jean told our story and then our host walked with us to the next house. At the school, we admired the four new classrooms built by parents round the football pitch and we climbed to the Bible Institute which housed the *foni* or radio. The headmaster suggested we contact Boga Mission to let them know of our whereabouts. I returned at six o'clock, the designated transmission time, and tried to get through for a quarter of an hour without success. Perhaps the storms were to blame.

On my way back, I was met by a shrieking mob of children, careering downhill with three blonde heads among them. It was the local sport of wooden-bicycle racing. Like Pelo's, these bikes were a wonder of design – strong enough to speed down a stony road, yet falling apart when picked up. Orlando had tried them all for comfort and explained the advantages of a straw seat and strips of rubber nailed to the wheels. Joseph's favourite had a tin headlight fixed to the handlebars.

Jean showed us our home for the night, a derelict European house which had once belonged to a Belgian coffee manager. The verandah was daubed with *Castro* and *Dallas*. The front room contained a four-poster bed and an oil-drum with *Mr and Mrs Epp, A.I.M., Congo* stencilled in red.

'Were Mr and Mrs Epp the Belgians?' I asked.

'No,' Jean said, 'they were missionaries. AIM is Africa Inland Mission. The Belgians ran away from the *Simba* rebels.'

I drew back the curtains and they fell apart in my hands. Charlie tested the bed.

'Great,' he said. 'Two thick mattresses, just like in *The Princess and the Pea*. I'm going to sleep right now: I'm whacked.'

Jean opened the oil-drum and took out four musty blankets and an enormous bolster. I gave Charlie a good-night kiss. The children were all outside, chasing a piglet.

'Quiet now!' I called. 'Your father is trying to go to sleep.'

'It's starting to rain, anyway,' Daisy said.

The thunder of raindrops hitting the tin roof grew to a steady roar. Jean looked up anxiously and disappeared into the kitchen. He came back with pots and pans and I helped him to arrange them under the drips.

A procession of umbrellas arrived from the village, led by the churchwarden. He placed a candle on the dining-room table and set out dishes of steamed plantains, fish heads and *pondu* – pounded cassava leaves. Plantains are dry and powdery on their own but the *pondu* was delicious and helped them down. Joseph hated fish but, in front of six solemn men watching his every mouthful, he did not dare to refuse it.

Jean wouldn't hear of us going to bed without a wash, even though the children were nodding off.

'We have a bathroom in the yard.'

'But it's still pouring out there.'

He looked so disappointed that I gave in. We were shown to a grass-walled enclosure, where a bowl of hot water was steaming in the rain. A bar of Imperial Leather soap and a towel were laid out on the stone beside it.

'Oh look,' Daisy exclaimed. 'It's the soap like a telly from England!'

It made her day. We lathered, sang and splashed each other; then tiptoed back through the mud to our beds.

Charles. . .

I dreamt we were chasing two mischief-makers. I caught hold of them in the stairwell of an old building. 'I know you!' It was Daisy and Orlando. Someone said, 'The window – that's the traditional punishment!' I opened several layers of glass and saw we were at a dizzy height above the city. A doctor was at my elbow, asking if I had the right to make them stand on the sill. 'It's not me,' I said, 'it's not me.' I looked into Daisy's eyes and she looked straight back at me, trusting but scared.

A breakfast of beans, sweet potatoes and tea arrived before dawn and we were on the road by seven. Jean said the elders would not accept payment so I left a contribution in the church box.

The road went up a tormenting incline between a graceful avenue of trees. My rucksack was an ordeal: it made my shoulders ache, my chest felt tight and I worried about twisting an ankle or knee. The pretty cottages and lawns of Chiyekele soon gave way to more tatty, ramshackle smallholdings, but they were still 'main road' houses with tin roofs and a wooden front door. The road twisted and plunged and we trudged from sunlight into shade. A lorry went by. We took a path which cut off the corners. Soon we were going straight up hills too steep for any vehicle to climb. We came out on the top in wild country.

'Dad, did you notice that lady's teeth?' Joseph said. 'They were pointed like a saw.'

'She had filed them,' I said.

'Why?' asked Daisy. 'It must be incredibly painful.'

'It's probably just a custom now. Originally it was cannibals who filed their teeth so that they could pull the stringy human meat off the bone.'

'Do you think she's a cannibal?'

'I hope not.'

We were resting at a crossroads in the shade of a giant clump of bamboo when a strange man stopped and began to take an interest in Janie and Daisy. He stood swaying from side to side, his hand searching in his clothing. Daisy let out a shriek.

'Mummy, he's got out his *thing*!'

'Go away, go away you nasty man! We don't want you here!'

'He's crazy,' Daisy said. 'Leave us alone!'

'Charlie, please help!'

A woman came out of her house and called urgently. By this time the fellow had hold of my hand, his face an inch from mine, the spittle bubbling between his teeth. The woman came up behind and kicked his legs away. The lunatic fell in a heap, sat up and roared.

'You must get away from here,' Michel said.

171

We grabbed our belongings and fled.

'Why did you shake his hand?' Janie demanded crossly.

'I didn't. He took hold of it.'

The madman's shouts pursued us.

'Is he following us?'

Daisy looked back.

'No, the woman's blocking his path. She's whipping him with a stick.'

We found a cool stream for lunch. As usual, Michel and I got there ten minutes before the others.

'What was wrong with the last stream?' Janie asked.

'This one has a waterfall. Michel thought you would prefer it.'

'Joseph nearly got trampled to death.'

'How?'

'Some cattles trapped me.'

'They had horns a metre long,' Daisy said.

'Joe was in the middle of a stream and they came stampeding down the bank to have a drink.'

'They were very thirsty,' Joseph said.

'What did you do, Joe?'

'I ran away.'

'You didn't cry?'

'No,' Janie said, 'he was very brave.'

We ate some sardines and rice and lay in the sun. Michel taught the children to count in Swahili and joined in a game of floating plastic bowls down the rapids.

'I wish we could stay here all afternoon.'

'Look at the sky.'

The thick white cumulus was beginning to turn grey along its bottom edge.

'More rain,' Michel said.

Wearily, we hauled on our rucksacks and set off again. The path eventually led downhill across open ground and the village of Bukaringi appeared in a hollow. We picked up a companion in a white doctor's coat, who introduced himself as the choir-master.

'*Safari wapi?*' he asked.

'Boga. How far is it?'

He looked doubtful. About thirty kilometres?

172

'Heavens!' Janie said. 'We'll need another day at least. Charlie, you told us the people at Nyankunde walked it in two!'

'I know, but just look at Michel.'

He was striding out half a mile ahead, his shirt-tails flapping in the breeze and Janie's rucksack balanced jauntily on his head.

The storm had built up behind us. For a time we were lucky and the squalls raced to left and right: then we were caught in a downpour and ran to a small settlement. The hut we entered was entirely covered in thatch, like a large mound of hay. The interior was very dark and partitioned into a living and cooking area, a bedroom and a goat pen. The family exchanged greetings and then ignored us. The rain poured in and made puddles on the floor. There was a bleat outside, someone opened the door and four kids and their mother trotted in.

When the cloud-burst was over, we made a triumphal entry into Bukaringi. The choir-master went in front in his white coat. People took the children's bags and someone hoisted Joseph onto his shoulders. A little boy came up with a toy camera and squirted water at us. A group of teenagers in conscript uniform stopped drinking to turn and stare. Although we were bone tired, there were customary courtesies to be observed.

'This is my school,' the choir-master said.

'Do you want to visit the priest in his house?' asked Michel.

A pretty nurse detached herself from the crowd.

'Vous êtes les Anglais?'

'Oui.'

'I have been waiting for you. Please come. Mam'zelle Pat will be here soon.'

'Pat Nickson is coming here?'

'Yes, in the Land-Rover.'

'Kids! We've got a lift to Boga!'

'Whoopee!'

The nurse took us into her clinic and gave us tea and a plate of beans.

'How did you know we were coming?' Janie asked.

'I heard on the *foni*. We have been expecting you for two days. At Kamatsi, they cooked a meal for you but you never turned up.'

'Kamatsi?'

'It's on the road,' Michel explained.

173

The crowd at the window shifted its attention for a moment.
'I think Pat is here.'

A Land-Rover pulled up and Pat climbed out, clutching a baby girl under her arm.

'Hello Janie, hello Charlie. *Karibuni*, welcome. Has Elizabeti looked after you? We've been hearing all about your adventures on the *foni*: you're the talk of the district. The children must be exhausted.'

They were dashing round outside, playing tag.

'Come on kids. Time to go.'

An hour later, we rolled into Boga hospital compound in darkness.

21

Orlando. . .

I woke up in my own comfortable bed. Dad was shaking me.

'Come and look at the snow!' he said.

I went outside and looked round the garden in the sunshine.

'You're mad,' I replied. 'I'm going back to bed.'

'No, come on,' Dad said. 'It's hidden by the banana-trees.'

He led me down a path and across a field. We came to some rough bush where no one had planted.

'Where is this snow?'

'Just a bit further,' he said.

We climbed to the top of a slope and looked down into an enormous valley, the biggest I had ever seen.

'The Great Rift Valley,' Dad said. 'You can see this from outer space.'

'What's that lake called?'

'Which person is everything in this country named after.'

'Mobutu?'

'That's right; and over there is the snow!'

He pointed to some mountains. I could just make out a white patch on the highest one.

'The Ruwenzori,' Dad said. 'The Mountains of the Moon.'

'How far away are they?'

'About sixty miles.'

'Are we going there?'

'We haven't planned to. They're very steep and wet.'

Through the day the mountains changed colour from purple to green to brown to orange to black.

Janie. . .

We met up with Pat for supper soon after dark. She lived in a whirlwind, running the hospital and a network of clinics, training nurses and midwives, performing operations, learning French.

'Why French? How has she coped all these years?'

Rosemary, a veteran nurse and her colleague of two months, explained:

'Pat's a fluent Swahili speaker but the government has just given the nursing school accreditation and the exams are in French. It's a bore.'

'*Tu dois m'aider à parler Français!*' Pat called from outside where she was filling the paraffin lamps. Rosemary opened the oven door, releasing clouds of wood-smoke, and pulled out two perfectly baked loaves and a cake. We were tucking into pumpkin and peanut butter when a timid knock came at the door and a dozen students entered.

'They've come to sing a welcome to you,' Pat said.

'How delightful. Could I record them?'

'Most certainly. They'll sing all evening if you like. We have our own composer, Kahambu. She had a tremendous thrill a few months ago: we came second in a competition on the World Service. I was working in the pharmacy with the radio on in the background when suddenly I thought, I recognise that song! It was our girls.'

'Well done!'

We turned our chairs round and listened.

'*Karibu-ni, Karibu-ni!*' the girls sang.

'Thank you, *merci beaucoup*, that was wonderful!' Charlie was appreciative. 'They've got the most intricate counterpoint I've heard yet.'

'It sounds even better in the open air,' Rosemary said.

Pat took me round the wards next morning. There were thirty beds made from strips of cow-hide nailed to a wooden frame: all were occupied. Pat greeted each patient like an old friend. A girl in white uniform was taking temperatures.

'*Habari Mam'zelle Pat?*'

'*Mzuri sana.* Nyangoma and her twin sister, Nyokato, are my chief allies. They're descendants of Apolo Kivebulaya.'

Nyangoma was attending to an emaciated boy.

'How old is he?'

'We think about ten. He doesn't speak any language we know. He came from Uganda on his father's back. It's TB I'm afraid. I don't hold out much hope but we can but try. I'll bring him some peanut butter later.'

'How do the patients get fed?'

'Their relations cook for them in the courtyard. They used to sleep under the beds but we've just built a visitors' shelter.'

A woman sitting beside her husband got up as we approached and presented Pat with two large pawpaws.

'A present?'

She laughed. 'I wish they were! His leg was badly gored by a wild pig. We're putting raw pawpaw on the wound. It's a natural antiseptic and speeds up the healing process.'

A girl who was no more than sixteen lay on her side, weeping quietly. She had been in labour at her home for three days. There was no road to her village and her relations carried her several miles before they found a Land-Rover to take her to Boga. Pat had performed a symphysiotomy – cutting through the pelvic bone to make room to get the dead baby out.

'Why not a Caesarian?'

'That's a major operation. Remember, I'm a nurse not a surgeon. With this method, she will be less at risk if her next confinement is at home. Poor darling: she's so upset. As you can see, she needs to eat too.'

'Do you get much malnutrition?'

'We shouldn't: there's plenty of rain and the soil is good. We tend to find it in pockets, like near to the gold workings.'

'You'd have thought they would be the most prosperous.'

'Oh I'm sure the men are! They get about Z 45 for the weight of a matchstick in Bunia or Butembo. Very little of the money finds its way into children's stomachs though.'

'We met women cooking for the miners.'

'Yes, exactly, and then they don't have time for their fields.'

We came to the end of the ward round.

'If I hurry I can get an operation done before lunch,' Pat said.

'Can I watch?' I asked.

'You can help. I'm sterilising a woman. She had a difficult twelfth delivery five days ago. I'm worried that she may wriggle when I give her an epidural.'

We left our shoes outside the theatre. The light over the

operating table was powered by a car battery. Pat scrubbed up and a student helped her on with her gown. A rubber glove split.

'That's what happens when you have to re-use them.'

The patient sat very still while two students washed her. Before injecting the anaesthetic into her spine, Pat asked the woman if she was a Christian. She nodded and we prayed together that everything would go well.

I had never been present at an operation before. I held the woman's hand throughout, while the student took her blood pressure. The clamps on the blood vessels were like a tangle of lace-making bobbins: there wasn't much room left for getting inside. The first fallopian tube had been tied and cut and Pat was fishing with her finger for the second, when Nyangoma put her head round the door and asked for the first aid box. Outside the Land-Rover was revving up.

'It's our rule that the flying squad must leave within two minutes on an emergency call,' Pat said. She finished sewing up the abdominal muscles and left the student to tidy up the fatty skin.

Early the next morning we received a summons to report to the immigration office. It was full of shouting men. The official leafed very slowly through our passports and asked me why they had not been stamped at the last town.

'I'm taking them,' he said.

'You can't,' I answered. ' I refuse to give them up.'

'Foreigners are not permitted to wander around at will. I will have to investigate your case.'

I got away as fast as I could and went into the market. A stream of people were panting up the escarpment, sacks of coffee balanced on their heads. A young man in a straw boater was sampling the beans for quality.

'They grow this coffee in Toro district in Uganda,' he explained.

'How far do they have to bring it?'

'About twenty miles.'

'The sacks must be heavy.'

'They weigh twenty-five kilos.'

'Why don't they sell the coffee in Uganda?'

'There is too much tax to pay: it's less here in Zaire. Also we can get nothing with our money in Uganda.'

'What happens to the coffee now?'

'It's bought by businessmen and taken to Goma in trucks. Then it's transported through Rwanda, Uganda, Kenya to the sea at Mombasa, where ships carry it to Europe.'

'What a long way round!'

I looked at the sacks with new respect.

The usual smell of drying fish hung over the market in spite of a stiff breeze. Men were ladling thick red palm-oil into bottles and a blood-spattered butcher chopped his way through a haunch, watched by an anorexic cow tied to a tree. I bought pats of butter wrapped in pumpkin leaves and some second-hand clothes – an embroidered silk dressing-gown for Z 30 and a gold brocade waistcoat with diamante buttons for Z 10. They cheered me up no end.

Charles. . .

I went to bed for a few days, complaining of a temperature: I hated to admit I was exhausted. We were staying in a comfortable thatched house belonging to Tim, an English engineer, who was away building a road: Judy, his young wife, was camping with him. Opposite the bed was a painting by a Zairean, made from their wedding photograph. The artist had caught the texture of the church wall with loving care but the figures of the newly-weds in morning dress and white he could not understand: their faces were blurred and unreal.

I discovered two books on Tim's and Judy's shelves which addressed the doubts I had felt at Mandima and Nyankunde. The first was *The Primal Vision, Christian presence amid African religion*, by J.V.Taylor. The author was General Secretary of the Church Missionary Society (he performed the dedication of the new church at Boga to Apolo Kivebulaya) and later Bishop of Winchester; a man working within the established church who had the courage to pose tough questions. Was Christianity what it claimed to be – genuinely a religion for all peoples? If so, could it rid itself of European culture?

How many of the missionaries and teachers who have fun with

179

African hymns and paintings recognise that a truly African worship is going to seem queer and distasteful to European Christians?

Christ has been presented as the answer to the questions a white man would ask, the solution to the needs that Western man would feel, the Saviour of the world of the European world-view. But if Christ were to appear as the answer to the questions that Africans are asking, what would he look like?

The answer, Taylor believed, was to be found within traditional African belief systems. He surveyed them in his book, acknowledging what was fearful and destructive but showing that a desire existed, in Africa as elsewhere, for a loving and accessible God, and that such a presence was not incompatible with a world dominated by spirits or with ancestor worship.

The Primal Vision was published in the 1960s, when African politics were in a ferment. The hope it expressed for an emergent African Church has not been widely realised since then. Perhaps Taylor's questions were posed too late. The power structures of European Christianity were already in place and a generation of mission-trained Africans, some more conservative than their European counterparts, has filled the offices of bishop, archdeacon and rural dean. Boga was a case in point.

The second book, *Christianity Rediscovered, an epistle from the Masai* by Vincent J. Donovan, took this missed opportunity as its point of departure. Why on earth do Africans cling to European ways? Donovan asked. The Church has failed in its mission. Its strategies for winning converts have been disastrously dishonest: buying slaves from the Arabs, only to enmesh them in an equally alien culture: bribing natives with medicine, education and jobs in the bureaucracy: most damning of all was the continued struggle to win converts after 150 years of permanent mission! St Paul never spent more than two years in one place, often it was only a few weeks, yet a whole Church grew from his words.

To test his convictions, Donovan turned his back on all established forms of European Christianity and tramped the Serengeti for six years, telling the Masai, one of the proudest and most resilient tribes in Africa, about Jesus Christ. He spoke in their language and to their culture. He did not tell them how to worship or pray or sing hymns: everything to do with forming a church he left entirely to them. After a year with each clan, he reached a point where they either formally accepted Christ or rejected him. His mission rôle was then ended and the growth and nurture of the Masai church was left largely in the hands of its own chosen leaders. Here at last was an indigenous Christianity.

It was a strange kind of Mass. No church building, not even any special, fixed spot where it took place. As a matter of fact it moved around all over the village.

Grass was a sacred sign among the Masai. Since their cattle, and they themselves, lived off grass, it was a vital and holy sign to them, a sign of peace and happiness and well being. So, as the Mass began, I picked up a tuft of grass and passed it on to the first elder who met me, and greeted him with 'the peace of Christ'. He accepted it and passed it on to his family, and they passed it on to neighbouring elders and their families. It had to pass all through the village.

The Mass was not just a ceremony but a special day in which the whole life of the community – herding, fetching water, cooking, repairing huts, caring for the children, the sick and the elderly, worrying about the future – was offered in dance and music.

I never knew if the eucharist would emerge from all of this. The leaders were the ones to decide yes or no. It was not easy to achieve the eucharist. It was not an act of magic accomplished with the saying of a few words in the right order. And if the life in the village had been less than human or holy, then there was no Mass. If the grass had stopped, if someone had refused to accept the sign of peace, there would be no eucharist.

At other times the will was there to override the weaknesses in the community, the will to ask the Spirit to come on this community to change it into the Body of Christ, so that we could say together, 'This – not just the bread and wine, but the whole life of the village, its work, play, joy, sorrow, the homes, the grazing fields, the flocks, the people – all this is my Body.' Ite, Missa est. Go to it. It is the Mass.

The title Donovan chose for his book was no idle boast.

On Sunday morning, we went to mass at Apolo's church and sat patiently through the English liturgy translated into Swahili. Kahambu's choir sang. There was a long address. I was invited to say a few words and tried to express our gratitude for the hospitality we had received. Afterwards, Pat showed me the photographs of Apolo, an old man with wrinkled eyes and a woolly beard. He was wearing a white cassock beneath a dusty single-breasted jacket. (Kivebulaya means 'he who wears the European thing'.)

'Isn't it unusual to dedicate a church to a person not long dead?' I said.

'From the stories one hears,' Pat replied,' he was a marvellous man with his own God-given convictions; strong-willed yet gentle, a very simple and straightforward person. He was great friends with the pygmies.'

'But don't you think he must have been a bit of an Uncle Tom, a stooge of the European missionaries? It's hard to believe that an African was able to by-pass the Church seventy years ago, to reach his own faith as it were.'

'Apolo was not just a preacher and a pastor, though I think he was very good at both. He had powers his own people could recognise. He was as disciplined in his spirituality as the very best witchdoctor. He spent an hour or more in prayer every night around two o'clock. He healed the sick by prayer. He was able to reconcile warring factions within the tribe. He was brave. Once in the early days, they all ganged up on him and armed men surrounded his hut, but he cowed them by the force of his spirit. He survived all sorts of adventures with animals. The wild pigs were afraid to touch his garden.'

'You're not serious?'

'Yes I am. The gardens round here have to be protected with thick thorn hedges: children sit up all night round a fire when the crops are nearly ready. Apolo's garden had none of this but his vegetables went unharmed. In the morning, the villagers would trace the pigs' tracks in the earth: when the footprints reached his boundary, they always stopped short and went off in a new direction.'

Janie. . .
Pat came out of the *foni* room looking grim.

'Bad news I'm afraid.'

'What is it?' we asked.

'The Commissar is coming from Bunia tomorrow to instal the new chief. We'll get no work done at all.'

'Does he throw his weight around?'

'He *will* insist on eating with us. We'll have to use your house, I'm sorry. It's not really our responsibility at all: the *collectivité* should feed him.'

'Are the chiefs still important then?'

'The old boy was a sweetie: everyone loved him. Sadly, he got caught up in cattle rustling and they gave him the push.'

The Commissar flew in with his wife shortly after breakfast: he had been expected for eleven o'clock. Nyangoma and Nyokato, who were pounding plantain and peeling sweet potatoes at the back of the cottage, reacted with panic.

'Quick Madame! Make the beds, send the children out to play!'

Five minutes later, there were voices outside and the party made its entrance. The Commissar was in early middle age, his skin smooth and shining with oil. He wore a courtelle *abacos* with a paisley cravat and matching handkerchief, white silk socks and snakeskin shoes.

'He looks just like Mobutu,' Orlando muttered.

'Shush darling. Go and join the others.'

Even the Commissar's heavy-rimmed spectacles were modelled on the President's.

His young wife stepped carefully over the threshold. Her hair had been straightened and her eyebrows plucked into thin lines. She was dressed in an ankle-length gown of shimmering grey with coordinating clutch bag and court shoes. Just the thing for a day in the country.

Bringing up the rear were a high-ranking army officer in green breeches and a male secretary whose job was to hold a silver ghetto-blaster which supplied the Musak. Anticipating this, Rosemary had brought some cassettes.

'Mozart or Beethoven?' she said brightly.

'I think Beethoven writes very enjoyable stuff, don't you?' the Commissar replied.

Rosemary put on the Fifth Symphony.

Nyangoma brought in tea and we made polite conversation

about Northern Ireland and Mrs Thatcher.

'I like Africa,' the Commissar opined, 'because here we are free.' Outside the mission lay silent in the sunshine. The school was closed for the day and the hospital waited. Even the market had been called off.

The young chief came in and was so over-awed that he made his excuses after two minutes and fled.

Pat announced lunch was ready. Among the various dishes were Rosemary's precious European supplies – white rice, tuna and tinned baked beans. The officer helped himself to a bit of everything before we had even sat down. Was he testing it for poison?

'I hope this is what you like,' Pat said.

'Well actually, I prefer our Zairois menu – cassava, *pondu*, fish, plantain.'

'Oh dear, I'm sorry.'

'I like bacon and eggs,' the Commissar joined in. 'A big plate of bacon and eggs is the best food you people know how to make.'

Pat chose this moment to mention our difficulties with the immigration officer. She was careful not to criticise him. (He's on the make, she had told me earlier. He's only been here a few months but the taxes go straight into his pocket and everyone is fed up.) The Commissar listened but gave no reply: he continued eating and acknowledged her with a wave of his hand.

I tried asking him about the women we had seen with filed teeth.

'I don't know,' he said. 'Why do they have filed teeth?'

'Is it because they are cannibals?'

He laughed and bit delicately through a potato.

'The meat of man tastes very good,' the officer added and he looked at me as if I was an appetising titbit.

Daisy. . .
We had good fun at Boga. There were lots of children and we played at building pygmy houses out of branches and leaves.

Mum went riding on a stallion which had come from Sudan with an Englishman. He had to leave the horse at Boga because it kicked a statue of President Mobutu and got into trouble. The police said it was a spy and had eaten some secret papers.

Pat said we could borrow the horse for the next stage of our journey through the forest to Butembo. I thought it would be fun but Mum said the stallion was wild and bit her leg too often: also the rivers were now too swollen for us to cross.

Just then Marshall from MAF (motto 'On Wings of Love') dive-bombed our house in his airplane and dropped the mail into the garden. He told Pat on the *foni* that he could take us to Butembo the next day.

'Hurray!'

After breakfast, we walked to the airstrip and waited in the International Departure Lounge – a grass hut. The priest who had taken the Sunday service was ploughing with a pair of oxen. He got very cross when Mum tried to photo him. Marshall arrived. The plane was tiny and we squashed into the back with a fat African woman and her baby. Pat gave Marshall a glass of milk, a sandwich and a banana. Then we said goodbye and took off over the Rift valley.

22

Orlando. . .

I have always wanted to be a pilot, but going to Butembo I was sick into a black polythene bag. The others were all sick as well: only Dad, Marshall and the African lady escaped. Some Canadian women were waiting at Butembo to take our places.

'I'm afraid we've used up all the sick bags,' Dad said. He dumped them behind the hangar.

We nearly had a crash on the plane. We were landing in a village in the forest. The runway went in between the houses. Our wheels touched the ground and we were taxiing along when a motor-bike raced across in front of us. Marshall was very angry and told the people so.

'If you want us to fly in here, the deal is that you keep the runway clear,' he said.

When we were ready to take off again, there was a small dark shape on the ground. Marshall slowed down and went to investigate. It was a kid playing in the grass.

'Right, that's it!' Marshall said. 'I'm not coming here again.'

Despite feeling sick, it was fun seeing the Ruwenzoris and the forest stretching to the horizon on our right. The pilots have no radar beacons or weather forecasts, so they follow the roads across the forest. They know how to do their own repairs.

Charles. . .

Butembo was bustling and prosperous. The streets were full of bicycles and we saw cars – the first since Kisangani: there was even a bus service to Goma.

'Good roads from now on, kids!'

'*On achete de l'or ici,*' said a sign above a doorway.

'*Ets. Mongala et Fils, Négociants en Café.*'

From his office, M Mongala could see his coffee growing on the surrounding hills.

Restaurant Zoo.

'Let's have lunch,' Janie said, 'and replace what we've just lost.'

We went into the grubby shack and sat at a table. The usual poster of the President in a leopard-skin hat was pinned to the wall. There were original paintings too.

'Look Mum, whites whipping blacks!'

'And slaves in chains.'

'I don't get it,' said Joe. 'What is it?'

'It must be scenes from Zairean history,' I said. 'Look, here's a mission being burnt to the ground.'

The waitress brought boiled meat and rice and asked us if we would like some coffee.

'Yes please. It should be good.'

She went behind her counter and put two heaped spoons each of sugar, dried milk and fresh coffee grounds into a cup: then she poured on warm water. It was undrinkable.

'I can't understand it,' Janie said, 'surely she must know.'

'Perhaps she thought it was Nescafé,' Orlando suggested. 'It's kept in a Nescafé tin.'

'They would never serve instant coffee: no one can afford it except missionaries.'

'Perhaps she thought it had turned into Nescafé.'

We went shopping. Daisy bought herself a new hat from a man behind a sewing-machine.

'What's he making?'

'Can't you see? They're a long string of brassieres.'

'*Vous voulez acheter* – for your daughter? Citoyen Musavaka ex-André at your service.'

'You're very kind: she's too young.'

'Why did he call himself ex-André?' Daisy asked.

'André was his European name. Mobutu banned them but people don't like to give up that easily. Mobutu used to have European names too: he was called Joseph Désiré.'

'Orlando's disappeared,' Janie said.

'He was here two minutes ago.'

'There he is!'

He was surrounded by a crowd of teasing children.

'Orlando, leave them alone, just ignore them!'

'They've no manners. They're asking for it.'

'Calm down. They think you're strange, that's all.'

'Come on,' Janie said, 'it's time we left.'

The bus had gone, so we walked to the edge of the town and found an empty pick-up going to Kanya-Bayonga. How wonderful, we thought. Speed, comfort and room to stretch our legs.

When would we learn?

A hundred yards up the road, we halted beside a waiting group of people. An old man got on first with two rolls of barbed-wire, a 25-kilo sack of flour, a box of nails and a bundle of clothing. Seven other passengers joined him and then we returned to town to collect some cement. We ended up perched round the edges, with our legs dangling over the side.

The road went for a hundred miles through a maze of steep hills and wooded valleys. Gum-trees had been planted along the verge to prevent traffic falling into the ravines. I held Joseph tight as we screeched round each hairpin. Was it better to hit a tree or plunge over the edge? I could not forget the stories Paul had told us in Kinshasa.

'Bodies all over the road, Charlie! One minute they're swaying past you, singing their hearts out: the next, you come across these ghastly scenes. It's fatal to stop. In Zaire the person with the money takes the blame.'

It was a beautiful afternoon. A treacly golden light spilt through the clouds. The eucalyptus bark glowed a fragile pink. The hills piled into each other in exhilarating chaos and the road writhed like a snake in their clutches, skimming a ridge, cutting a col. We passed many villages of conical huts. It rained slightly at Lubero and a rainbow spanned the sky. A sign flashed past.

L'Equateur.

'I thought the equator was flat,' Joseph said. 'It was when we crossed it on the river. If it's a straight line, surely it must be flat.' He looked about him doubtfully. 'It's very bumpy round here.'

188

Orlando with a pygmy mother

Arriving at Nyankunde

Janie playing noughts and crosses with Pelo

Joseph on bicycle at Chiyekele

Waiting after the crash

Lunchtime between Chiyekele and Bukaringi

Pat and Rosemary in the departure lounge, Boga airport

Gukunda holding Nyakarima, Parc de Volcans, *Rwanda*

Rainbow over the equator at Musienene, Eastern Zaire

Masai children, Ngorongoro, Tanzania

Happy's Land-Rover, Serengeti, Tanzania

Dawn on Lamu Island

Gilman's Point, Kibu Peak, Mount Kilimanjaro

The idyll in the forest

It grew dark and we got stuck behind a huge yellow truck growling along at walking pace.

'What's the matter with him?'

The driver was hanging out of his cab, shining a torch beam onto the road ahead.

It was nine o'clock before we reached Kanya-Bayonga. To our delight, we were dropped at a brand-new, well appointed business hotel.

Janie. . .

We looked in wonder at the white walls, varnished wood, gold door-knobs and terylene rose-printed sheets on the beds. We took two rooms but because of a paraffin shortage there was only one lamp available between them. The shower in the yard was supplied by a bucket in a wheelbarrow. We ate a large helping of egg and chips and tucked the children into bed. Then Charlie and I returned to the lounge for a nightcap. The chair-covers were crocheted in fluorescent orange and green.

'I like the hunting nets,' Charlie remarked.

We ordered beer and the waitress poured a little into our glasses and set them before us. Whenever we took a sip, she crossed the room from the bar and refilled them.

'This is service!' I said.

'Very civilised, I must say.'

'I shall miss Zaire, though I'm glad it's nearly over.'

A lorry rumbled past. On the radio, Tabu Ley gave one of his characteristic whinnies.

'It gets into your blood, that music.'

'Perhaps,' I said, 'the Commissar at Boga was right after all. It is a free country.'

'Free to go mad perhaps?'

'I was thinking of free to run hospitals, free to *disappear* – like the pygmies. It's how I imagine the Wild West used to be.'

'I shall feel happier,' said Charlie, 'when I can look back on it from the outside.'

The next morning, we wandered through Kanya-Bayonga looking for the market-place. It was strange to see thousands of mud huts making a town. Did all these people live off the land?

If not, why were there no signs of a cash economy – tin roofs, a general store, a bar or two? The only shops were portable rabbit hutches. We could see the wares through the wire-netting but the owner would only unlock it once your money was in his hand.

All the lorries in the market were going north, so we sat down to wait. Charlie became entangled with a Jehovah's Witness and I got out my diary. A face peered over my shoulder.

'*Que faites-vous?*' he asked.

'I'm writing. *J'écris.*'

'What are you writing?'

The Zairois are suspicious of spies.

'I'm writing a letter,' I said, 'to my mother.'

'May I see?'

'Certainly not.'

'But you must show me! I'm a secret policeman.'

I giggled.

'You're not very secret, are you!'

He had already lost interest.

A truck coasted down the hill and stopped nearby. It was a British Leyland – one of the first we'd seen: the paintwork was still fresh. The driver went round to the bonnet and peered inside.

'What's up?' Charlie asked.

He pointed to a fuel leak and gave a thumbs down. His mate pulled a strand of hemp from a sack: they undid a nut, wound the hemp round the thread and tightened it again. The driver turned the engine over.

'No good,' Charlie said. 'Diesel is gushing out. What about making a washer?' He turned to me. 'The insole of your shoe might do.'

'A rubber mat would work even better.'

We took the mat out of the cab and cut a washer to fit. It worked perfectly: the driver was very pleased.

'We're going to Goma,' Charlie said. 'Can you take us?'

He thought for a moment.

'Z 250?'

'Okay.'

We threw our luggage up to the other passengers. There were

only a few: the lorry was carrying palm-oil in large drums.

'*Eh, m'zungu!*' The driver put his head out. Charlie laughed.

'He wants to know if we can mend punctures too.'

'*Un pneu est foutu à l'arrière.*'

'What did he say?'

'I didn't catch it.'

Hammer blows were resounding from the rear axle.

'I hope we're not going to break a spring again,' Daisy said.

'I doubt it. The truck's almost new.'

'Besides, it's British.'

Shortly afterwards we set off.

Daisy. . .

Dad woke us up to look at the view. We were on the edge of the Rift valley. You could see for miles. Another lake gleamed on our left.

'That's Lake Amin,' Dad said, 'and look at the volcanoes dead ahead! That's where we're going.'

He sounded very excited, but then Dad always is. The bottom of the valley was covered in tiny dots.

'There's a game park down there,' Mum explained. 'It's too hot for humans. Those are animals you can see.'

I watched for a bit but then I felt drowsy and went back to sleep.

Charles. . .

As the truck slowly made its way down the escarpment, Janie and I were discussing travel books.

'It must be so difficult to know how to sustain interest,' I said. 'Adventures don't just happen to order.'

'What I find boring,' Janie replied, 'is writers' dreams: they're such personal things.'

I smiled. She had told us a dream in great detail the week before at Boga.

We slowed down to edge past a truck which had boiled over on the way up. Our driver was hugging the inside of each bend, cutting so close to the bank that the sand scraped his paintwork.

'He seems to be trying to avoid the camber,' I said.

191

Janie lay back and closed her eyes. A gentle breeze blew across the great valley. I looked fondly at the sleeping children: all three had wedged themselves in tightly. The lorry reached the next bend, its engine protesting, its springs creaking. I watched it nudge into the low bank. Stop. Slip forwards. Stop again.

Then my mouth went dry. I put my hands beneath me and prepared to jump. I think I called out but it was a small, futile sound, lost in a slow-motion roar of tumbling barrels, screams and smashing glass.

Janie. . .

I jerked awake at Charlie's shout and just had time to pull my legs out and land safely. Behind me, Daisy lay pinned beneath an oil-drum, her face twisted in shock. Orlando hung upside-down. Charlie was throwing his weight against the roof bars, roaring:

'Get Joseph out. Get him out!'

The driver crawled through the windscreen and stood shaking. A passenger heaved the barrel off Daisy and helped her to her feet.

'Get Joseph out!!'

Charlie was desperate. The lorry lay half on its back with all four wheels in the air. We found Joseph right underneath, trapped across his waist and ankles. He was very still. His head and arms were hanging loose and his face was hidden. There were so many screams that I couldn't tell if his was among them. I thought, Joe's dead! We pulled him out and, thank God, he was screaming too.

Charlie must have realised then that his strength was not equal to holding the lorry up. He let go and lifted Orlando clear. The cargo was still creaking and spilling. Orlando's face was stained with orange palm-oil and his clothes were encrusted with wheat. He was crying with pain. Carefully we laid him on the ground.

'My leg, my leg.'

His shin and ankle were blackened and swelling. Joseph couldn't walk either. Daisy appeared the least badly injured.

I looked up, my heart pounding, and saw a mother

running down the hill, shrieking over her baby.

'Where were they?'

'In the cab,' Charlie said.

Another woman sat in the road, sobbing with shock. A youth walked round in dazed circles, blood pouring down his face, wads of hair hanging about his ears.

I went back and rummaged for my rucksack. What do you do when the first-aid worker is herself in shock? My hand was shaking so badly that I couldn't undo the straps. We were carrying a respectable supply of local anaesthetic, sutures and dressings, but then I realised we had only half a bottle of water. Charlie pointed out that there was plenty of beer. Could we wash wounds in beer?

I set to work with cotton-wool, fetching out grit and wiping off the palm-oil. Charlie handed out homeopathic pills for shock and dabbed gentian violet on the baby's grazed forehead. We were sitting in the shade cast by the cab.

'We should disconnect the battery,' he said suddenly. 'For all we know, the engine could explode. Where's the driver?'

Another truck had pulled up behind us. The passengers came crowding round, clicking their tongues.

'How many dead?' they asked.

'Bugger off!' Orlando yelled through his tears. 'This isn't a zoo!'

'Couldn't they take Orlando?' I said. 'He needs a doctor.'

The lorry came past and Charlie tried to wave it down. Our driver leant out and grinned.

'Not this one, *m'zungu*. I fetch help. Bye!'

'That man is a criminal,' the young mother said. 'We will have him arrested. We will write to the magistrate in Kisangani. You must help me.'

'What actually happened?' I asked.

'It was a puncture,' Charlie said. 'One of the back tyres was flat at Kanya-Bayonga. He tried to tell us. He thought he could get away with it because the wheels are in pairs. We simply overbalanced.'

'They should never have put oil-drums on top of wheat.'

Bruises were spreading over both Joseph's knees. He stared at them sadly. We waited another hour until a near-empty pick-up gave us a lift.

193

'You never know your luck,' Charlie said, looking out over the game-park. 'Another mile down the road and we could have been eaten by lions.'

Charles. . .
After Daisy was born in Ludlow at three o'clock on a June morning, I was driving home, my heart full to bursting, when suddenly I was forced to stop the car. The road ahead was thick with wild rabbits. Now, just when her young life had been threatened, Mother Nature showed up again. Gazelle, impala, wildebeest and zebra grazed in their hundreds. Beside the track, a lioness with two cubs sunned her stomach and lazily switched her tail.

Orlando. . .
I lay on a sleeping-bag. The truck had tall sides and I couldn't see out. My leg hurt a lot when it jolted. We stopped at the game-lodge but the clinic was closed. There were lots of baboons in the car-park. Daisy brought me a Coke from the bar and said she'd seen the driver there. So much for getting us help! Mum gave me a painkiller and they allowed me into the cab for the rest of the way.

Janie. . .
My children had nearly died. I wondered guiltily why we had not checked the tyres or noticed the top-heavy load. I could hear my mother's voice —*You're so irresponsible. A wicked parent! How dare you play like that with your children's lives!* Then I remembered the dream at Boga and my guilt receded. It was one of those rare, sequential dreams. I had woken up remembering every detail and the strength of it haunted me all day.

The whole family was driving very fast in the back of a pick-up through the mountains in Zimbabwe. The truck tipped and fell over sideways but it continued moving until the bushes on the verge stopped it. Orlando was underneath. Nobody was badly hurt but later I had my right foot amputated just above the ankle. This worried me because I have slim ankles and it seemed a pity to lose one. I woke just as I was being fitted with a wooden foot.

Perhaps someone up there was looking after us: perhaps it was our destiny. I trembled with relief that we were still alive.

We spent the night at Rutshuru in a friendly, white-washed hotel. The bedrooms were arranged round a flower garden with a thatched bar in the middle. We washed and changed and carried Orlando and Joseph to a table.

'What would you like?' Charlie asked, looking at the list which covered a whole wall. 'There's Primus from Kinshasa, Kisangani, Gisenye or Bukavu. There's three types of whisky, French wines, London gin. . .'

'Only Skol or Coke,' said the waiter.

'What is there to eat?'

'Goat and chips.'

The children's faces brightened. When the waiter returned, I raised my glass.

'Now,' I said, 'a toast – to us.'

'The Hampton Family,' Charlie added. 'I'm proud of you all.'

Then we talked over each minute detail of the day.

23

Janie. . .

Goma is a large trading-centre at the head of Lake Kivu. We arrived there the following evening on top of another lorry, laden with coffee and dozens of people. My hands went clammy and the children yelped every time it lurched into a pot-hole, even though Charlie had examined the tyres carefully.

I made a mistake when it rained and they pulled a tarpaulin over us. I pointed my camera into the crowded darkness and took a flash. At once, angry exclamations broke out and the covers were thrown back. A man seized my arm.

'How dare you! That is my woman. Did you ask permission?'

His girl-friend smirked into her hanky. Charlie calmed things down.

'Please accept my apologies for my stupid wife,' he said. 'She doesn't know what she's doing. I expect the camera went off by mistake. How can she see in the dark?'

The man looked at him.

'Which tribe are you from, *m'zungu*?'

'The English people.'

'Who is your chief?'

'We have two, Queen Elizabeth and Madame Thatcher.'

'You allow yourself to be ruled by women?'

'No. That is why I am here in Zaire.'

He laughed.

'I agree: why concern ourselves with the foolish creatures? You are my friend. Now, you must take my snap also.'

The road went past the volcanoes. Mikeno was the most dramatic, a needle of rock towering over the landscape. Nyiragongo was still active. The most recent eruption had

196

plugged the crater and caused a smaller mountain to blow a few miles down the chain. The lava flow had left narrow embankments which looked like a new motorway: the soil beneath was very fertile. Lonely banana-trees grew in holes hacked through the lava. The passengers bought bundles of leeks and carrots from a wayside stall. We gorged ourselves on strawberries and passion fruit.

Goma was important enough to have an honorary British consul, a Belgian called de Bruyn, who lived close by the lake.

'Turn left by the bent lamp-post,' someone told us.

Daisy and I walked down there while Charlie looked after the boys in the hotel. Goats grazed in the centre of the street and soya beans grew on the verge. The lamp-posts had only recently been installed and children had signed their names in the wet cement. Sure enough, one was bent at right angles, twenty feet above the ground.

'But how did it get like that?' Daisy asked.

'They must have put it up already bent.'

The consul was just leaving in his Mercedes.

'Come with us,' he said. 'I'm taking my daughter to a riding lesson.'

M de Bruyn was a gruff, red-faced man who owned a coffee factory, a fishery and several shops. He listened as I told our story.

'We don't know if his leg is broken or just bruised.'

'There are no X-ray machines in Goma,' he said. 'You will have to go across the border to Gisenye.'

'Is it far?'

'Not at all: two and a half kilometres. But you will need a visa to enter Rwanda. These can only be obtained in Kinshasa.'

'We have them already.'

He looked pleasantly surprised.

'Good. Then I will drive you there tomorrow.'

'That's very kind of you. Thanks.'

We arrived at the stables and watched his daughter being led round the paddock on an enormous black horse. In her jodhpurs, she looked the very image of a Pony Club girl, blonde curls escaping from her riding-hat. De Bruyn lit a cigar.

'How long have you been in Goma?' I asked.

'Twenty-eight years.'

'How many people live here?'

'About a hundred and fifty.'

Daisy looked puzzled. 'Does he mean *thousands*?' she asked me.

'No,' I muttered. 'He means *whites*!'

Charlie was waiting for us in the restaurant. We told him our good news.

'There's decent grub here,' he said. 'Let's celebrate.'

I had been looking forward to a good meal but suddenly the world seemed a glum place. Instead of perking me up, my sherry tasted vile. The brown décor appeared quite ghastly, the children twittered inanely, the menu was boring, the service was slow and the seats were hard. I chose steak but when it arrived I took one mouthful and burst into tears. The adrenalin had stopped flowing. Charlie helped me out of the dining-room and tucked me into bed with a sleeping pill. I lay curled up, shaking and gulping. Headlights arced across the room. The events of the crash repeated themselves more and more slowly until finally I fell asleep.

Charles. . .

Goma border-post is reputed to be one of the most difficult in Africa. With a Union Jack fluttering on the bonnet, we sailed through the formalities. At once, the different atmosphere of a new country became apparent. Gisenye felt like a resort. The lake glittered through the trees. Flowers grew where goats might have eaten them. Houses smiled at us across open lawns. There were no fences: could this mean no thieves as well?

'I think you'll find this place comfortable,' de Bruyn said, stopping outside the Hotel Edelweiss, a Swiss chalet perched above the road. He left with a wave of his cigar.

We checked in and wandered down to the beach. Joseph was hobbling by this time and Orlando rode on my back. While the others swam, I took him on to the hospital. The first X-ray they made was of the wrong part of his leg. After a whole day's wait, they discovered a small crack in his shin-bone.

The doctor took me aside.

'Can you get me an eight track, reel to reel, Grundig tape-recorder?'

'Well I'll see what I can do.'

'I have no plaster. You will have to buy him an elastic bandage. And keep the boy in bed for three weeks.'

'But that's impossible.'

'He can play cards if he wishes.'

Further objection was pointless. As soon as we were out of earshot, Orlando said he wanted to go swimming.

Gisenye was far too expensive a place to spend three weeks, so I decided he must have a pair of crutches. We made enquiries and found a furniture factory who measured his arms and said they would build him a pair.

Back on the beach, we found Janie talking to a European couple. The man was very tall with blond, curly hair. Their freckled children were splashing in the lake with Daisy and Joe.

'This is Wieland and Claudia,' Janie said. 'Claudia is a nurse and Wieland writes for a German newspaper. They would like us to stay with them on a mission south of Kigali.'

'Perhaps we could come in a day or two. We have to wait for Orlando's crutches and then we want to visit the gorillas.'

'Wieland has been,' Claudia said. 'They are very interesting but it's tough going.'

Wieland stood up to check on the children.

'Till! Not too far out!' He turned to us. 'Do not allow your children to depart from the shallow water.'

'Is it dangerous?'

'People drown here every year. Volcanic gas rises from cracks on the lake-bed and sits on the surface of the water. A swimmer enters unawares, passes out and drowns. It is especially dangerous in the early morning, before the air warms up.'

'How sad,' Janie said, gazing at the sparkling waves. 'Why is water in Africa always so dangerous? If it's not gas, it's bilharzia or crocodiles.'

'Were you here when the last eruption happened?' I asked.

'No,' Claudia said, 'but there will be another one soon, I think.'

'Why?'

'The local people say the bats have come back. They have left their caves in the mountain and moved into town. This is a sign.'

The food at the Edelweiss was delicious and we looked forward to each evening with relish. It had a Swiss proprietor and a dozen or more of his compatriots were staying there. They were touring Africa in a fleet of dormobiles, sticking together for mutual support. A law in Rwanda forbids camping of any kind so they slept discreetly in the hotel car-park. Their main concern was that a vehicle might be tampered with or stolen: this anxiety bordered on neurosis. During dinner, one or other of them slipped away between each course to make sure nothing had gone amiss. They had been on the road for five months.

The next day the crutches were ready. The factory had made them out of hardwood with upholstered leather arm-rests and brass studs; they refused all offers of payment. Orlando was delighted and hobbled all the way to the bus-station. The family was mobile once more. We squeezed into a minibus going to the *Parc National des Volcans* at Ruhengeri.

Janie. . .
It was an American, the late Dian Fossey, who fought for the preservation of the last 240 mountain gorillas in the world, living in this corner of Rwanda, Uganda and Zaire. (There are none in captivity.) Her campaign for a national park led to a conflict of interest with the local peasant farmers who resented their exclusion from the land. Heavy fines now discourage the Rwandans from selling gorillas' heads, hands and feet to tourists but there is still a danger from poachers who set snares for antelope. If a gorilla is caught in the wire, it dies slowly of gangrene. A team of government rangers keeps a daily check on each of the gorilla families, their wages being paid out of the high fees charged to tourists – about twenty pounds a person for an hour's viewing. The time limit is strictly observed: no one wants the gorillas to become so tame that they lose their fear of poachers. Children are not allowed so Charlie and the kids stayed behind at the hostel.

I rose at four a.m. to walk the ten miles uphill to the park.

Banana groves gave way to fields of beans and the silver-leafed pyrethrum flowers from which mosquito coils are made. At the headquarters, I met up again with the Swiss from Gisenye and we followed our guide, Jonas, to the foot of the volcano Gahinga. Here we rested and Jonas gave us careful instructions. We could not smoke or use a flashlight camera. 'Does anyone have a cold or flu?' he asked. 'The gorillas have no immunity.'

When we met them, we were not to speak or point. Any movements we made should be slow and gentle. If a gorilla came close, we should on no account touch it. If the silverback – the male head of the family – approached us, we were to crouch down, look at the ground and eat some grass. Meeting his gaze would be understood as a challenge and he might charge.

For the next two hours, Jonas hacked a path through thick bamboo and stinging bushes. First he had to find the spot where the gorillas had been the day before and then follow their trail of chewed twigs and droppings. We passed several large nests in the bamboo above our heads but there was no sign of inhabitants. We were feeling tired and demoralised when Jonas signalled us to stop on the edge of a small clearing. Ahead a branch was shaking. A black hand came out, delicately picked a leaf and disappeared again. We crept forward and there in the bush sat the silverback. He looked at us and grunted. Jonas grunted back and he relaxed. They had known each other for several years.

Mulifi was much wider and shorter than I had imagined, with a fat belly and a massive, ugly head. It is the hands and feet of gorillas that are so human. Entranced, I didn't notice that little Kwachum was sidling up to me from behind. I held my breath when he appeared at my elbow, nibbling a green shoot. I was sorely tempted to stroke him but the firm hand of Jonas pushed me aside.

We followed them to another clearing where one of Mulifi's women, Zahaboo, lay on her back so that baby Kampanga could suckle, watching me with big, staring eyes. Her brother Toto was picking fleas from his mother's legs. Gukunda, wife number two, ambled in and chose the bush beside me for her next meal. Her daughter Nyakarima was only one month old and her hair was still shining and wavy. She clung to her

201

mother's grizzled curls and blinked in the sunlight.

After a while, they all stopped eating and lay in the sunshine, farting and grunting. Mulifi stood in the background and never took his eyes off us. Our hour was over and reluctantly we backed away. I felt so elated that the long journey back passed unnoticed. It had been a privilege; I only hope the gorillas are still there for Daisy's children to see.

Charles. . .
Rwanda is a small, mountainous country. Its population of nearly six million is the most densely settled in Africa. The hillsides are carved into terraces and food grows in every available corner. Since 1959, when the Hutu and Tutsi tribes fought for power, the government has been stable and receives aid from a wide variety of sources. The ruling party is financed by both the North Koreans and a West German foundation. The Chinese have built a splendid highway to Kigali, the capital, and can still be seen in their coolie hats, directing the gangs of labourers who clear the landslides.

Our minibus spent a fruitless half hour touring the streets, trying to fill up with passengers. For some reason, people were reluctant to ride with us. We discovered why, later that afternoon. The day before, an American had approached the minibus rank and become involved in a wrangle between two bus crews over who should take him. He was pulled into the leading vehicle which was already overcrowded. It took off as fast as it could and the rival bus gave chase. Both drivers became so angry, they lost their wits and left the tarred road, careering along a mountain track with horns blaring. The passengers, jam-packed and sweating with fear, were thrown from side to side, fainting, screaming and trying in vain to open a door and throw the American out. Word of this crazy misadventure had spread through Ruhengeri and, not surprisingly, no one wanted to travel with *wazungu*!

Wieland met us beneath Kigali's pride and joy, the only set of working traffic lights in Rwanda. We transferred to his jeep and drove south to Ruhango. He was a strange person to find on a mission, an atheist and a communist who had left his university studies to work for six years in a factory, assembling televisions.

'German Protestant churches are very liberal,' he explained. 'We attended a training seminary for six months before coming here, but no one asked us any questions.'

Now he was researching the history of the German occupation of Rwanda.

'It's a story of how to colonise a country with three people,' he said. 'Graf von Goetzen arrived here in 1884 with two friends and introduced himself to King Rwabugiri as an explorer. He did not tell the king that Rwanda was already German as a result of the Berlin Conference. The king never found out because he expired soon afterwards. It is not known whether this was voluntary. The first German expedition resulted in two deaths: both von Goetzen's sausage dogs were attacked by wasps.

'Rwabugiri's successor was only a child and three years later his mother invited Hauptmann von Ramsay, the pacifier of Tanganyika, to be their protector. The German government and the Protestant Church now combined to civilise the country. The Protestants established a mission on Lake Kivu and collected money for a steel boat which they transported all the way from Dar-es-Salaam. When the First World War broke out, they put a machine-gun into the mission boat and attacked the Belgians. For this act, they lost the territory at the Treaty of Versailles.

'At the height of the occupation, there were never more than forty Germans in this country. Their memory was cherished by the Rwandans who invited Hitler to help them when he came to power.'

'What is the President like?' I asked.

'Habyarimana is a nice man. He drives around incognito without any bodyguards and makes surprise visits to his schools and clinics. He gives people lifts in his limousine. What impressed me most was his refusal to accept a television station from the French. He said to them, "This is useless for my country. I would like you to spend the money on rural development."'

'And did they?'

'No. It is not so easy to find a prestigious project in the countryside.'

Janie. . .

'We are nearly there,' Claudia said. 'I hope you are not feeling sick. These roads never get repaired.'

Small boys were driving long-horned cattle home to the kraal. Women in colourful tartan wraps sat gossiping in their doorways, pausing to raise a clay pipe to their lips. We passed a sick man being carried to Claudia's clinic in a basket suspended from two poles. Ruhango Mission came in sight, a collection of European buildings on a hilltop overlooking a vast, mosquito-infested swamp.

'That,' said Claudia proudly, 'is the source of the Nile.'

'I've heard that one before,' I said.

'Please allow us to be right,' Wieland said. 'It gives me a reason for putting up with malaria once a month.'

We unpacked and Claudia made a pot of tea.

'My gardener would like to meet you,' Wieland said. The Rwandan greeted us with a formal hug. We admired the vegetable patch, the goat-pen, the well which he and Wieland had dug and the duck-pond. Under a shelter smothered in Morning Glory, Till, Nele and Joseph were playing in a sandpit. Joseph had made a road and was re-enacting our crash with a toy lorry.

'My gardener has just opened a bar,' Wieland said, 'with money his wife made by brewing banana and sorghum beer. This is a good example of how development projects go wrong. Since coffee was introduced into this area as a cash crop, the peasants have got plenty of money to spend. Their bellies are always thirsty for beer, which the women are happy to sell to them. This has led to an increase in malnutrition among the children. Bananas and sorghum are the basis of their diet too, but now there is not enough for them to eat.'

Round the garden Wieland had planted a thick hibiscus hedge.

'It keeps out the neighbours.'

'Are they troublesome?'

He grimaced.

'American Baptists. We don't see eye to eye.'

'You must meet Stan,' Claudia said. 'He buys converts with rabbits.'

Orlando. . .

I am the family rabbit expert. In Zimbabwe I had a hutch on top of the chicken run, where it was shaded by a palm-tree and out of reach of dogs. The rabbits' names were Rosy-Primrose, Peter, Snowy, Sunshine and Killer Punch.

I explained all this to Stan and he told us that he used to be a farmer in Tennessee. When Jesus came into his life, he sold his farm to his brother and flew to Africa to teach people there about agriculture.

Stan was unhappy because of all the cows in Rwanda. Everyone had a cow and there wasn't enough grass for them to eat. The grass had worms in it which made the cows thin and his job was to cure the cows by giving them medicine. The trouble was, as soon as he got rid of the worms, they came back again because there was no worm-free grass to eat. Stan thought it was very stupid and it made him fed up.

Then he had a bright idea. He would give everyone rabbits instead! They didn't need nearly as much space and grass as cows and they were nice to eat. He worked out how to make mud rabbit-hutches with clay pots inside for the doe to have her babies in. If he could persuade some people to grow rabbits, it would reduce the number of cows and gradually solve the problem. The trouble was, nobody wanted to give up *their* cow, because having one made them feel rich. Some people even worshipped their cows! So Stan decided the only way he could persuade them to take his rabbits and get rid of their cows was by telling them about Jesus too. He reckoned that belief in Jesus would replace their old beliefs and Jesus, as everyone knows, was dead set against being rich. Stan told the people that if they came to him for a whole week to learn about Jesus, he would give them a free pair of rabbits and show them how to look after them properly. He said it had worked very well. In one year, he had given out three hundred pairs.

Daisy. . .

At Ruhango, people gathered round and stared at us if we did African-type things, such as going to the market to buy meat. The butcher gave Joseph and Till a fresh cow's horn each. You could hardly see the meat for the flies buzzing all over it. There were so many people crowding round us that the butcher was forced to flick blood at them with a cow's tail to drive them away. They came back though, just like the flies.

Wieland told us a good story. Some Frenchmen came to a village near Ruhango called 'Common Market' and put up some solar panels which are a clever invention for making electricity from the sun. Now you can have lights in your school, they said. They were very pleased with their job and went home.

After they had gone, someone's cow came and sat on a solar panel and damaged it. This was a great shame since each one cost over a thousand pounds. So the village people met and decided to build a fence to keep the cows out. A tall tree near the house was shading the panels with its branches and preventing the sun from making electricity. If we chop the tree down, they said, we can make a strong fence out of the wood. So they cut the tree down. Unfortunately, it fell on the solar panels and destroyed them completely.

Charles. . .
Back in Kigali, we sat poring over the map while our stomachs grumbled after a disastrous Chinese meal. (The road engineers remained, but the cooks had clearly all gone home.) Orlando's injury had reduced our options and now we wanted to get to Nairobi as soon as possible.

'The people at the Ugandan embassy were very relaxed,' I said. 'They claimed the country was quiet.'

'Let's not hang about then,' Janie agreed.

24

Janie. . .

The road to the Ugandan border followed a long valley filled with tea plantations. Teams of pickers walked between the rows, wearing all-enveloping plastic aprons made from fertiliser-bags, and carrying giant baskets on their backs.

We walked across no man's land at Gatuna, Orlando swinging gaily along on his crutches, and found no one to stamp our passports. An Asian businessman knew where to find the official, who emerged, rubbing the sleep from his eyes.

'Welcome to Uganda. I hope you enjoy your stay.'

It was good to hear English spoken again. The businessman put us in the back of his pick-up with sacks of carrots and cauliflowers. We left the steep valleys and entered cattle country: a buzzard wheeling in the sky, gentle hills, knee-high tawny grass and isolated huts surrounded by waving banana fronds. The road was straight and tarred and the driver knew where to expect the pot-holes.

We were dropped off at Mbarara and found beds in a Christian hostel at 60p each. Joseph made friends with a young man called Francis, who wore a fur tea-cosy on his head. He said he could tell our fortune by the shape of our nose.

'The psychological aspect of Orlando's nose ensures by its width that he will be a scientist. Daisy has a political nose.'

'What about Joe?'

'His nose is not yet developed sufficiently.'

'Francis wants to be my pen-pal,' Joseph said later. 'He's the third this week. What a pile of letters will be waiting at home!'

The hostel was protected by tall iron gates and a high wall. Prayers were said at six in the courtyard and then we went out to find a meal. Many of the buildings in Mbarara were empty

207

shells and ugly maribou storks brooded on the rooftops. We ate boiled sweet potatoes in a café. The women's dresses must have been modelled on what the missionaries wore eighty years ago: puffed sleeves, a square neckline and a full-length skirt. The material was shabby and they lacked the style of Zairean women.

Charles. . .
'What is Obote doing?' I asked a young man in the café. We were sharing a bottle of Scotch which retailed at the astonishing price of £3.50. I never discovered how this was possible. The Ugandan currency had devalued so rapidly over the past five years that £10 notes issued when Amin fell now exchanged for £1.

'Obote is piling up his cash outside the country. The government is quite bad, quite unpopular. He knows it cannot last very much longer.'

'What will happen when he goes?'

'Who knows? Amin is waiting but only a few people in his own tribe want him back. Museveni's guerrillas are very well behaved. They took my friend's car and he thought not to see it again. But they brought it back and they even put in petrol! Museveni would make a good leader I think. God save us from more bad times.'

Editorial, National Mirror, *Kampala, 15th May, 1985.*
The National Mirror *most resolutely and unreservedly condemns the cowardly assassination attempt on the life of the Secretary-General of the Uganda People's Congress, Dr J. Luwuliza-Kirunda.*

The dastardly attempt raises once again the spectre of the idea of governance by men of violence, as opposed to governance by the ballot for peace, prosperity and people's welfare.

The will and power of the people shall not allow the men of violence of any category whatever to plunge Uganda once again into the darkness of the seventies, to misbehave with impunity.

From the bus to Kampala next day, we got occasional glimpses of the bays and inlets of Lake Victoria. We passed several roofless, burnt-out schools and, nearing the capital, the road-blocks increased: soldiers every two miles and a police station every ten.

'The fares have gone up a lot,' the man next to me said. 'We pay for the army's wages, soon no one can afford to travel.'

The road surface in Kampala was the worst I have ever seen. The traffic climbed nose-to-tail over the ruts and bumps. The pavements were crowded too and drains with missing covers yawned suddenly at your feet. The buildings were desolate and decayed, their windows smashed or boarded up. Reconstruction work had long since been suspended for lack of funds, and creepers grew on the scaffolding. We stayed at a cheap hotel near the station. Next door was the 'Departed Asians Property Board, Custodian and Head Office'. The clients on our floor earned a noisy living by night. A sweating customer grabbed me on the stairs, put his scarred face close to me and repeated:

'Uganda is a beautiful country, a beeyootifool country!'

After supper, the children insisted on going to the cinema which was showing *Kelly's Heroes*. The bulb in the projector was so dim that you could barely make out what was on the screen. The film had broken and been spliced together so many times, and in such random order, that it made an anarchist's collage of the plot. The kids sat it out, even though the floor was wet and smelly and most of the seats were broken.

Our last day in Uganda passed on a train, across the Nile at Jinja and through Basoga country to Tororo. It was clean, slow and very cheap – 125 miles for £1.50. Every carriage had a soldier on guard in the corridor, though I can't imagine why some thought it necessary to wear gas masks.

At the border town of Tororo we carted Orlando from the station in a hired wheelbarrow to another boarding-house, where they served us a big plate of *matoke* (pounded plantain) and meat. The washtub had a scum on its surface and the beds were flea-ridden. In the morning, we walked past a kilometre of lorries queueing in both directions. It was the main route from central Africa to the coast. Some drivers had been there a week, waiting for customs clearance.

Obtaining currency at an African border is a very informal affair. There are no banks and no bank-notes may leave a country, so you do a black-market deal in no man's land and hope you haven't been fleeced. Janie approached a youth and asked for Kenyan shillings, only to realise to her embarrassment that she had asked a policeman. He was very polite and pretended not to hear.

We were both in a muddle that morning. Perhaps it was the relief at reaching Kenya that caused us to relax. While the opportunity offered, we only bothered to change £10 and the rest of the weekend took shape on the basis of this miscalculation.

As soon as we bargained with a *matatu* driver, we realised that it wasn't enough. (*Matatus* are Kenya's privately-owned taxi-buses.)

'Never mind,' I said. 'We'll change some traveller's cheques in a bank.'

It was a Saturday and the banks closed at eleven. The driver assured us we would get to Bungoma in time:

'It's only ten miles.'

He carefully loaded a three-piece suite onto the roof. We set off, ran into a police road-block and at ten fifty-eight, with Bungoma in sight, waited while a goods train crossed the road in front of us, stopped and shunted back again. I dashed to the bank, arriving just as the doors were closing, and tried exerting my charm through an open window without effect. Business in Kenya is done in proper fashion.

At Eldoret, forty miles further on, Janie visited half a dozen Asian stores, which had always been willing money-changers in the past. The owners listened to her, looked at the floor and turned away. Increasingly desperate, we realised we could not reach Nairobi. The *matatu* dropped us at sunset in the dingy industrial town of Nakuru.

A receptionist at the Midland Hotel looked disdainfully at our grubby, haggard faces.

'We can accept American Express for your accommodation,' he said, 'but not for your food.'

'But that's ridiculous!'

'It's terribly expensive anyway.'

By this time, I was in a foul temper, most of it directed at poor Janie.

'Why oh why didn't you change more? What good is £10? The

kids are tired and hungry. We've got perfectly good money in our pocket. We're surrounded by goodies of every kind and quite unable to pay for them!'

'Oh shut up!'

We sat on a low wall in the car-park as darkness fell. Young couples in chic evening wear were arriving for a disco contest. Orlando hobbled around, thwacking an empty can with his crutch and complaining. Oh God, I thought, I've failed my wife, I've failed my children, I've failed.

Then Janie spotted a European getting out of a car. He was too old for the disco and dressed in a faded safari suit.

'I'll give him a try,' she murmured.

'You can't just go up and ask a stranger to change money.'

'May I remind you that the situation is desperate.'

She went over and started talking. The children watched anxiously and I sat, my head buried in my hands. Shortly after, Janie reappeared with two men, the second an Arab. Her eyes were gleaming.

'This is Abdul al Bari. He *owns* this hotel.'

'You want change money?' the Arab was saying. 'Sorry, it's not possible. No change in Kenya now except at bank. The police lock up Abdul, even they find him with one pound note English.'

I opened my mouth to speak, and he held up his hand.

'You want money, no problem. I lend you till Monday, banks open. How much you want, one thousand, two thousand shilling?'

He looked down and smiled broadly.

'Ah, you have chillen. What a pretty girl. They come from Uganda too?'

He saw Orlando.

'What is matter my darling? He break his leg? Tcha! You hungry? No food in Uganda, eh? Come inside. Come, come. This is Abdul's hotel. I drink a few beers, you eat. Tony – this my friend, Tony – take the boy's bag, poor little bugger!'

We followed him back inside. The receptionist was called to take our rucksacks, which the grinning children heaped into his arms. Led by Abdul's portly figure, we padded across the dance-floor and into a panelled board-room, where he sat down

211

at the centre of the table and clapped his hands. Waiters appeared and laid a white cloth. They brought in a dozen *Tusker* beers, a bottle of vodka, lemonades and Cokes, followed by fish and chips, steak, salad, banana splits and ice-cream. The children could not believe their eyes and fell on the food with yelps of delight. Tony told us he was a Catholic priest from Belfast. He had just retired from teaching at a Nairobi high school. Abdul meanwhile never stopped talking.

'You second people Tony and I rescue this day. We find young girl, she pilot her own plane, land at golf-course from Nairobi, lunch-time. Very nice girl, had small engine trouble. I very kind man, Abdul is kind to his friends, drive her into town, find spare part.'

'It's quite true,' Tony said, 'he's very kind, a very generous man.'

'He's very nice man, Tony. He my friend. We meet every Saturday, have a few drinks. Tony have the vodka. I no like. Abdul drink beer. Abdul Moslem.'

'You shouldn't drink at all, in that case,' Janie said.

'My father no drink. He say Abdul bad boy. I no care, old man now. My wife no like me neither. So I decide buy this hotel, enjoy drink in private with my friends.'

He stopped to crunch some raw onions and open another beer. I was fascinated by his hands. The fingers, podgy and bejewelled, rested in a row on the edge of the tablecloth, rising only when required to perform the trick of despatching a waiter in a single, neat, imperious gesture.

'I am Nakuru Tanners. Tanners, my dear. Hides and all that. Goat, sheep and cow. We make coats, slippers woolly for your English winter, ladies' handbags. You'll see. Abdul's son show you round factory. Tomorrow we go out in car. Mohammed come. We kill goat. I show you how the rural folk live in Kenya. Have some beers. Maybe visit flamingos. You seen them? Very good. Millions pink birds.'

He noticed that Joseph had fallen asleep with his head in his plate and sent Tony to reception.

'You stay here tonight. No matter, I pay. Mummy, you are Minister of Home Affairs. Take your children up to bed. You can bath them in the morning. Go now. Charles stays here to drink with me.'

'Oh Abdul you mustn't, you're too kind.'
His hand went up, forbidding argument. He hiccuped.
'Abdul *very kind man!*'

Orlando. . .
On Sunday, Abdul took us to Lake Baringo. Tito, Abdul's
chauffeur, drove us in the Mercedes. Mohammed took Abdul
and Mum in his Lancer Turbo. We drove along and came to the
equator. Abdul said we must all get out and sit on it for photos.
Then we went to a little wooden bar called the Tip Top for
drinks. Abdul bought a goat and Mohammed took it round the
back of the shed and killed it. Mum was watching and got blood
all down her legs. She screamed a bit. We roasted the goat and
tried to eat some but it was too tough. Before it had a chance to
cook properly, Abdul decided he wanted to leave. He and
Mohammed had an argument about this which Abdul won. Tito
put the smoking goat carcass in the boot.

We went back across the equator and took another road to
Lake Baringo. The country was hot and dry. We crossed the
equator for the *third* time and came to a bridge that had been
washed away by the floods. The way round it was very rough
and we saw a lorry lying on its side.

Then Abdul and Mohammed had another argument about
which lake to go to. Abdul wanted to go to Lake Bogoria, which
is where the flamingos lay their eggs. Mum locked herself into
Mohammed's car. Abdul lay down in the road and said he
would not move. We settled for Lake Baringo.

When we got there, it was about five o'clock. There was a
beautiful club, the sort that used to be for whites only. We swam
in the pool and had cocktails and chips. Abdul jumped in in his
underpants: it made a big splash! Tito took us to see the hippos
in the reeds. Sometimes they come up onto the lawn and scare
the guests. We wanted a ride on a camel but it had gone home.

Then Joseph got lost. The manager found him and took him to
his office but Joe got frightened and locked himself in a
cupboard. He refused to come out until Daisy climbed in there
with him.

Mohammed now said that he didn't want to go back to
Nakuru in the dark because of the bandits. Abdul was very

drunk and Mum said she wouldn't spend the night at Baringo with him. Mohammed whispered to us that he wanted to go home too, but Abdul always did the opposite of what he wanted, so he was pretending. It worked and we did drive back. I was in the front of the Mercedes. Abdul was asleep in the back between Mum and Dad. We crossed the equator for the fourth time. Four times in one day!

Joseph. . .

Tito and Mohammed took us to the lake at Nakuru on Monday. We saw thousands of flamingos, pelicans and cormorants. Tito drove the car down onto the sand. It was great fun making the flamingos take off in a pink cloud. We paddled with the pelicans. I was worried for them because Mohammed said there was no fish. I picked up some long feathers and did a pelican dance. We drove right round the lake looking for lions but they were all asleep.

Daisy. . .

We went to Abdul's factory. It smelt *vile* and the floors were covered with dirty water, so we had to jump from one place to another. Abdul was not there, he was in bed with a headache, but his son showed us round. We saw the skins being soaked in salt, the big tubs with paddles that removed the hairs, and the 'wet blue' stage where the skins are soaked in chemicals. The grading is done according to the number of holes and knife cuts. The best skins are sent to Europe still wet. The rest of the factory makes products for the shop. Abdul's son gave us a pair of slippers each and Mum a new bag. She put our passports and money in it but then she left it at the bus-station. We reached Nairobi and rang up Mohammed in a panic. Fortunately, he found it and we got everything back.

Janie. . .

I could not get used to the pace of life in Kenya. The beautiful highlands sped past like a silent film. We saw a woman carrying a wardrobe on her back, held by a leather strap over her forehead: I wanted to call to the others but she was gone in a flash. The other passengers in the *matatu* sat silently, not talking to each other: for once there were empty seats between us.

Katie Halford had been my father's secretary in the war. She kept a small hotel in a Nairobi suburb where we received a courteous welcome in the best Kenyan colonial style. The house was Edwardian tudor with a rose garden and a lounge full of comfortable chintz. The cooking was fresh, thoughtful and delicious, there were flowers on every sideboard and pressed linen sheets on the beds. The bar was a watering-hole for the type whose views about natives became franker after the fifth whisky.

The Nairobi Hospital was just down the road and I took Orlando there for a final check up. We realised it wasn't a government hospital when we saw a sign saying 'Chauffeurs set down your passengers here'. The doctor said we could throw away the crutches. Orlando wondered if anyone else might need them but I told him to be patient: this was not the place to ask.

'It's a good job you came now and not in a month's time,' Katie said a day or two later. 'Every bed in town is booked and double-booked. First there is the UN Women's Conference and then the Pope flies in.'

'That sounds fun,' Charlie said to me. 'Perhaps you could stay and do some reporting.'

The same afternoon, I went to the offices of the BBC and met Mike Wooldridge, the East African correspondent.

'Janie Hampton? Well I never. We heard you on the radio only yesterday, on a train in Zaire. Yes, you can cover the conference if you like. I'm going on leave. It's complete chaos at the moment, as you would expect. You'll have to get yourself press accreditation. Why don't you all come to lunch tomorrow and I can do an interview for Woman's Hour. Your journey sounds most exciting.'

'Do you know anyone who could make use of Orlando's crutches?'

'My wife works in a clinic in the Mathare valley. I'm sure she can find a home for them.'

I noticed the offices of Associated Press on my way out and

215

put my head in there too. I returned to Charlie flushed with triumph.

'AP and the Beeb have both offered me work.'

'Excellent, well done. I think I'd better fly home with the kids while you get on with that. It's time I found a job too.'

'We've got three weeks till the conference starts. I suggest you go to Lamu tomorrow night and I'll join you there in a couple of days when I've got a press card. We can spend ten days or so on the coast and then go to Tanzania so that you can climb Kilimanjaro. I'll take the kids on safari.'

'We can be *real* tourists for once,' Orlando said.

Mike did an interview with us and Charlie took the kids on the night train to Mombasa. The next day was a Sunday and Katie invited me to the races at Ngong Hills.

'It has been a part of the social scene since Nairobi was a row of tents,' she said. 'You'll love it.'

The members' enclosure was guarded by police in khaki with white puttees. Nannies sat in the shade beside their prams. Katie's name was painted on a reserved seat in the owners' stand.

'It's so sad,' a lady said to me in the members' bar. 'In the old days there was racing every Sunday: now so few people can afford it.'

We placed a bet with a bookie called 'Surrey Racing' and watched through leather-covered binoculars as Hot Gossip outpaced Star Wars on the final furlong. Katie's horse came in fourth. It was almost a shock when I met the jockey to realise he was black.

25

*I saw this one throwing me many eyes. I returned a smile. He was
tall, with a pipe in his mouth, and he did not look as old as the others
whose face-skins fell into many folds. He spoke Swahili well, but in a
funny way, and would add one or two English words. He was a
mtalii from Germany and he had come to the country on a special
mission. He was looking for a certain girl from Kabete. She had been
taken to Germany by another German with promises of marriage.
But she found she had been tricked and he wanted her to start a trade
with him, for he and others had figured that if* watalii *could pay all
that money for aeroplanes and for hotels at Malindi on account of
having seen an advertisement of an aged white man with a young
African woman with the words: For only so much you can have this:
they would pay even more willingly if Malindi was brought to
Germany.*
From *Petals of Blood*, a novel by Ngugi wa Thiong'o.

Charles. . .
We arrived in Mombasa early on Sunday morning. The
American navy had just left and the streets were empty. We
passed the notorious Castle Hotel and the children were
disappointed to see the terrace deserted. The whole town was
sleeping off a week's binge. We were with a young painter, a
Kenyan white man, who had sat up with us till late on the train.
He was slowly killing himself with heroin, cocaine and vodka.
He took us to his beautiful house in the Arab old town, down a
narrow alley and overlooking the harbour entrance. The central
room was open to the sky: it contained a fountain, potted palms,
a throne, cushions and carpets. On his balcony was a water-bed
with a brass hookah beside it and stacked around the walls were

217

pictures of his dreams, which he sold to tourists. The women were either red or blue.

We left him after breakfast and looked round Fort Jesus, built by the Portuguese three hundred years ago, and the Victorian Anglican cathedral, designed by a Scotsman to look as much as possible like a mosque. The service was in Swahili and the children soon got bored. We walked across town, bought bread and fruit and caught a bus to Malindi.

Janie. . .
The ticket office was closed at Nairobi station and a porter told me to buy one on the train. The carriages were brand new, with bright chrome and formica everywhere. I found a compartment with two Moslem women, put my bag on a couchette, and went to find the bar.

Two middle-aged men were leaning against the counter, looking as if they owned it.

'Evening love,' said a North Country accent, 'where are you from?'

'I was born in London. Are you English?'

'Oh aye.'

'If the frame took a very long screwdriver, crossed end, down the side behind the facia, that might do it. I reckon they'd have a job getting in there, at any rate.'

'They might, Sam. God knows, we've tried everything else!'

'Are you something to do with the train?' I asked.

'We're British Rail engineers, love. Out on a two year contract with rolling stock.'

'Did you build this carriage?'

'Well not me personally,' said Sam.

'Derby workshops,' said the other. 'Export order job, this.'

'Would you like a beer?' said Sam. 'Neville, buy the lady a beer.'

'What were you talking about just now,' I asked.

'The speakers in the compartments. They keep nicking them.'

'They're only worth about fifty pence but they fetch a good price out here.'

'Personally I'm rather glad mine's missing,' I said. 'I can't stand Musak.'

'Their stuff's dreadful, isn't it? We usually bring our own.'

'Fancy some dinner?' asked Neville.

'I wonder if Walter's on.'

'Yes, I saw him earlier on.'

'I'll just pop back and fetch a tape then.'

'He'll like that.'

Neville led me to the dining-car where the head-waiter greeted us with a shy smile.

'Jambo bwana.'

'Hello Walter. Table for three please.'

Sam joined us and handed the waiter a cassette. 'Never fails to please him,' he said. 'He'd like us to give it him I think, but then we might not get the same service.'

Walter returned, a smile on his face and after a short pause we heard the deep, confident tones of Roger Whittaker:

'Have you seen the old girl, who walks the streets of London,
Dirt in her hair, her clothes in rags. . .'

Our table was laid with starched linen and heavy Sheffield plate. Overhead, a dozen whirring fans jerked on their axis in a mechanical ballet. The menu blew onto the floor and Neville bent to retrieve it.

'We had fun last week. Every time the train stopped, the fans went round faster. We were sitting in a gale in here; waves on the soup. Took us ages to work that one out.'

We ordered chicken à la king and more beers.

'Where else do you export trains to?'

'Tanzania, Gabon,' Sam said. 'It's a part of British Rail that actually makes a profit. We construct the carriages to local specifications.'

'This line's historic, you know,' Neville added. 'Took them years to build. They kept thinking the coolies were deserting, till they found out the lions were eating them. Lions held up work for a whole year.'

'The modern designs are not as good as the old ones. Look at the kitchens. They're far too narrow. There's no room to wash up, no proper ventilation. The locals are afraid of the steam-heaters so they wash up in a bowl in the passage.'

'I'm leaving on a jet plane. . .' sang Roger Whittaker

We returned to our compartments, stepping over a man

cleaning plates in the passage. The two women I was sharing with had locked up and gone to bed. My cries went ignored or unnoticed. I tried several other doors before an American woman let me in.

At dawn, we broke down somewhere in the Tsavo National Park. Antelope grazed beside the line and a herd of giraffes undulated in slow motion above the scrub. Within a few minutes someone had set up a Coca-Cola stall beside the track.

Roger Whittaker was still singing.

'I'm going to kill whoever put that bloody music on,' said my companion.

The dining-car was packed. I squeezed in next to a Kenyan and ordered some coffee.

'Allow me to pay for it, madam,' he said. 'Did you sleep well?'

I told him I'd been separated from my luggage.

'And your ticket? I am the inspector.'

'I boarded the train in a hurry. Can I buy one from you now?'

I handed over the money and he returned half of it.

'That will be enough.'

He gave me a sly wink and the cash went into his top pocket.

The bus journey along the coast is long and wearisome: those who can afford it fly. I found myself next to an American family from Nyankunde.

'Hello!' they said. 'What are you doing here? This *is* a coincidence!'

It wasn't a very great one I later discovered. Africa has a limited supply of holiday resorts and we met several other acquaintances from our journey during our stay on the coast. The Americans got off at a luxury hotel outside Kilifi. A notice in German and Italian asked the guests not to go around naked: I smiled at the prospect of my missionary friends doing any such thing.

Between Kilifi and Malindi the bus travelled for twenty-five minutes through one sizal estate. It was dusk when we got to Malindi and I booked in at a cheap hotel for the night. Ramadan had just started and children were out in the streets selling fast-breakers. Swifts screeched and swooped above the rooftops. I bought some samosas and wandered down to the beach. The sand was white and fine, the sea a deep green in the setting sun.

A cargo ship was anchored offshore. While I was eating a samosa, a man came up to me and asked if I was going to Lamu.

'Why, yes,' I said.

'Come in my ship then,' he said. 'I will charge you only eighty shillings and we shall be there in twelve hours.'

'But I have a bus ticket.'

'The bus is no good. The Tana river is flooded. It cannot take you all the way.'

I thought how impressed Charlie would be if I turned up in a ship. The man was tugging my arm urgently.

'Give me your deposit now,' he said. 'Forty shillings and I will go and tell the captain.'

I said I'd pay him in the morning. I had almost fallen for it!

Next morning, the bus charged down the dirt road from Malindi to the Tana ferry, clogging our throats with dust. The driver kept up a steady 60 mph for fear of bandits. Five armed soldiers were squashed into the gangway. One of their comrades had been shot in the foot the week before – by the Somalis, they said. It's convenient to blame one's neighbours. The Sudanese merchant beside me was making scathing remarks. No one could explain, he said, how the soldier came to be wounded when he was lying on the floor at the time.

We crossed the Tana river and boarded another bus, waiting to take us to Lamu. The flooding was very extensive here. Vultures preened themselves in the trees and ostriches sprinted across the road. Three British students in Laura Ashley dresses shrieked with delight when they saw them. They were sitting at the back, chattering with the carefree energy of people on holiday. I found myself irritated at the way they were munching their sandwiches: in Ramadan only children eat during daylight. They made a dreadful fuss later when the bus had a puncture.

Lamu is a small island with a largely Moslem community of Arab descent. Some of the buildings date back to the fifteenth century. Fishing and boat building were the main occupations before the tourists came. Trading dhows crossed the Indian Ocean to Bombay and mangrove poles from the surrounding swamps are still carried along the Red Sea coast to be used as building materials.

Lamu has attracted Europeans in search of *bhang* (cannabis), sexual freedom and sunshine for nearly a century. A group of Utopian socialists called 'The Freelanders' were among the first in 1890. They intended to start a commune on the slopes of Mount Kenya but got no further than Lamu's palm-fringed beaches. Their women shocked the Moslems by their immorality and the men were responsible for introducing alcohol. In the 1960s, wealthy pop stars came here and they were followed by a hippy invasion. Things got out of hand and the local council were forced to expel the hippies and ban them completely. They passed a law forbidding any islander without a trading licence from even talking to a tourist. Lamu still has a reputation as a place where white girls can find themselves a boy-friend for a week.

A launch took us across the lagoon as night was falling. The woman beside me had a skin like dark chocolate, her eyes outlined with *khol* and cherry on her lips. She was holding a cheroot in nicotine-stained fingers. A crowd waited for us at the town jetty. I climbed the steps and looked around.

'Charlie? Are you there?'

'I'm here, Chalis am here. I come for you.' A young Kenyan grabbed my bags. 'You stay with me. Nice room, very cheap.'

'No, you're the wrong Charlie. I'm looking for my husband.'

'I can be husband Chalis. I make good husband.'

'I've already got a husband called Charlie. He's got three children with him. Have you seen him?'

'Oh *Chalis*. With Daisy?'

'That's right.'

'They are staying at Shela with Ali. You cannot go tonight.' He pulled a finger across his throat and grinned. 'Stay with me to the morning.'

'Janie?' said a cool Scandinavian accent. 'Do you remember me? Jens. We met in Rwanda, at the gorilla camp.'

'Goodness. Hello.'

'It's a small world, yah? Charlie has asked me to take you to our house for the night. My wife has a meal ready. Charlie waited until six, but could not return to Shela after dark.'

We walked along the quayside. The tide was out and the dhows lay on their side in the mud. A crowd of Europeans was sitting on the terrace of Lamu's one licensed bar, half-listening to a guitar. In the narrow alleyways of the town, the mullahs had just called the end of the fast and hawkers were out selling samosas, pikoras, fried fish and dates. We bought a kebab fresh from the grill and a doughnut from the top of a pyramid. Chalis walked past with a sun-tanned girl on his arm, humming to a Walkman. He feigned not to notice me. The girl stopped and slapped her ankle.

'Ouch! A mosquito just bit me!'

Chalis' laughter, unnaturally loud because of the music in his ears, echoed down the crowded passageway.

Charles. . .

Shela is a tiny village on the edge of the dunes. Being winter we had it almost to ourselves. Donkeys wandered among the flat-roofed, white-washed houses. Peponi's hotel was closed. The children speared jelly-fish and dug tunnels on the beach. In the evening, we played cards on the terrace with Ali. Every conversation ended with something for sale.

'Your children happy?'

'Yes thank you.'

'They not bored? I take them for ride in boat?'

'Knave of clubs. It's your trick. Do you want to go sailing, kids?'

'No thanks. We went yesterday. Joe gets scared when it tips over.'

Ali tried again. 'You like lobsters?'

'Yuk,' said Daisy.

'Everyone like lobsters. Crabs? Prawns? I bring you some tomorrow.'

'What's that you're chewing?' Orlando asked.

'It's called *miraa*. You like to try some?'

Ali pulled a stalk out of his bunch and put it in Orlando's mouth.

'Ugh, it's bitter.'

'You should take bubble-gum at the same time.'

'What do you chew it for?'

Ali tapped his temple.

'It makes him feel good,' I said.

Ali fished some jewellery from his shirt pocket. 'Ruby. Very old.'

'Where did you get it?'

'Police gave it to me. Reward. I catch thief.'

'Really, where?'

'Thief hide in dunes. When woman go into sea, he take their clothes. I get him this night on the road. Big fight. He have knife. I take it, so . . . and so . . .'

Orlando's eyes opened wide as Ali showed him a scar on his stomach. It had been there a long time.

'When your wife come?'

'Soon.'

'You buy this for her? Nice present?'

'No thanks.'

'You tell her what Ali says. No go bath in dunes. Many thief. Ali no catch them all.'

'We don't have any valuables to lose.'

He looked at me narrowly and put out his cigarette.

'I bring prawns in morning?'

'All right.'

When Janie arrived, the larder was so full of crustaceans, you could hardly move.

'We'll never eat all that.'

'I just couldn't resist them.'

'How much did they cost?'

'Only a few bob.'

'Are those crayfish still alive? Couldn't we put them back in the sea.'

The whole family slept together on the roof where the warm wind blew in off the ocean. Daisy and Fatima, Ali's little sister, festooned it with perfumed jasmine. The mosquito-net was anchored with bricks from the parapet; a white, wildly tugging cocoon against the stars and the rustling palm fronds. Every night at one a.m. the loudspeaker came to life in an ancient mosque next door. (There were nine mosques in Shela).

'*Allah akbar, Allah akbar, ashhadu an la ilaha illa Allah, ashhadu anna Muhammadan rasulu Allah, hayya ala as-salah, hayya lalal-falah, as-salatu Khairun mina al-Naum, Allah akbar, Allah akbar, la ilaha illa Allah.*'

'Oh God,' Daisy exclaimed, 'when will they shut up!'

'Come to pray,' I sang.
'I don't want to pray. I want to sleep.'
'Prayer is better than sleep.'
'Not you too, Charlie!'
'God is great.'
'Belt up, Dad!'

One night we took up Ali's offer and went for a moonlit sail in a small dhow. The timbers of the hull bore the cut marks of an adze. They were heavy and looked immensely strong: the bulkheads had been cut in one piece out of the fork of a tree. It was a wonder how the builders achieved the sleek lines and watertight accuracy. The crew was a man and a boy. When the wind blew, we heeled over sharply. There was no keel, only a sack of stones to act as ballast and a long pole to sit out on. Every time we went about, the boy had to shin up the mast to untangle the lateen sail.

The night was lustrous, magical: the lights of Lamu winking across the lagoon, a full moon and scudding clouds. We lost the wind in a mangrove creek and drifted silently across the oily water.

'Where's the Southern Cross?'
'There, see, next to the Centaur.'
Orlando was asleep in the bottom of the boat.
'What happens if we capsize?'
'We don't, I hope. She'd go straight to the bottom.'
'I suppose they could heave the sack out.'
'If there was time.'
'It's beautiful, isn't it. Just look at the moon now.'
'It's perfect.'

The novel *Petals of Blood* has a bleak thesis. Kenyan society is divided and alienated, Ngugi says. The European bears responsibility for the poverty and squalor of Mathare valley, for the one-party state, for the drug barons and the prostitution rackets. His fraudulent Christianity destroyed indigenous culture, his capitalism held a deadly appeal. Now Kenyan exploits Kenyan with ruthless zeal. After the book came out, the author was held without trial for a year, then sent into exile.

'You don't want to believe Ngugi,' the young addict on the

train told me. 'That Commie! Kenya's going through changes. Society is adapting. We must expect a rough ride. There's nothing basically wrong here.'

If only I could believe he were right.

Daisy. . .

Jens and his family took us to a deserted beach on Manda Island for a swim and a picnic. They were very brown and not afraid of the sun. Mum and Jens' wife went topless and poor Mum got sunburnt. We went to the hospital to get some cream.

'Now we're here,' Mum said, 'let's ask if we can look around.'

The first ward was full of men, coughing and wheezing.

'What's wrong with these people?' I asked.

'TB,' the nurse said.

'Perhaps we shouldn't hang about in here,' Mum said in a hurry.

We looked at a baby who lay with fists clenched, struggling for breath.

'Pneumonia,' said the nurse, 'and brain damage we think.'

Most of the children were recovering from measles. The mothers who had new babies beside them looked proud and cheerful, all except one who was asleep.

'She's a funny colour,' I said.

'What's wrong with her?' Mum asked.

'Oh, she's dead,' said the nurse. 'We got the baby out alive.'

We heard the sound of wailing and her relatives came in with a stretcher covered in black cloth. They wrapped up her body and carried it away.

Orlando. . .

We left Shela after a week and stayed two nights with Charis at the Pole Pole Hotel. The name means 'take it slowly'. Every room had one of his girl-friends in. We went to watch the dhows being built. This skill is dying out because few people bother with dhows any more. Dad said he'd like to sail one back to England.

On 4th May we set off to go to Tanzania. Usually there is a ferry across the Tana river, but the water level was too high and we had to leave the bus and cross by canoe. They were leaking, twisted old dugouts which wobbled and frightened the tourists because the water came right up to the edge. A German woman refused to kneel down in the wet bottom and the boatman had to shout at her. The current was very strong. Upstream, a boy was beating his cattle to make them jump into the water and swim across. The cows were not very good swimmers and their eyes, just above the waves, were wide open with fear. The boy swam with them, holding onto a horn. When they got to the middle, one of these cows was swept sideways into a canoe and tipped it over so that the men fell in. They couldn't swim but they managed to grab hold of the wire, stretched across the river, which the ferry normally uses. They hung on there until they were rescued. Their trunk bobbled away downstream to the sea. Mum was in another canoe taking photographs. She didn't see the wire coming and it nearly knocked her over too.

Janie. . .
We had a day to kill in Mombasa and found a field above the estuary where a commercial laundry had hung out hundreds of sheets and towels to dry in the breeze. We chose a row of red blankets labelled 'Memorial Hospital' and sat in the grass to eat our cashew nuts, avocado pears and passion fruit. The smell of cannabis drifted over from a clump of trees. The mud-flats beneath us were strewn with car tyres. A cascade of rubbish littered the bank. The children rummaged through it and found matchboxes advertising a competition to win a radio. Only when they had collected enough for several entries did a boy translate the Swahili and reveal that the closing date was in April. In disgust, Orlando threw them into the air and the updraught took them to the circling kites and carrion crows.

The square in front of Mombasa station was overgrown and untended. Tramps lay asleep under the trees. We came upon a little girl squatting in the long grass. She popped up, smiled at us and said *Jambo*, then got down to her business again. Outside the station, the ground was swept and weeded. A sign beside an orange tree in a tub, said, '*Do not sit on the flower pots.*'

The children discovered some waste ground where a man was hiring pedal-cars and bikes to race round a track at two shillings for five minutes. They had no brakes and often collided, but the man was strict with anyone who messed about and gave Orlando a good telling off.

At seven o'clock, we caught the train to Voi. A Kenyan came into our compartment.

'Hello,' he said. 'I was on the bus with you yesterday.'

'Were you visiting relatives in Lamu?' Charlie asked.

'I was going there for my work,' the man said, 'but when I got to the Tana river, it was flowing very fast. I heard this boy' – he pointed to Orlando – 'telling someone how the canoe had turned over and I decided it was too dangerous. I took the bus back to Mombasa with you.'

'What is your work?' I asked.

'I am working for an American development agency. I am to report on famine relief in Lamu.'

'Famine in Lamu?' Orlando said. 'You can say they've got plenty of prawns and lobsters to eat.'

The express arrived at Voi soon after midnight. The connection to Taveta didn't leave till seven and people rushed to grab a space in the shelter. It was already full of sleeping bodies so we decided to look for a room. 'Transport of Corpses and Ashes', said a notice in the left-luggage office. '9/- per km. Minimum 288/-'. We left our rucksacks there and walked in pitch darkness towards the town. I was gloomy about finding lodgings at that hour but Charlie strode ahead, whistling confidently.

'We won't get mugged here,' he called. 'We're passing a police station.'

'Perhaps we could sleep in a cell.'

A face appeared behind a glowing cigarette.

'Hello, can you help us please? We're looking for a room for the night.'

'That would be my pleasure,' said a kind, resonant voice. 'There is a guest house in Voi. Please to follow me.'

He led off and then stopped so abruptly I bumped into him.

'Excuse me. Allow me to introduce myself. I am Police Constable Samuel Phiri. I am a bit tipsy.'

It was a lovely morning, bright and not too hot. The Taveta

train – tongue-and-groove planking on the outside of the carriages, mahogany panelling within – rattled across the Tsavo plains, stopping frequently. I thought of Sam and Neville's forbears. Slender Masai herdsmen swung aboard wearing tartan *kikoyis* and a dagger in their belt. Charlie was hanging out of the doorway, waiting for his first view of Kilimanjaro. It appeared when still seventy miles away, the snow-cap quite distinct above the clouds.

'Heavens, have I got to go up there?'

His brother had climbed to Uhuru peak the year before and set a challenge.

I decided that crossing a border was the right time for a change of image and Daisy helped me to dye my hair with henna in the folding sink.

Taveta was full of people for the weekly market. Hundreds were tramping the three miles of no man's land. We bought Joseph a pair of sandals made from car tyres. The maker fitted the strap to his foot and secured it with a nail. Some tall, bony Masai women, looking immensely arrogant, pushed past spitting on the ground to keep ordinary folk at a distance. Their version of the tyre sandal was a rectangle of tread, held on with a piece of string.

Once again we were entering a new country on a Saturday, but this time we made no mistake. Tanzania had a black-market rate of five or six to one, which meant the dealers were everywhere. A small boy selling meatballs bought our Kenyan shillings through the fence. Parked nearby was the very same overland truck which had refused us a ride at Kisangani. This time they agreed to take us the twenty-five miles to Moshi. It was an unpleasant journey spent fending off a diesel barrel and trying to breathe through a narrow air vent. On arrival, we booked into the clean, modern YMCA which was celebrating its 25th anniversary that weekend.

'Meet the Bishop,' Charlie said. 'His Grace Alpha Mohammed.'

A video of *The Ten Commandments* was shown after supper with a running commentary in Swahili. It's a very long film and, during the third tape, the two tired commentators disagreed about the plot and nearly came to blows. The manager turned it off and, much to Orlando's fury, sent the audience home.

26

Charles. . .

'Thousands climb Kili' every year,' Paul told me in Kinshasa.

'Did you manage to?'

He nodded. '—But don't under-estimate it: even more have to turn back. The altitude is a pig to cope with. There are three staging huts where you spend a night and allow your blood cells to catch up. Drink all the tea you can. It's only twenty miles or so across the ground but you climb eleven thousand feet. The summit's a lot higher than anything in Europe. Your body slows right down until it takes a minute just to move a leg. I warn you, it's bloody cold. They like you to reach the top just after dawn. The cloud usually lifts then. It means a one a.m. start from Kibo hut, which is nasty.'

'There are two peaks, aren't there?' I asked.

'There's Mawenzi at the other end of the saddle. It's a rock climb; very difficult I should imagine. Kibo is the crater. Gilman's Point is the summit you reach first at the top of the scree. Uhuru is the top-top, round the other side of the crater. It can be a nasty walk if the conditions are against you. Which month will you be going in?'

'June.'

'Not the best. If there's a lot of snow, you have to put your feet in the holes left by previous climbers. It'll probably be blowing a gale and, if you're like me, you'll be feeling as sick as a dog.

'When I went, we met a party of Aussies carrying a hang-glider. They lost the pilot. As soon as they got him strapped into the thing at Gilman's, he took off straight upwards, and didn't stop. The wind was funnelling up the side of the crater. I should think he blacked out; his heart or his lungs would have packed in.'

There are several hotels in Marangu, on the lower slopes of the mountain, which equip climbers who arrive with only a tropical shirt and a pair of shorts. We found the YMCA's package was cheap and efficient. A guide, a porter, three meals a day and a bunk in a hut at the day's end could be bought for about £35. We hired boots, thick socks, long johns, ski trousers, two jerseys, a quilted jacket, a waterproof, gloves and a balaclava from the National Parks office. Our guide was called Moses, a small wiry man in his late forties with a shy smile, who told me he had been to the top over three hundred times.

Climbing with me were Clare, Erica and Matthew. Clare and Erica were social workers from London who had been touring Africa for the past six months. Clare had slipped on a wet concrete floor in Malawi and damaged her knee: she hoped it would hold up. Erica was absorbed in flirting with Matthew who was good-looking, charming and arrogant. On a warm morning, we set out through the tangled, dripping forest to Mandara hut.

Janie. . .
Erica and Clare had told us enthusiastically about their 'Star Tours' safari to the Ngorongoro crater and Serengeti. An Asian in Arusha had fixed them up with three nights in hotels, a Land-Rover and a driver called Happy. They had seen masses of animals and visited the Olduvai Gorge where man began.

The day Charlie left, two Americans appeared in our room.

'Hi, my name's Jerry and this is Arnold.'

'Mine's Janie. I'm very ill.'

'Hi. Listen, we have a problem. We hear you want to go safari, right?'

'We wondered if we could string along together, share costs.'

'That would be nice,' I said, 'but right now I have flu.'

'The problem is, we really have to leave today because Arnold flies home on Sunday.'

'So whadda you say?'

I realised I wasn't going to get any better with the children shouting and rampaging around me. Reluctantly, I hauled myself out of bed, swallowed a couple of aspirin, packed our essentials into two rucksacks and went with Jerry and Arnold to catch a bus to Arusha.

Lunch was bought through the window. We could not help staring at the Masai in the next seat; two teenager warriors, tall and strikingly handsome in their blood-red robes, holding spears bound with copper wire. Their ear-lobes hung down in long loops festooned with wire and beads, bits of baked-bean tin cut into arrow shapes and their rolled-up bus tickets. They had more beads and a chrome digital watch on each wrist.

Arusha has a large international conference centre, built when the ink was still wet on Nyerere's famous declaration of African freedom, and opulent gifts flowed from European governments grateful to relinquish their responsibilities. Now there was no money to reglaze the windows and most of the rooms were either empty or let out as offices. We found Star Tours in one of them.

'Oh yes,' said Mr Shah, 'I can assure you most certainly, the driver is a bloody experienced game expert and my Land-Rovers are in tip-top condition.'

'We still need one more passenger,' Jerry said.

'There is an English teacher staying in town who wants to go,' Mr Shah said.

Briefly I had cold feet. We had always avoided travelling in company. Did I really want to be with these people? Arnold and Jerry had clearly been best friends from the cradle. Both were slightly built with well cut hair. They wore matching sneakers, navy trousers and red sweatshirts and carried identical cameras, binoculars and rucksacks. They were both terrified of mosquitoes and crocodiles and made terrible jokes all the time. Hilary turned out to be a tough, capable girl who had just finished a two-year VSO contract. Oh well, I thought, it's only for four days.

The Land-Rover came to collect us the next morning and the driver grudgingly piled our luggage into the back. We decided that all Star Tours drivers must be called Happy. Ours was deeply and permanently miserable.

We set off along a straight road beneath grey clouds. When we reached the entrance to the Ngorongoro park, we found we had to pay, not only for ourselves but for the driver and the car as well. Arnold and Jerry were furious.

'What was all that money we just paid your boss for?'

232

Happy shrugged and scowled at the ground. After much arguing, we agreed to divide the cost and demand reimbursement.

By this time the day had warmed up. There was no drink on sale and between us we had one bottle of water.

The road climbed steeply up the side of the crater. Masai children screamed at us as we chugged past. They were all dressed up in beads – on their heads, their arms and round their necks too. As they shouted and gesticulated, the wide discs round their necks bounced up and down.

'What a noise!' said Hilary.

'What do they want?' asked Orlando.

'They want you to take their photo,' said Happy; his longest sentence yet. 'Their parents send them to make money.'

'Stop,' said Arnold.

I was torn between getting a snap of the children standing next to my own and registering my disapproval of them selling themselves. But wait, I thought, fashion models get paid: and these families have been forced to join the tourist industry by being evicted from their homes in the crater to make more room for the game. I got my camera out. The group was controlled by a boy of about twelve who negotiated terms. He had no beads, only a plastic bag on his head. Arnold and Jerry were showering the kids with coins and snapping away. I gave a handful of change to the smallest child. Instantly the boy snatched it from him, barred him from my view and asked for more.

We got back in the car and drove on. The road went round the lip of the crater, climbing higher all the time.

'Is that a rhino?' asked Jerry, squinting through his view-finder.

'No it's a hippo,' said Arnold.

'You don't get hippos on top of craters,' Orlando said.

'It looks more like a cow to me,' Joseph added.

Ngorongoro Crater Lodge was like a hotel in the Scottish Highlands surrounded by damp trees dripping with moss. The effect was depressing. We stopped for lunch and then drove on.

'When do we go down into the crater?' I asked Happy.

'On way back.'

I had not realised we would drive to the Serengeti plain in one day. It grew hotter again and very dry. We had to pay once

233

more to enter the second national park. On the wall was a notice giving details of the number of animals in the 1981 survey.

Wildebeest	1.5 million
Zebra	200,000
Grant's and Thomson's gazelles	1 million
Buffalo	74,000
Impala	75,000
Giraffe	9,000
Lion	3,000
Hyena	4,000
Elephant	5,000

The yellow landscape was completely flat. It was quite easy to believe that if you ever reached the edge, you would fall off. Giraffe were nibbling the flat tops of the acacia-trees and gazelles wandered through the scrub. When they heard our engine, they panicked and zig-zagged in front of the vehicle, racing along beside us and leaping high in the air. Safaris are meant to be fun but after an hour of this I began to feel bored and disenchanted. Jerry and Arnold were snapping away. Perhaps animals gain excitement from their rarity, and there were just too many of them around.

There had been no rain for weeks and dust billowed up through the cracks in the floor. We took it in turns to poke our heads out through the roof. Orlando began to worry me by wheezing with asthma. Where were we heading? Mr Shah had been vague about our itinerary. You will camp at a hostel in the Serengeti, he said. For four hours we saw nothing but dry flat scrub and wild animals by the thousand. Occasional piles of rock broke the horizon. Sometimes these turned out to be elephants. In the fading light an outcrop somewhat larger than the rest amazed us all by revealing a modern hotel, built within its caves and crevices.

We were the only guests. The manager showed us to a room which was more luxurious than anything we had stayed in for weeks. The French windows kept the migrating herds ever before our eyes. We had the latest in pink bath-suites and the first loo paper I had seen in Tanzania. The roll had been sawn in half. By the time I got Orlando into bed he was wheezing, vomiting and whimpering. I gave him Phenergan and he dozed off.

Daisy. . .
The dining-room was a cave. It looked like a set for *Doctor Who*. Little furry animals were scuttling around in the rocks.

'They're rock rabbits,' Mum said.

'Hyrax,' said Arnold. 'Descended from the mammoth.'

I picked up a baby, so young that its eyes were still closed.

'Can I keep it?' I asked a waiter.

'Sure,' he said. 'Take it and its mother. Take the whole family. They're eating the curtains.'

Orlando. . .
I woke up vomiting in the middle of the night. The generator had gone off so Mum felt around for a candle. Nothing. She opened the door and I heard her cry out.

'What is it?' I asked.

'There's a buffalo outside,' Mum said.

Charles. . .
I was happy; stepping from boulder to boulder in the sunshine, above the tree-line, above the clouds. The meal Moses had prepared at Mandara tasted like a feast. I drank a quart of black tea. We were sitting at communal tables in semi-darkness. A party of Italians were growing wildly excited as they passed the brandy round.

'They'll never make it,' the young man opposite me said. The skin on his face was red. Dried barrier cream flaked off his nose. There was salt rime round his lips.

'Where did you get to?'

'Uhuru. It was very cold.'

'Did you enjoy it?'

'Great fun.'

His eyes shone brightly and every ten seconds or so he opened his mouth to yawn. We stared at each other in amusement, two refugees from the world, freed unexpectedly from petty anxieties. But whereas I did not yet know if the mountain would be kind to me, he had been in its presence. Its spirit resonated in him.

Moses and the six porters were way ahead up the path. They went barefoot, carrying our rucksacks, a sack of food, cooking-pots and firewood. There was no fuel where we were going; no water even. Above Horombo hut, the col was like a moonscape. No plants could live in the thin air.

The human system begins to stop too, the young man had warned me. You lose your appetite, you can't relieve yourself, your thoughts drift, nausea and vicious headaches arrive mysteriously and without warning.

'You call that fun?'

Why was I feeling so happy?

Janie. . .

I lay awake at dawn wondering what to do. It had been a sleepless night and I was still feeling the effects of the flu. Orlando couldn't cope with another drive through the dust. A light aircraft had landed near the hotel. Should we fly back to Moshi and claim on our travel insurance?

After breakfast, things didn't seem quite so bad. It had drizzled a bit and dampened the dust. Arnold, Jerry, Hilary, Daisy and Joseph set off for a drive around the plain and we went back to bed. Orlando was cheered by a rabbit which peered at him through the window. I hung out some clothes but thought better of it when a baboon sidled up and tugged at my trousers.

The others returned for lunch in a bad mood. Every time they had spotted some animals, Happy drove towards them at high speed and then braked suddenly, revving the engine. I don't think he liked our party much.

We ate a meagre meal of dried soup and tinned fruit which would have cost a law-abiding tourist £50. Then we set off across the plain to the Olduvai Gorge. We drove past a lion lying on the branch of a tree. This is something Tanzania is proud of: lions don't lie in trees anywhere else. A cheetah shot across our path to shrieks of delight from Arnold and Jerry. Happy set off in pursuit but it easily outran us. The Olduvai Gorge was a deep gash in the ground. It looked more like a gravel pit than Eve's birth place. We peered at some maps inside a locked hut. Happy could tell us very little.

We got back to the Ngorongoro Lodge around four o'clock. Reception was deserted and Jerry called out:

'Honey, I'm home!'

The girl appeared.

'Could we have some tea please?' said Hilary.

They had run out of milk. Cold fog swirled round the chalets. I managed to extract a dribble of tepid water from the boiler, had a bath and went to order chips and fruit salad. On the menu was zebra stew, which seemed strange for a national park. I overheard an Indian asking the waiter if it was really zebra.

'If it is beef disguised as zebra, I cannot eat it.'

When the food arrived, the portions were tiny and left the children feeling hungry. The fruit salad consisted of two chunks of pineapple and a slice of orange. When we got back to our room, it was so cold that the children tucked themselves up in one bed. I was freezing too and pulled Joseph in with me: even then, I could not stop shivering.

Ngorongoro Crater is the remains of a vast volcano, ten miles wide and half a mile deep. It contains one of the biggest concentrations of game remaining in the world. We drove down a steep, rocky road and then circled aimlessly in the long grass looking for rhino. We saw a lake, pink with squawking flamingos and eighteen lions lying on the bank. A family of hippos swelled out of the water like submarines; the young turned over onto their backs and revealed pink tummies and funny wiggling tails. Arnold and Jerry were ecstatic and took roll upon roll of film.

Our guide was bossy and uncooperative. We were not allowed to sit on the roof or look out of the roof-hole: we couldn't even open the windows in case we were eaten. He ignored the children's questions. Lunch at a picnic spot was particularly miserable. We were still not allowed out, though another party were perched happily on their roof. The packed lunches for which we had paid £4 each contained a measly ham roll without margarine, two bananas and an orange.

'I paid a 10% service charge for this,' I raged.

'That was for putting the things in the box,' Hilary said.

My headache seemed to be getting worse; the bananas tasted like cardboard. I decided it must be the high altitude: we were over 10,000 feet above sea level. When we go down from here I'll feel better, I told myself.

Mr Shah had said the last night of the safari would be spent in a very nice government lodge, cheap and comfortable, near Lake Manyara. In heavy rain we slithered and ground our way out of the crater and headed off downhill. With every foot we travelled, I prayed that my headache would go, but instead it got worse. I was feeling hot and thirsty and we had nothing to drink. One of the nuts had fallen off the back wheel and it was rattling badly: every few miles we stopped while Happy tightened them up. The road was too bad to go fast.

We reached a village and parked in the courtyard of a bar.

'This is it,' said Happy, pointing to four huts surrounded by broken bottles and empty tins.

I fell out and collapsed beside a wall.

'What's the matter Mummy?' Joseph asked.

'I think I've got malaria.'

My headache fitted the description.

'Please find me something to drink.'

Daisy helped me inside and sat me down on a narrow iron bed. I tried to take my shoes off and burst into tears. The young man in charge stood at the door and stared.

'What is matter with madam?' he asked kindly.

'Mum's got malaria,' Daisy explained. He took off my shoes and spread the blanket over me.

'This village is called the "Place of the Mosquitoes" in Swahili,' he said.

'I'll go and look for a doctor,' said Hilary. 'You need a Chloroquine injection.'

A doctor out here? Hilary was gone a long time.

'They say he'll be along soon,' she said.

'That could mean months. I don't believe there is one.'

'We've got some tablets for malaria,' Daisy said. She counted out four. 'Take these now and four more in the morning.'

They tasted vile.

'Here's a painkiller,' Hilary said.

238

Every time I moved, tears sprang to my eyes at the hammering inside my skull.

Jerry was ranting outside in the yard.

'We can't stay here,' he screamed. 'There is only one mosquito net!'

Charles. . .

In the late afternoon, we reached Kibo hut at the foot of the volcanic cone. Sixteen thousand feet above sea level; three and a half thousand more to go. Queen Victoria gave this mountain to the Kaiser of Germany as a birthday present. Did he come here to play with his gift?

'You rest here until midnight,' Moses said.

He brought me some tea but I couldn't drink it.

'You look green,' Clare said. 'Are you feeling all right?'

'No. Weak, dizzy, pretty awful. It's my own fault.'

I'd made an elementary mistake. After the long plod across the col, I'd seen the hut appear and made a playful run towards it. Ten minutes later, I threw up. Now I lay on a bunk staring at the graffiti on the wall and trying to keep a grip on myself.

> *Grant Turner '85. Uhuru in 4 hrs 30 mins.*
> *Cathy woz sick right here.*
> *In memory of Rex Jardine, '76.*

Even reading nauseated me. My mind was swimming. I felt truly scared and out of my depth. Darkness fell, sleep brought frightening dreams and I was grateful when a muffled figure came in with a hurricane lamp.

'Time to go,' Moses said.

We slowly dressed ourselves in layers of clothing, fumbling with our buttons in the candlelight. Another larger party was going up at the same time. They had flown out directly from New York at huge expense: a guide had been hired for every single person.

'I want your agreement, chaps,' Matthew said. 'If any of us have to turn back, they do it alone.'

'What if my knee packs in?' Clare said.

'You can have Moses,' Erica replied. 'Whoever carries on will have to keep up with the other party.'

Moses came back.

'Ready?' he asked.

'Yes,' I said, 'I'm ready.' I felt a little better.

'Can you help me with some toilet paper?' Moses asked.

We stared at him in astonishment. Clare, ever practical, produced a packet of tissues from her bag.

'My precious supply,' she whispered.

Moses gave me the hurricane lamp to hold and stuffed paper into the cracks.

'Right, let's go.'

Thus equipped, we set out into the night.

My watch said one a.m. There was no moon. The path led through a mile or two of massive rockfalls at the foot of the slope. We trudged along in single file in the pitch darkness, unable to see where our boots were landing, following the shoulder of the person in front silhouetted against Moses' swaying lamp. A cold wind set the tiny flame flickering. The other party were grunting and calling encouragement to one another.

'You there Rodge?'

'I sure am Bill.'

'You're doing fine Nancy, just fine.'

'Oh shit,' came Erica's voice close behind me. 'I keep stumbling over things. Can you walk a bit slower Charlie?'

'We have to keep up. Are you feeling all right?'

'I'm okay.'

Every fifteen minutes or so, we rested on Moses' orders. At two forty-five, we reached the bottom of the scree. The stops were lasting longer by this time: Matthew was growing impatient.

'We have five hours to reach the summit. Either you make it in time or you give up. It is dangerous to spend too long at this altitude.'

The Americans were off ahead of us. Wearily I got to my feet.

'Right, on we go.'

The conditions immediately became very difficult. We were climbing a slope of some forty-five degrees in zig-zags about fifteen yards long. Underfoot was soft volcanic ash. If you strayed from the path in the darkness, your feet sank in up to the ankles. After half an hour of this, Erica collapsed.

'It's my bloody legs,' she said tearfully. 'They won't do what they're told. I seem to have lost all control.'

We looked at each other. The other party were three or four zig-zags ahead: we could see their flashlights and hear their feet crunching in the ash.

'I'm going on,' Matthew said. 'I've got to go now, or I won't be able to catch them up. Goodbye.' He turned away, and added as an afterthought, 'Good luck!'

'What do you want me to do?' asked Clare.

'I take her down,' said Moses. 'You go on too. Go.'

Erica was a foot taller but he lifted her onto his back and set off down the slope.

With no lantern and no guide, Clare and I turned back to the mountain. We tried to follow the path and keep up with the others but the cold and dizziness numbed our brains. We lost our bearings and kept floundering off into the ash. The nausea was returning. I reached for my water bottle to take a sip and found the contents had frozen and split the metal open. We seemed to be making no progress at all.

'This is hopeless,' I said.

A few steps further on, the nausea swept over me. I sat down, choking and shaking, my head between my knees and bile dribbling from my lips. The flashlights and muffled voices receded. I was all alone. The moon rose, revealing a bed of fleecy clouds, the huge barren col and the jagged peaks of Mawenzi.

'It's no good,' I thought. 'I'm exhausted. I can't go on.'

A figure stirred on the periphery of my vision.

'Clare? Is that you?'

'Who do you think it is?'

'What are you doing?'

'I'm waiting for you, aren't I?'

'Oh.'

'Are you ready yet?'

'Give me a bit longer.'

I took a long, deep breath. Perhaps I'd been going too fast again.

'I shall need to take it very slowly.'

'Don't worry,' said Clare, 'so will I.'

241

'A rest at the end of every zig?'

'And every zag.'

'All right, you're on.'

We climbed slowly and steadily for another hour. It began to grow light. We noticed snow among the rocks beside the scree. The Americans were only twenty yards above us.

'Look at them,' I said, 'so close and yet they're probably half an hour ahead.'

'Save your breath,' Clare said.

The scree is a little over a mile long: we climbed it in seven hours. The summit arrived suddenly. The ash turned to rock, we scrambled over loose stones, squeezed between boulders and looked down into the dazzling snowfield inside the crater.

'Phew!'

We hugged each other with delight.

A whistle came from above.

'Up here you guys!'

It was Matthew, sitting astride Gilman's Point, smoking a cigarette and listening to his Walkman. We clambered up the final knoll. Too fast: same mistake again! More bilious vomiting followed quickly. I noticed with distaste it was bright green.

'A cigarette?' Matthew said lightly.

I looked at him through watery eyes. The Americans were hollering and cat-calling among the rocks.

'They had to carry one of the girls up here,' Matthew said. 'She got her value for money. Look, there she goes now.'

Two guides were dragging a dumpy, senseless form back down the scree. They ran pell-mell in a straight line, sending up clouds of dust.

'Are you going on to Uhuru, Matthew?'

'No ways. There's been a fresh snowfall, you can't see the path any more. It's a shame Moses isn't here.'

'There's a place here to sign your name,' Clare said. 'I haven't got a pen. Matthew, have you got a pen on you? Charlie? Never mind, I'll take some photographs.'

I looked around me at the snow and the clouds, glowing pink in the morning sun; at the white pole snapped by the wind and the box full of tattered pages covered in names. I felt my heart would burst. I wanted to laugh. I wanted to cry.

'My God!' I said, 'my God! Here we are! We've made it! I don't think I've ever done anything so bloody stupid, so pointless in all my life!'

Janie. . .
I drifted in and out of consciousness. It was morning. We were in the back of the Land-Rover again. Someone had placed a sleeping bag around my shoulders. I heard Happy say:
'Only two hours' drive; all good road now.'
A car came towards us flashing its lights. We stopped.
'What's happening? What's going on?'
'They're taking our spare tyre,' Hilary said.
'Why? They can't! Supposing *we* have a puncture?'
Arnold was listening to the driver's conversation.
'One of Shah's other vehicles has rolled over in Ngorongoro,' he said. 'I guess they've got one spare for the whole fleet.'
'Hell,' said Jerry, 'they must have been there all night.'
I was trying to make plans for our arrival in Arusha. I was too weak to make it to Moshi by bus and almost out of cash. Charlie had the remaining dollars and only he could change the traveller's cheques. I tried to count the days since we parted. We had agreed to meet back at the YMCA.
Happy dropped us outside the New Arusha Hotel and went off without a word.
'See you around,' the others said. I sat on my rucksack and drew breath. A cup of strong coffee would help. The boys carried the bags into the lobby. I would ring Moshi, then find out how much it cost to stay here.
'I'll meet you in the garden,' I told the boys. 'Daisy, sit on the bags while I go and enquire.'
'But I thought we hadn't any money.'
'We might have enough if we don't eat anything.'
There was a crowd at reception. An American safari had just arrived. I worked my way to the front.
'Do you have a double room please?' a woman was saying.
'Certainly madam.'
The price was double what we could afford and they required a full night's deposit. I found my legs wouldn't move. The clerk looked at me.
'How much is a room with three beds?' I asked, stalling for

time. He seemed to be swaying and I didn't hear his reply. A form appeared in front of me. I tried to read it. The ground was slipping away. I grabbed at the smooth desk but there was nothing to hang on to.

I became aware of a man with a French accent shouting in the darkness:
'Is she alive? Does anyone know this woman? Call a doctor!'
I was surrounded by legs.
'Do something, man!' said the French voice.
A waiter picked me up, threw me over his shoulder and dumped me in an armchair.
The manageress stood in front of me.
'Have you got anyone with you?'
'No,' I murmured. 'My husband is on a mountain.'
I couldn't remember its name.
'What happened?' she asked.
'I don't know. I think I have malaria.'
'We'd better get you to hospital. Where's your luggage?'
'Daisy is sitting on it. I want her with me.'

Daisy. . .
We got Mum into a taxi. The manageress came along too and left us at the hospital. Mum lay on a couch and fell asleep. I held her hand until a doctor appeared. He asked me how much she'd had to eat.
'Not much,' I said.
He explained that Mum had fainted because the Chloroquine pills caused low blood sugar. He tried to find a vein in her hand for a glucose drip. The pricks woke her and she sat up and said:
'I'll drink it, if you don't mind.'
Then she started coughing.
'Let me listen to your chest,' the doctor said. 'Hm. You have bronchitis as well as malaria. You will need antibiotics. Stay in bed for a few days.'
The manageress returned.
'Are those your boys?' she said. 'They have eaten a big tea. We have put you in a nice family suite.'
'Oh dear,' I thought. 'How are we going to pay for it?'

Mum explained that Dad was waiting for us in Moshi.

'Don't worry,' the manageress said. 'We have a sister hotel in Moshi. We will get a message to him.'

Charles. . .

I came down the mountain in ten-league boots, with giant sure-footed strides, whistling and singing. I breathed in deeply the clear blue air, surveyed my future below the clouds and laughed at its uncertainty.

When I got to Moshi, there was no sign of the others.

'Where are my family?'

'We haven't seen them,' said Reception.

'No messages?'

'None at all.'

By evening I was mildly worried. It was a Saturday. The phone at the YMCA was out of order. The post office was shut. I went to the big hotel in town and rang Star Tours. Mrs Shah answered.

'Mr Shah has gone to Dar. When did you say your family left?'

'Tuesday.'

'They should be back by now. Try the hotels.'

I rang them all, including the New Arusha. The person answering spoke Swahili so I gave the phone to the receptionist.

'Ask if my wife is staying there. Her name is Hampton,' I spelt it, 'with three children.'

After a long wait, she looked up and shook her head.

'Not there, sir.'

I had tried everything I could think of. Where could she be?

Janie. . .

The phone in the room next door rang and rang. I reached for the bottle of painkillers. Daisy had been out on her own and hunted round Arusha till she found Hilary. They came in together now. Hilary had an armful of Graham Greenes.

'I found these going cheap downstairs. Do you like him? Arnold's taking a bus to Moshi in the morning. He'll find Charlie. Would the kids like to come for a walk?'

'Thank you Hilary. You're a brick.'

I opened *Travels with My Aunt* but my heart was not in it. At nine p.m. I picked up the phone and rang the police.

'Can you find my husband please? Tell him I'm ill.'

'Yes madam.'

'Tell him I'm very ill. He must come at once.'

I had £7 in my purse. Our room was £40 a night. A fried egg cost £3. I was terrified the manageress would find out.

'Just sign the bill for breakfast,' I told Daisy, 'and eat as much as you can.'

Throughout that day and the next, the children played a game of travel agents round our room. They rang each other at their desks and made tickets out of the menus. Hilary came with fruit and bread and took them out for walks. I dozed and read. Where was Charlie? Was I in South America or Tanzania? Had Charlie fallen off the mountain? Was I part of a Graham Greene novel? It was hard to be sure.

Clare and Erica turned up.

'We bumped into Arnold outside. He said you were here.'

'Do you mean he's still in Arusha?'

'Yes.'

'Oh dear. He was meant to go to Moshi. Where is Charlie?'

'Waiting for you at the YMCA. He made it to the top. We all went to hear a Zairean band last night. He reckoned you would turn up today.'

'I can't.' I suppressed a sob. 'I'm a prisoner here.'

'What do you mean?'

'I can't afford to pay the bill. I can't afford to buy food from outside. We're forced to eat fried eggs and chips at £4 a plate. If Charlie doesn't get here soon, we'll never escape.'

'I can take a message to the bus station for you,' Clare said. 'I'll give it to a passenger.'

'Do you think it'll work?'

'Never fails. It's the modern bush telegraph.'

I picked up a laundry list and wrote, 'Help! Rescue us from New Arusha Hotel. Collapsed here with malaria, hypoglycaemia and bronchitis. We have no money. Please come soon. Give this person some money. Love Janie.'

At tea-time I remembered Bishop Alpha Mohammed and rang him at his office. He was very friendly.

'Don't worry, I'll send one of my priests round on his bicycle.'

'Soon?'

'Right now, my dear. Don't fret.'

Charles. . .

I was sitting in my room late on Monday afternoon when a knock came at the door. Outside was a policeman, a clergyman and an old man in a battered felt hat. They all started speaking at once. Three notes were thrust into my hand. I glanced at the sprawling handwriting and looked up, recognition dawning. The old man wanted money. I dug into my pocket.

'*Asante sana!* Thank you, now excuse me please. I have a phone call to make.' I dashed out of the building.

Orlando. . .

The next morning, Dad turned up. We jumped for joy. I wanted to tell him about our game but he wouldn't listen.

'Quick,' he said. 'We must pack as fast as possible. You do the bags while I help Mum dress. I've got us a lift to Nairobi in a lorry.'

'What about the bill?' Mum asked.

'That's paid.'

'I'll never survive a lorry ride.'

'It's a German hospital truck,' Dad said. 'I made friends with the driver at the YMCA. You can go in the cab.'

27

Charles. . .

Back in Nairobi, we tucked Janie into bed in a brothel. There was a barred iron gate at the top of the stairs and metal grilles on all the windows: guests fixed their own padlock to the door.

I rang the Hurlingham from a phone-box.

'Sorry Charles,' Katie said. 'No can do. We're booked solid till the end of August. Where are you now?'

'A boarding-house off Latema Road. I've found two rooms.'

'Well you're lucky. I should stay there.'

When she saw Janie's pale drawn face, the proprietress was sympathetic and found three extra pillows. She showed me where to do the washing.

'Don't let your children out in the street on their own: and tell them to be quiet in the morning. The girls like to sleep till midday.'

They were a friendly crowd around the tub on the flat roof. Our torn and faded T-shirts joined lace panties and skimpy bras on the washing-line. A baby was passed from hand to hand. At five o'clock, the girls on the evening shift appeared in calf-length boots, see-through bodices and leather jackets. Once this uniform was on, all men became their prey and I got down to some serious scrubbing on Orlando's trousers.

Latema Road was actually a square with bars, a market, a taxi rank and pavements that supported every known form of city life. While Janie read her way through Graham Greene and slowly got stronger on chicken take-aways and hot chocolate, the children and I explored the streets in a cautious huddle.

Joseph had a photograph taken of his shoes being shined for a mere £5.50. Nearby, a young man was break-dancing beside a ghetto-blaster with exquisite agility and rhythm, causing a crowd to form for his friends to pickpocket. It was an economical outfit because the music was all inside his head. The cassette player was a balsa-wood toy.

I lost £15 on the old three card trick. He had the knave and two other cards face down on the pavement and shifted their positions with lightning speed. Even so, it was possible to bet with certainty where it finished up. The first time, my attention was distracted by an accomplice in the crowd. The second, he actually got me to put my foot on the knave and place another bet. I reached into the tight pocket of my jeans, rocking back ever so slightly on my heels: my eye strayed for an instant to the 50 shilling note in my hand and the knave escaped.

Janie listened to these adventures with weary resignation and hoped we would not be bankrupted before she could get up. One night, she rose and went to the mirror beneath a red bulb in the corridor and, ignoring the rhythmical squeaks from the door behind her, hacked off all her hair with the Swiss army knife. In the morning, we surveyed the mess and agreed to an appointment with the *salon de coiffure* at the Hilton. She was getting better.

A night or two later, we returned from a movie to find we had locked ourselves out of our room. A large man wearing only his vest and pants emerged from the toilet.

'Excuse me,' said Orlando. 'Do you think you could break our door down?'

He looked at us quizzically. We reassured him that the catch was not very strong and it was our room.

'You could perhaps put your shoulder to it?' Janie said.

'I don't think that would do at all,' he replied. 'But I tell you what: could you get me a place at Manchester University?'

Not much else happened to the kids and me in Nairobi. The days passed slowly until our flight. Three times we went to the railway museum and found it shut. Orlando and Joseph discovered a boating lake in the park and forgot all about their triumphs and their trials, paddling a tub round an ornamental island. Daisy had her ears pierced. I fought off more Jehovah's Witnesses and rejected the Anglican cathedral in favour of the much jollier Catholic one.

Finally, at seven p.m. on 24th June, after a further twelve

249

hours delay caused by engine failure, we elbowed through the crowds of tarts outside the hotel and boarded the airport bus. Janie stood on the dark pavement to wave us goodbye.

'Cheerio Mum! Take care of yourself.'

'So long darling. Enjoy the conference. Be good.'

'See you all in a month's time. Bye children. Look after Daddy for me.'

With a crashing of gears and a honk on its klaxon, the bus took us away through the garish streets, past the slums and across the sleeping veld to the airliner: then Africa released us into the night sky.

Janie. . .

After Charlie and the children left, I moved into the Iqbal, a Moslem hotel in Latema Road. It was cleaner but no more expensive and there was a friendly mixture of customers. Cheap, tasty food was served all day: my favourite was a glass of fresh yoghurt and *bhajias* – potato fried in spicy batter. For the first time in months I had a permanent base and I decorated my room with postcards and bunches of flowers.

Next morning, I found I couldn't get out. The door handle had broken and I was firmly trapped inside. I tried shouting through the key-hole but no one came. I looked out of the window: I was three storeys above the crowded street. A woman walked past on her husband's arm and gaily answered my wave. I wrote a note and wrapped it round a matchbox: it was kicked into the gutter. The next one landed in the fire of a man roasting maize. I tied my washing line to a bottle and stuck a note inside. *'HELP! I am locked in room 36 of the Iqbal Hotel. Let me out.'* I dangled it in the doorway of a sweet shop below. At first no one took any notice: then people began to read it, look up at me and laugh. Some walked away, others swung the bottle or hit it. I was nearly in tears, waving and shouting at them. Eventually the shopkeeper came out to see why such a crowd had gathered, read the note and rescued me.

From my window I could follow the comings and goings outside the notorious Green Bar. When Charlie was asked to take me there, he had politely declined: now I wanted to see for myself. The interior was bleak and unattractive. The walls, the ceiling and even the bare light-bulbs were stained with nicotine. The girls looked like overdressed dolls, propped lifelessly round the wall. I was besieged with offers of drinks from leering men but someone with a Grace Jones haircut pulled me down next to her.

'Get out the way, you,' she jeered at the onlookers. 'I'll look after you, honey. Mirabelle is my name: what's yours.'

At a glance, she could have been attractive: but as she talked, I realised that her clothes were too tight and her shoes worn out, her nails bitten to the quick and her eyes red and tired. The Green Bar attracted the poorest of the prostitutes, those who needed all the clients they could get, just to pay the rent. Mirabelle was full of girly jokes and she made me feel safe. I wondered why she wanted to spend her time talking to me, until she put her hand on my knee.

'Do you think I'm attractive?' she asked, stroking my thigh.

'I like your haircut,' I said. 'How do you keep it that shape?'

I had never been propositioned by a woman before, let alone a prostitute. Perhaps Mirabelle thought a white client was a good catch, whatever the sex. I bought her a couple of drinks and made my excuses.

I hadn't lived on my own in a city for over ten years. Without the children, I found I needed much less sleep but there was a yawning gap which only work could fill. The BBC sent me a telegram.

'The time has come for Network Africa to investigate the goat: its role, mythology, culture, life style and bleat.'

Today the goat, I thought, tomorrow the world's women. I read up what I could, interviewed the goat officer at the Ministry of Agriculture and decided I needed a few bleats to complete the recording. A young man named Kululu offered to help and we took a *matatu* to the Mathare valley.

'You must leave your watch and your money behind,' Kululu warned.

The government would like to think this terrible slum does not exist and provides the bare minimum of water-pipes, clinics and schools. Some of the worst houses are owned by the council, which charges such a high rent that two or more families are forced to share a three-roomed shack. Many of the

251

dwellings we saw were benders covered in plastic bags.

The goat market was in a patch of wasteland. Goats are to the festival of *Id* (the end of Ramadan) what turkeys are to Christmas, so prices were high and the turnover fast. The animals stood tethered in anxious groups, resigned to their fate and resolutely dumb. Kululu explained that I wanted to record a bleat and somebody twisted the ears of a billy until it moaned in a quite ungoatlike fashion. Eventually I paid a boy ten shillings for his very passable imitation.

The day before the conference started, I walked down Kenyatta Avenue, Nairobi's main thoroughfare, and wondered if I was in the same town. Gangs of council workers had repainted the signs, cut the knee-high grass in the central reservation, covered the road with fresh tarmac, carted away piles of rubbish and swept the pavements clean. All the shoe-shine boys, fruit-sellers, beggars and prostitutes had disappeared and armed policemen with alsatians were patrolling outside the hotels.

Normality was waiting for me round the corner of Tom Mboya Street. The Iqbal was part of the danger zone where tourists were assumed not to go.

In 1975 the United Nations declared an International Decade for Women at a conference in Mexico *'to eliminate all forms of discrimination against women'*. Nairobi was the venue for the end of the decade, *'to review the achievements and obstacles encountered and to formulate strategies for the future'*. The UN reports suggested there was plenty to discuss.

Under 10% of the world's professional civil servants are women. 3 out of 170 Kenyan MPs are women.

47% of the world's agricultural labour force and only 2.9% of its agricultural advisers are women. 75% of agricultural labour in Africa is done by women.

In Rwanda, a village woman's work takes three times as long as the work done by men.

As I talked to the organisers, however, I realised that the poor and downtrodden were not going to have it all their own way. Professor Eddah Gachukia was the Kenyan chairwoman of

'Forum 85', the get-together for non-government organisations which coincided with the official conference.

'Our constitution guarantees equality between men and women. What has been lacking is the ability of women because of certain constraints, such as the nature of women.'

'You don't think there might be cultural or political reasons why Kenya has only three women MPs?'

'There was an idea brought here by the Western press that women wanted to be equal. We don't believe in the liberation movement or desire women to be equal to men. Women are created different. There was a misguided trend where women were removing their bras so that they could be like men. We want to be women and stay that way.'

Her colleague, Muthoni Lilimani, was more practical.

'If you are working you can always get a girl to help in the house. I don't wash my own clothes, I have a girl. There is day-care for the children. African women don't want men to cook. I can't stand a suit in my kitchen. I like it if a man changes the tyre on my car. So in Africa there is always a division of work. We like it that way. Why should I fix a nail and my husband cook the soup?'

What would they make of Betty Friedan and Angela Davis?

Both 'Forum 85' and the official conference lasted a fortnight and overlapped by a week. The Kenyan government had planned for 8,000 participants and 15,000 turned up. UN staff arriving in advance from New York found they had no offices, telephones or transport and were forced to share single hotel rooms.

'Forum 85' got going on the university campus. The women of one hundred and fifty-one nations filled every corner: blonde crew-cuts from Scandinavia, dreadlocks from Chicago, veils from Iran, peroxide spikes from London and bowler-hats from Peru. Those who couldn't communicate by talking, sang or just held hands. A dancer from Boston pegged hand-dyed silk bags to a washing line and invited us to place our 'fears, wishes and desires' in them. Betty Friedan set up shop under a flowering tree and held forth to her admirers on 'The Feminine Mystique'.

'We are all beautiful and the women's movement is exploding all over the world,' she croaked, and hugged a frail Indian woman to her teddy-bear figure.

Over a thousand workshops, recitals and exhibitions took place, ranging from 'Afghan women for peace' to 'Women fishing in Alaska', 'Women laughing in living colour' and 'Dramatic readings of the celebration of menopause in religion'.

West German peace activists hired a marquee for discussions between warring nations. The meeting on South America melted away when a Chilean official was recognised taking down names. The Iranians and Iraquis threw lemonade at each other: the Iraquis claimed their peace resolution had been returned and the Iranians said they never received it.

'We want large families to achieve world victory!'

The eleven Iranian delegates popped up everywhere, parting their veils to scream 'Imperialist Devils!' at passing Americans.

The sexual discussions were among the most interesting. Western women were horrified by a detailed description of different types of female circumcision, illustrated with a plastic model. The lesbians weathered an official campaign to silence them as 'un-Kenyan' and held a daily caucus on the lawn. Apart from laying into a *Newsweek* photographer who wouldn't down his camera, they were a good-natured lot and dealt gently with the crowds of intrigued Kenyans, both men and women, who wanted to know how they made love.

The International Prostitutes Collective drew up a petition to the Kenyan government, objecting to the arrest and eviction of their Kenyan sisters. It was learnt that they had been driven into the deserted northern region and dumped there: the more enterprising were already trickling back.

Any Kenyan man who thought he was going to make hay soon discovered otherwise.

'This is obviously a sexist meeting against men,' a student raged at me. 'Women must remember that we each have our duties. Men should not go in the kitchen. We stay outside to protect our women.'

Jaja from Sudan claimed he was enjoying every minute of it.

'I'm a feminist too,' he said, 'but all these discussions won't solve anything. What we need is more dancing and eating together. The women don't want castrated men. They want us to be partners.'

'Are you sure you're from Sudan?' I said. 'Your accent sounds rather Californian to me.'

254

When the official UN conference opened at the Kenyatta Centre, Maureen Reagan, the president's daughter and head of the American delegation, threatened to walk out if Palestine, apartheid or disarmament were discussed.

'Politics is not a woman's issue. If we debate these issues, then we have robbed women.'

'We do not want any confrontations,' Eddah Gachukia stated in her address. 'We are here to discuss and solve problems. There will be no rows because all women agree on the path forward.'

Baroness Young of Farnworth added her own weight.

'The conference should not be thwarted on divisive political matters.'

Next day, her colleagues on the British delegation admitted that they did not really understand the resolutions they were busy passing.

'We do know that we are not legally obliged to implement any of the "Forward-looking Strategies".'

The Wages for Housework Campaign knew exactly what every resolution and square-bracketed paragraph meant. They had been battling for thirteen years to get women's work included in the Gross National Product and at last had scored a symbolic victory. They were a frank and friendly bunch, based at King's Cross in London. Carol, who had shaved her temples and hung a bleached plait over her forehead, called herself a raspberry ripple (cripple) and wobbled along on a stick, her palsied legs zippered into tight punk trousers.

'Black is not just a skin colour,' she said. 'It's a state of political consciousness. Have you written it down with a capital B?'

I realised I had a lot of catching up to do when I got back to Britain.

At the official party at the High Commission, a young black woman stepped forward and read a statement.

'The British delegation cannot be described as representative of British women in age, occupation, income, race or any other social category. The Decade for Women has achieved nothing for women in Britain.'

Three freshly scrubbed young men sought diplomatic immunity behind a Martini shaker.

'You must try to understand,' said one. 'I'm not a man in this

255

context, I'm merely a symptom of my organisation.'

'Yea, like a boil on yer bum,' Carol replied.

'I do not believe that male delegates need justifying,' said another. 'We are here to discuss equality. Discrimination against anyone is wrong and, besides, we can't expect Lady Young to run around doing hard routine work.'

'You take care of the cooking and washing up, do you?'

At the end of 'Forum 85', a massive celebration march was planned through the city but the police refused permission, saying all public demonstrations had been banned since a coup attempt in 1982. Instead, over 10,000 women joined hands at the university and sang 'We Shall Overcome' while balloons filled the sky. Standing next to me, a Kenyan policewoman bit back her tears.

There was still a week until my scheduled flight home by Air Sudan, but now the fun of the 'Forum' was over and the official conference had only two days to run. I had reported all I could and realised I was missing Charlie and the children. The next day was our fourteenth wedding anniversary. On an off-chance, I called to enquire if there was an empty seat to London that night. The travel agent was doubtful.

'It's very short notice. There are only a few hours before the plane leaves.' He shuffled his papers around his desk. I felt in my bag.

'Here, take this.' I handed him a bar of chocolate.

'I'll do my best. Come back in an hour.'

When I returned, he grinned and presented me with a new ticket.

'Oh thank you!'

I gave him another bar of chocolate and a kiss on the cheek, ran to the Iqbal, packed everything, left notes saying goodbye to my friends and took a taxi to the airport.

The plane touched down at Khartoum for two hours after midnight. I had a Sudanese visa and decided to use it. Outside the airport, a group of taxi drivers were smoking by their cars.

'Who will drive me round Khartoum and back here within an hour?' I asked, waving a $5 bill.

They all pounced at once and the winner pushed me into his car saying:

'I speak Ingleesh.' They were the only words he knew.

I was surprised to find that traffic drove on the right. The President had issued a decree to this effect after a visit to America in 1976. Many of the older people still found it difficult to adjust. My driver had little trouble keeping to the side, however, because his taxi had to slew into the kerb in order to stop. He took me to the Nile and I peered over the edge of the parapet at the inky darkness. Only the smell told me there was a river below. General Gordon's palace was floodlit and surrounded by soldiers.

Back at the airport, Immigration found it hard to believe that I was leaving again, after only an hour in the country. The plane sat till six a.m. on the tarmac.

Charlie had sent me newspaper cuttings in Nairobi about Live Aid, the enormous concert held jointly in Britain and America to raise funds for famine relief. I handed them round to the Sudanese.

'This is excellent,' said a portly businessman. 'I am glad the world is celebrating our glorious coup d'etat.'

In the past, I had felt guilty about flying over drought-stricken Africa while tucking into duck à l'orange and a bottle of Beaujolais. On Air Sudan, the conscience-stricken passenger could rest assured. The meal arrived in the usual pre-formed plastic, but inside was a piece of bread and some goat's cheese, with water to drink.

England on a sunny July morning was a great shock. Everything was so green. I found a bus to Oxford and marvelled at its smoothness and speed. Never had a motorway seemed more beautiful: the fields were laid out to perfection, their hedges neatly trimmed, the poppies as brilliant as on our wedding day. The people looked pale and unhealthy but they spoke my language. I knew what they were thinking. I couldn't persuade myself that I had a right to be there, that I was no longer a visitor or an observer.

Charles. . .

Fernando from Barcelona and Louisa from Warsaw were

257

struggling with irregular verbs when the phone rang on the wall beside the blackboard.

'Hello?'

'Mr Hampton, your wife is on the outside line. Will you come down to the office.'

'My wife!'

I raced from the classroom and tore through the building.

'Hello darling.'

'Hello, it's me. Happy Anniversary.'

'It's a fantastic line. Aren't these satellites marvellous. Are you all right? How's the conference going? We're missing you like mad, can't wait till next week.'

'You don't have to,' Janie said. 'I'm in Oxford market.'

APPENDIX 1

Bibliography

Practical

Bradt and Bradt, *Backpacker's Africa*, Bradt Enterprises, 1987.
Suggested walks in Eastern and Southern Africa.

Crowther, Geoff, *Africa on a Shoestring*, Lonely Planet, 1982.
The information is often out of date but the fact that someone
once went from A to B by train gives you the confidence to
begin at A, even if the train no longer exists. A heavy book,
covering the whole of Africa. We cut out the countries we
weren't interested in.

Dodwell, Christina, *The Explorer's Handbook*, Hodder &
Stoughton, 1985. Some good ideas based on the author's own
experience of solo travelling.

Werner, David, *Where There Is No Doctor*, Macmillan, 1979.
Everything you need to know about tropical diseases, deliver-
ing babies or mending fractures with no equipment.

Non-fiction

Dodwell, Christina, *Fortune's Travels, An African Adventure*,
W.H. Allen, 1979. Inspiration for the inexperienced traveller
because the author was quite unprepared for her four years of
roaming Africa.

Donovan, V.J., *Christianity Rediscovered*, SCM Press, 1978.

Fossey, Dian, *Gorillas in the Mist*, Hodder & Stoughton, 1983.

Greene, Graham, *In Search of a Character: Congo Journal*,
Penguin, 1961.

    A Burnt Out Case, Penguin, 1970.

Miller, Charles, *The Lunatic Express*, Ballantine, 1971.

Moorehead, Alan, *The White Nile*, Hamish Hamilton, 1960.

Naipaul, Shiva, *North of South*, Penguin, 1980. A visit to Kenya, Tanzania and Zambia.
Taylor, J.V., *The Primal Vision*, SCM Press, 1969.
Turnbull, Colin, *The Forest People*, Jonathan Cape, 1961.
   The Lonely African, Chatto & Windus, 1953.

Fiction

Conrad, Joseph, *Heart of Darkness*, Penguin, 1982.
Katiyo, Wilson, *Going to Heaven*, Longman, 1982.
Naipaul, V.S., *A Bend in the River*, Penguin, 1980.
Wa Thiongo, Ngugi, *Petals of Blood*, Heinemann, 1977.

APPENDIX 2

Equipment We Took

*Worth taking   †We wouldn't bother again

*Rucksack. Don't choose one so large that you can't carry it when full. Janie's internal frame rucksack unzipped all the way round, which made finding things easy. Beware of putting valuables in outside pockets.

*Kagoule. Choose the largest size. Few kagoules are truly waterproof in an equatorial downpour but they will keep you warm.

†Umbrella. Our golfing umbrella was good for shade but little else.

*Sleeping-bag. Synthetic fibres dry quicker.

*Cotton sleeping sheet. Janie made sleeping sheets that doubled as mosquito nets. They were in the form of a bag which fastened with velcro along the top. A window of netting allowed you to breathe and see out.

*Foam sleeping mats. Cut these to individual lengths from head to hip.

†Tent. We carried an extra light tent and only used it once. When it was warm enough we slept outside. When it is raining heavily or there are dangers, a tent is no use. A hut or a cheap hotel is better.

*Universal bath plug – the kind that fits any size hole. Lighter still is a piece of inner tube.

†Collapsible water carrier. Ours punctured in the first week. On long dry journeys, a two-gallon solid plastic container is better.

*Aluminium water bottles. Very useful and virtually indestructible. Will keep tea or coffee warm for some time if wrapped in clothes.

*Camera – the smaller the better. We had an Olympus XA2 each, with flash attachment. They are automatic and so small that they can be used before anyone notices. Large cameras excite the interest of spy-catchers and by the time you have focused, the perfect shot has either melted away or stood to attention. Keep your camera on a strong cord round your neck to prevent theft.

*Camera films. Available in Kenya and Zimbabwe but expensive. Not available in most places. Take more than you think you need.

*Maps. Michelin are good.

*Swiss army knife. Keep permanently attached to your belt. The minimum required is a blade, scissors, tweezers, corkscrew and tin opener.

*Ten yards of nylon rope. This has endless uses – tying your rucksack to a truck or bus roof, guy lines for a sunshade, washing line, etc.

†Torch. Tiny Duracell ones are good. Candles sometimes melt.

†Cooker. We lugged a paraffin pressure cooker around and it didn't really pay for itself in extra weight. Camping Gaz is difficult to find. In most places there is cheap ready-made food and drinks. You can usually make a fire.

*Matches. Keep in a container to avoid humidity.

†Assorted dried food. We found this tasteless and expensive. We carried packets of stew halfway round Africa, waiting for the appropriate moment to eat them and finally gave them away.

*Clothes. These should be ones you really like and feel comfortable in. Some people make a cult of looking as scruffy as possible. It may be chic to look poor in Europe but many Africans find it insulting. Look as smart as you can, especially when dealing with officials. Short hair for men is advisable: in Malawi immigration officials cut men's hair if it reaches the collar.

*T shirts – avoid political slogans.

*One smart shirt or dress makes getting visas easier and you *may* be invited to an embassy cocktail party.

*Cotton trousers or a longish skirt. Jeans take too long to dry and are very uncomfortable when wet. Shorts can appear

262

provocative on women and either scruffy or colonialist on men.

*Cotton socks and pants. A fresh pair of socks makes anyone feel better.

*Light woollen or cotton jersey. In the night it gets cold, especially in high altitudes.

*Shoes or sandals. We found well-made trainers the best all-rounders for comfort. But many hotels won't let you in wearing trainers or sandals (or jeans or shorts). The children went barefoot a lot of the time. This is not advisable in towns or where jiggers and tapeworms are found.

*Flip-flop shoes – light to carry.

*Hat or eyeshade – one that doesn't mind being sat on and will protect both the eyes and the back of the neck.

*Swimming-pants or costume. The smartest you can afford should get you into hotel swimming-pools or exclusive beach clubs.

*Washing things – toothbrush, toothpaste, thin flannel, razor, comb, soap in a plastic box. Replacements are available everywhere. Quicker and friendlier service is given to sweet-smelling people. To the African nose, sweaty Europeans smell like wet chickens.

†Talcum powder – turns to mud when mixed with sweat.

†Tampons. Janie packed one month's supply of tampons and mini-pads into separate plastic bags. Sanitary towels are available in most places. Tampax is on sale in Kenya, Kinshasa and Zimbabwe, but it is expensive.

*Linen or cotton drying-up towel. It is lighter and dries quicker than a terry towel. A Kenyan *khanga* – printed cloth – can double as a towel, skirt, veil or sheet.

†Loo paper – heavy to carry. Use newspaper or leaves. Paper is not usually provided, especially in Muslim areas where bottoms are washed, not wiped. This is why eating or shaking hands with the left hand is considered rude.

*Fork, dessert spoon, wide-based cup with handle, bowl. *Backpacker's Africa* suggests using a frisbee, then you can play with it too. We found that bowls make good frisbees.

*Playing cards. A good way to make friends and pass the time waiting for transport. 'Othello' is easy to learn and to teach.

*Books to read – long ones. Swap with other travellers when

263

you've finished or use the pages as loo paper as you read them.

*Exercise-book and ballpoint pen – for notes, letters, diary. Cheaply replaced anywhere.

*A reference from someone on impressive headed paper may be needed at borders or to obtain visas.

*Twenty passport photos. Every visa requires at least two. They are expensive and time-consuming to acquire.

*Sheet of carbon paper for all the duplicate forms at borders, visas etc.

*Insurance certificate. Get insurance with good cover, including a flight home in an emergency. Keep ALL receipts and always go to a police station if anything is stolen.

*International driving licence. You never know when you might need to drive a vehicle.

*Money belt for traveller's cheques, passport etc. Never take it off, even in bed. Never take out a wad of notes in front of anyone else, however much you trust them. Take some US dollars for emergency exchange when the banks are closed.

*Sewing kit – needles, button thread, thimble, large nappy pins.

*Plastic bags to wrap your clothes in. Rucksacks are never wholly waterproof.

*Children's favourite small soft toy – very comforting in strange places and a good introduction to new friends.

†Plastic whistles for the children to wear round their necks for emergencies. Very irritating when blown in the night for fun. Ours were eventually bartered for home-made toys. Possibly good for lone women travellers.

†Things to give away – ballpoint pens, razor-blades, lighters, digital watches, fish-hooks etc. These can be found in most places now and people either want money or they are friendly and don't want payment. Cigarette lighters fascinate rural people but £1 goes a lot further as a gift.

First Aid Kit

Keep this in a tough waterproof bag. Camera film containers are good for tablets, but mark them clearly.

*Paracetamol, one container-ful.

*Chloroquine, for malaria in Zambia, Zimbabwe and Southern Africa. Take two tablets a week, starting one month before departure and finishing two months after.

*Fansidar (pyrimethamine) for malaria in Kenya, Zaire, Tanzania etc. Take one tablet a week, starting a month before departure. Some areas need both Fansidar and Chloroquine. Fansidar may have long-term side effects, but malaria is so horrible that I think it's worth the risk. Every doctor has different views on malaria.

†Sticking plaster – goes unsticky in damp heat.

*Antiseptic cream – cuts and sores go septic very quickly in the tropics.

*Antihistamine cream – imperative for mosquito bites. Some doctors say it's bad for you but scratching all night is worse.

*Antibiotic tablets for bronchitis, tropical ulcers etc. Take at least one full course of a broad spectrum antibiotic tablet, such as tetracycline. Those on sale may be out of date. Don't take antibiotics for diarrhoea – they make it worse.

*Insect repellant oil. Better than spray.

*Stero-tabs taste horrible. Worse still are sterilising drinking straws. If possible, boil water for at least three minutes. Be sensible – don't have ice in drinks or buy ice-lollies from street-sellers. Eat fruit that has been peeled by you. Take-away street food is okay if you can see it being cooked. Let your guts get used to the local germs gradually. Everyone has diarrhoea at some point. DON'T take anti-diarrhoea medicines – they just block the germs in. Drink as much as possible: Coca-Cola is good for diarrhoea and vomiting. (Drink it in small sips if vomiting.) Or – mix one cup of clean water with a large pinch of salt and three teaspoons of sugar. If possible, add the juice of an orange or mashed banana. Drink one cup for every visit to the loo. Use this recipe to prevent and treat dehydration from diarrhoea, vomiting , heatstroke, fever, etc.

†Worm tablets. Everyone gets worms eventually.

†Sunburn cream. If you avoid a tan then you won't need this. Most places are far too hot and uncomfortable for lying around in the sun but there is always the occasion when you forget to cover up. Old cold sores will reappear after too much sun. For bad sunburn take paracetamol and drink lots of fluids (see above.) If you have to sit in the sun all day, take

265

Vitamin A tablets, preferably in advance.

*Painkillers – strong ones like Ponstan in case of accidents.

*Seasick pills. Janie once had terrible seasickness in a dugout canoe on a lake.

*Sterile dressing packs for application next to a wound. Rip up a T-shirt for bandages.

†Thermometer – some people like to know exactly how high their fever is.

*Aching muscle ointment – invaluable if you walk any distance. It makes a safe placebo to rub into other people if they ask you for medication.

*Disposable syringe and needles – if you need an injection, hand these to the nurse. Her syringe may have been used several times before.

*Sleeping pills – for those dreadful nights when the temperature is unbearable or your room is next to an all-night bar. Alternatively, go to the bar and get drunk.

*Contraceptives – take as many as you will need. If you have problems with a coil or cap, most clinics have staff trained in family planning. Abortion is illegal in most of Africa and where it isn't the operation uses up valuable medical resources. Condoms are available in most places and usually cheap. Always use a condom when sleeping with strangers. Gonorrhoea is ten times more common in Africa and penicillin-resistant in many places. Then there is the dreaded AIDS.

Vaccines:

Cholera – one injection which may make you feel ill for a couple of days. Don't leave it until the last minute as it must be ordered from the hospital. Views differ as to its efficacy but some countries require a certificate, e.g. Zambia and Zimbabwe. Cholera is rare in Africa and if you are well fed and sensible about drinking water, you are unlikely to catch it.

Tetanus booster – a good idea wherever you go: tetanus is in the soil all over the world. It is available at any doctor. Two injections now and a third in six months gives five years' protection.

Yellow Fever – two injections give ten years' protection. Some countries insist on a certificate, e.g. Kenya.

Hepatitis – one painful injection of gamma globulin gives three

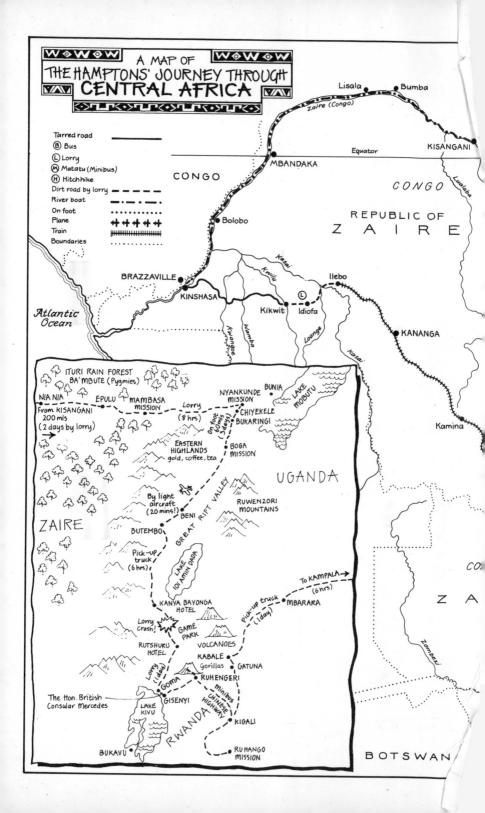

months' protection for 50% of receivers. Doctors disagree on its efficacy. Many people are immune, without knowing it. A blood test can show this.

Tuberculosis – one BCG gives life long protection. Worth having wherever you go, though well fed people are unlikely to get TB. You may have had a BCG at secondary school.

Typhoid, two injections give one year's protection. Some countries insist on a certificate, e.g. Zaire.

If you are genuinely allergic to any vaccine, get your doctor to give you a certificate anyway, otherwise some countries may insist on vaccinating you at the border, and you never know how often the needle has been used.

The countries that insist on vaccination certificates want to protect themslves from the disease, not you.